Praise for *The Six Disciplines of Agile Marketing*

"*The Six Disciplines of Agile Marketing* provides a comprehensive guide to the principles, practices, methods, and mindset of Agile Marketing. If you have a question about how a particular Agile approach (such as Kanban or Scrum) or Agile principle (such as embracing change) applies to the world of marketing, you are certain to find an answer here. Best of all, you'll never lose sight of *why* these ideas are so critical and relevant for modern marketers."

> —**Matt LeMay,** Cofounder and Partner at Sudden Compass,
> Author of *Agile for Everybody*

"This book distills years of experience practicing and teaching agile marketing into a pragmatic guide for leaders and practitioners. The insights within could only have emerged from an iterative process adapting the agile approach to marketing organizations and will help you speed adoption at your company."

> —**Roland Smart,** CMO/COO DBT Center of Marin,
> former VP of Social and Community Marketing, Oracle,
> author of *The Agile Marketer: Turning Customer Experience
> Into Your Competitive Advantage*

"Even with my twenty years of experience in the ad business, I have been inspired by Jim's amazing breadth of real-world experience and his drive to create real, forward momentum in marketing practices for today's complex environment. Jim's experience and foresight has produced a body of knowledge and practices that embraces not only a total business perspective but a practical "how to", both at a team level and at an organizational level. Get the book, study it and apply its many valuable lessons."

> —**Jeff Plowman,** Founder, The Super Market Business and Brand
> Consultancy, former EVP and Managing Director, McCann Erickson

"Moving beyond the buzzwords, Jim provides a down-to-earth yet deep and actionable take on what disciplined Agile Marketing looks like. Agile is the modern business operating system and this is a great guide to how to "install" and "tweak" it for your needs."

> —**Yuval Yeret,** Enterprise Agile Consultant, AgileSparks

"Jim Ewel's book *The Six Disciplines of Agile Marketing* provides a practical guide to implementing Agile Marketing in organizations of all sizes. How can companies survive and prosper in the most critical times, including the most recent COVID-19 pandemic? By using Agile to respond to changing market conditions and to innovate quickly. Read this book, as Jim brings his many years of experience to bear on the many problems facing marketing organizations today."

—**John Cass,** Digital strategist, founder, Boston Agile Marketing Meetup, former President, Boston chapter of the American Marketing Association

THE

6

DISCIPLINES

OF

AGILE
MARKETING

THE

6

DISCIPLINES

OF

AGILE MARKETING

PROVEN PRACTICES FOR
MORE EFFECTIVE MARKETING
AND BETTER BUSINESS RESULTS

JIM EWEL

WILEY

For general information on our other products and services or for technical support, please
contact our Customer Care Department within the United States at (800) 762-2974,
outside the United States at (317) 572-3993 or fax (317) 572-4002.

Wiley publishes in a variety of print and electronic formats and by print-on-demand. Some
material included with standard print versions of this book may not be included in ebooks
or in print-on-demand. If this book refers to media such as a CD or DVD that is not
included in the version you purchased, you may download this material at http://
booksupport.wiley.com. For more information about Wiley products, visit www.wiley
.com.

Library of Congress Cataloging-in-Publication Data is Available:
ISBN 9781119712039 (Hardcover)
ISBN 9781119712053 (ePDF)
ISBN 9781119712046 (ePub)

Cover Art & Design: Paul McCarthy

Printed in the United States of America

SKY10020778_082720

To my wife, Ann, whose support and encouragement made this book possible.

Contents

Foreword

I t has never been a better time to be a marketer.

The explosion of technology over the past 20 years has created myriad ways for us to attract, engage, and delight customers. Thousands of marketing and technology—martech—software companies vie to empower us in ever more innovative ways. Social networks and search engines give us virtually unlimited reach.

The digital world provides us a palette that holds an infinite variety of hues; we apply them, with every imaginable brush, knife, and sponge, to a canvas as expansive as our collective imagination.

And never have we seen greater demand for this power to create.

Marketing, once a peripheral function at many companies—the "arts and crafts department," as a colleague once lamented—now sits at the center of the organization. We are the heartbeat of customer experience, delivering customer engagement to the far reaches of the organization and returning rich insights to the management brain.

We who master the art, the science, the engineering of modern marketing, can have the world at our feet.

And yet.

And yet many organizations struggle to harness this awesome creative power that sits, seemingly, beyond their grasp.

It's not because they can't afford it. Most marketing tools are relatively inexpensive, especially when we take them for a test run—the ubiquitous "freemium" model of software-as-a-service (SaaS). And most cloud tools scale; we pay for what we use.

It's not because they lack the skills—at least the skills to wield the tools or execute digital tactics. Most digital marketing isn't rocket science: Vendors compete on user experience (UX), constantly making their products easier to learn, easier to adapt, easier to apply. And any how-to question you might have is answered instantly, from wherever you are, on Google or YouTube.

Paul Simon sang about it in 1986, and it's here now. *These* are the days of miracles and wonders.

So where is the struggle? What stands between marketing departments and digital paradise?

Management.

Of course, right? Who else takes the rap when something doesn't work?

But the problem here isn't the people in management. The problem is the process. Organizations manage marketing today with the practices and procedures of a bygone century. They yoke six horses to a jet airplane, and they roll across the prairie in a shiny metal stagecoach.

To soar in the twenty-first century, marketing needs a twenty-first-century approach; and that approach is, in a word, Agile.

The discipline of Agile management has evolved over the past two decades, from a manifesto in software-development circles to the rich set of methodologies that are now harnessed to nearly every discipline in our digital world. When applied to marketing, we call it Agile marketing. It's the secret to splitting and unleashing the power of the digital atom.

Agile marketing frees your teams to move faster and more efficiently. They'll adapt quickly to change, with little friction and fuss. They'll experiment in a focused and disciplined manner to discover opportunities. They'll continually improve—not just the work that they deliver, but the way they work together.

The teams will love their work. Really. In study after study, teams embracing Agile marketing report that they enjoy their jobs more. These happy, empowered teams produce better results.

Unlike splitting the real atom, anyone working in the digital world can split the digital atom. The intuitive principles of Agile marketing are easy to grasp and execute.

Implementing Agile marketing successfully—not just speaking the words or going through the motions of standups and Kanban boards—requires an understanding of the whole that is greater than the sum of its parts. It's a hill to climb; not because it's inherently difficult but because it's different from how you've managed before. Here, in your hands (or on your screen), is the guide to lead you to the top of that hill.

Jim Ewel, a pioneer of Agile marketing, helped forge the discipline over the past decade. He brings a wealth of experience as a marketing executive, a CEO, a university instructor in digital marketing, and an Agile transformation leader for top brands. He has pondered the "how" and the "why" of Agile marketing, has distilled his wisdom, and has placed it eloquently into this book.

The Six Disciplines of Agile Marketing is the new classic of marketing management.

Read this book. Embrace it. Practice it. Iterate and adapt it.

You'll soon find yourself standing on the other side; and, standing there, you'll agree:

There's never been a better time to be a marketer.

– Scott Brinker
Editor, chiefmartec.com
Author, *Hacking Marketing*

Preface

Why I Wrote this Book

Business has only two functions—marketing and innovation.
—*Milan Kundera, author of* The Unbearable Lightness of Being

I love marketing. It's one of the most difficult and most critical jobs in any company. It's also among the least understood jobs. It's sometimes the least respected. And the way many marketers plan, organize, and manage the execution of marketing is broken.

The traditional marketing plan serves little or no purpose. We sit in endless meetings, debating annual—or even worse, three-year—plans, without feedback from the market or from the rest of the organization. The resulting plans are long, inward-focused, detached-from-customer realities.

Do you file away those marketing plans the day you finish writing them, and never look at them again? If so, this book is for you.

The traditional marketing organization is broken. Many marketers work in silos, their loyalties and their point of view more closely aligned to their skill set (communication specialists, social-media specialists, SEO/SEM specialists, marketing technologists, advertising directors, brand managers, media planners and buyers, creatives, copywriters) than to the delivery of value to the customer. The traditional marketing organization frustrates marketers who are customer-focused and who want to get things done quickly.

Are your efforts to meet customer needs and to respond quickly to changing markets strangled by the conflicting priorities and endless handoffs and approval loops endemic to the traditional marketing organization? If so, this book is for you.

The typical campaign-based marketing approach doesn't meet the needs of modern marketers. Campaigns are planned over weeks or months, executed over months or years, and victory is declared with whatever metrics support the conclusion that the campaign was successful.

Are you frustrated by the endless meetings to plan campaigns, the vanity metrics pulled out of the air to support the conclusion that the campaign was successful, and the inability to take advantage of fleeting market opportunities? If so, this book is for you.

Marketing execution is broken. Too many meetings, too many status reports, too many work items in spreadsheets rather than tools to support modern marketing. The result is poor execution and an inability to communicate to the rest of the organization the value of marketing.

Are you the kind of marketer who wants to get things done and produce great work that is valuable to both the customer and the rest of the organization? If so, this book is for you.

Marketers face greater challenges than ever. The rapid pace of change, the shift in power to the buyer, the convergence of sales and marketing, and the impact of technology combine to make effective marketing both more possible and more difficult than ever. I'll cover these challenges in greater depth in Chapter 1, but here's a taste. Technology has made it possible to target marketing messages to specific audiences and to measure the effectiveness of that marketing message within days or weeks. It has also deluged audiences with a flood of marketing messages, most of which they ignore. This requires a new approach to marketing—one that is iterative and that measures effectiveness, not in status reports or weekly meetings, but in data visible to all. This new approach also requires new skills and greater responsibilities.

Do you long for rapid, iterative marketing that measures success based on business-focused analytics? Are you overwhelmed or frustrated by the ever-increasing demands being put on marketing, without matching increases in staff or budgets? I wrote this book for you.

Software developers faced a similar crisis at the turn of the millennium. Software was often delivered late. It frequently failed to meet the needs of the customer. Managers failed to make hard tradeoffs, those necessary to deliver quality software on a reasonable schedule. When software projects did work, it was only by dint of long hours and heroic efforts on the part of the developers. When demands became more complex, the then-current methodology, known as Waterfall, failed. Basic business requirements—quick turn, continuous deployment, and responsiveness to fast-changing user needs—went unmet.

Adapting Agile to Marketing

In February 2001, a group of software developers met at a ski resort in Utah. At the end of the meeting, they issued the Agile Manifesto, whose four values and 12 principles revolutionized software development. Today, Agile is the dominant methodology for planning, organizing, and managing the day-to-day execution of software development. Application of the Agile Manifesto's values, principles, and processes has raised not only software quality but also the productivity and job satisfaction of software developers.

Agile values, principles, and processes can also revolutionize how we practice marketing. We can realize commensurate benefits in productivity, quality, and job satisfaction. And, although we can't simply apply them as-is, we can take the values, principles, and processes developed by and for software developers and adapt them to meet the needs of modern marketing.

Many marketers today want to be Agile. The word itself is attractive—who wouldn't want to be agile? At the same time, they don't fully know what it means, and they don't know how to implement Agile methods and practices in their organizations. They may have taken Scrum master training designed for software developers; and while they're excited about the possibilities, they don't know how to apply Scrum or Kanban to marketing.

I've spent a decade figuring out how to adapt Agile to marketing. I've blogged about it, I've practiced it, and I've trained and coached many organizations through its adoption. I've learned—by making mistakes and realizing successes—what works and what doesn't. This book makes available to you what those years of learning have taught me.

The Six Disciplines and Four Shifts of Agile Marketing

To apply Agile to marketing, teams must master Six Disciplines and organizations must make Four Shifts in beliefs and behaviors (see Figure P.1). The Six Disciplines can be adopted at the grass roots and spread up and

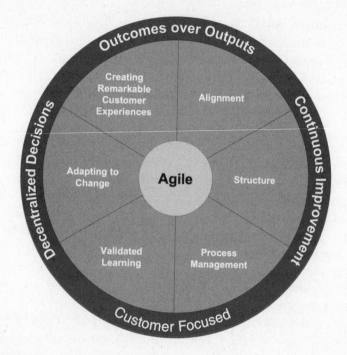

Figure P.1   The Six Disciplines and the Four Shifts of Agile marketing

out through the organization. The Four Shifts are different: They require changes to the culture of the organization, including parts of the organization outside of marketing. Marketing can often lead these shifts, and marketing is critical to their adoption in any organization.

The Six Disciplines vary in the degree of commonality they have with the corresponding disciplines practiced by software developers. The disciplines of structure and process management resemble disciplines mastered by developers as they apply Agile to software development. I summarize in this book some of the techniques and processes developed by software engineers and then discuss, in detail, the differences—subtle and profound—that we discover when we apply Agile to marketing.

Other disciplines, like alignment, validated learning, and adapting to change, create unique challenges for marketing. For these, I provide guidance on mastering them. The sixth discipline, creating remarkable customer experiences, requires that marketers collaborate with other areas of the organization, including software development, to create remarkable customer experiences. I provide guidance on how to begin mastering business agility and how to work effectively with others in the organization to master this discipline.

My goal is to help organizations and Agile practitioners adapt Agile principles to both the marketing function and to marketing-led businesses so that they can get more done, achieve better outcomes, adapt to change, and provide remarkable customer experiences.

Who Should Read This Book?

I wrote this book for marketers and marketing managers who want to apply Agile values, principles, and processes to the marketing function in their organizations. It is a *practitioner's* guide to Agile marketing, not a strategist's guide. While I spend some time answering the basic questions—What is Agile marketing? Why would you want to implement it?—I spend much more time focusing on the details of adapting Agile to marketing and practicing Agile in the marketing organization.

Senior leaders, including chief marketing officers, or CMOs, will find the concept of the Four Shifts helpful in implementing Agile in their organizations. Senior leaders who want their organizations to be Agile must guide the organization, and particularly the middle-management layer, to the changes in beliefs and behaviors necessary to realize the full promise of Agile. If they don't lead these shifts in beliefs and behaviors, both by example and by getting behind their adoption, Agile can have only limited effectiveness in their organizations.

Senior leaders play a primary role in leading the Four Shifts; they also have a role to play in mastering the Six Disciplines. CMOs and the most senior marketing leaders must support and involve themselves to an appropriate level in the disciplines of alignment, structure, adapting to change, and creating remarkable customer experiences. Working out whether the team adopts Scrum, Kanban, or something in between is less relevant to senior leaders; that is best left to the teams. The same goes for validated learning; the details are best left to the teams.

Organizations that succeed in adopting Agile and transforming their marketing tend to do the following:

- *Invest in training and coaching.* Thinking that simply attending a two-day training course will transform the organization is unrealistic. Organizations that succeed know that transformation requires time and follow-on coaching from experienced practitioners.

- *Persist.* They realize that major change takes time, and they do not stop for setbacks. They persist until they achieve results.
- *Experiment and embrace new approaches.* They are willing to change their existing ways of working and the way that teams are organized.

If you make the necessary investments, if you persist, and if you experiment and try new approaches, you can succeed in your adoption of Agile to marketing.

How to Use This Book

You can, of course, read this book straight through. It is organized into four sections: an overview, a section on the Six Disciplines, a third section on the Four Shifts, and a final section on how to succeed with Agile marketing.

If you're in a hurry to get started, you can take a different approach: I'd recommend reading the overview in Part 1, then Chapters 3 through 11 of Part 2, which cover the first four disciplines. You may also want to read Chapter 20 on getting started with Agile marketing. Once you have been practicing Agile marketing for three to six months, you can come back and read the remaining chapters. You will have more context in which to learn the final two disciplines and the Four Shifts.

If you're a senior marketing executive and you're more interested in the strategic and the change management issues of introducing Agile marketing in to your organization, I recommend reading the overview in Part 1, Chapter 3, as an introduction to the Six Disciplines, and then all of Part 3 on the Four Shifts. You may also want to check out Chapter 22 on the role of the Agile leader.

Benefits of Adopting Agile in Marketing

You who want to adopt Agile marketing have set a challenge for yourselves. If you're not management, you need to convince management. If you are management, you need to convince the individual contributors—they must buy in to new skill sets, beliefs, and behaviors.

Sounds like work; why bother?

- *Improved productivity.* This is the first reason marketers give when asked why they've adopted Agile marketing. The manner, however, with which marketers improve productivity is unexpected. It's not through working harder and getting more done in a typical eight-hour day. How do marketers improve productivity?

- They focus on what's most important to the customer and what's best aligned with the desired business outcomes.
- Unproductive work is eliminated.
- Long report-out meetings are replaced with short daily standups.
- They get agreement on the indicators of success and how to measure them.
- Their marketing is validated through experiments and testing.

- *Greater awareness of marketing's contribution.* "What is it that marketing does, anyway?" Every marketer has heard that question. When marketing is done well, its contribution is often overlooked. When marketing fails, everyone knows, and is quick to blame marketing. Because of Agile's inherent coordination with the business units and use of cross-functional teams, and because of the use of Scrum practices like Sprint reviews, the organization learns more about the contributions and the value of marketing. This raises the level of respect for marketing in the organization and makes it easier for marketing to get the resources needed to properly do its job.
- *Adaptability to change.* Marketers must adapt to and embrace change. While this isn't new, it's increasingly critical as the pace of change accelerates. Agile provides in-built adaptive mechanisms like emphasis on iteration, focus on customers, and the spontaneous emergence of requirements through experience rather than through fixed, up-front planning. And on top of the value of these in-built mechanisms, Agile marketers get to master the discipline of adapting to change, which leads directly to tremendous benefits to marketing and to the enterprise. This can be particularly advantageous for those organizations that include marketing in the creation of the customer experience. Marketing organizations that master this discipline sense changes in customer needs and help their organizations adapt quickly to these changes. Because they have tools and processes to adapt to change, Agile marketers embrace change.
- *Improved job satisfaction.* Both anecdotal evidence and rigorous scientific studies show that software developers in organizations that practice Agile have better job satisfaction than software developers in organizations that use more traditional development methodologies. Surveys also suggest that the same is true for Agile marketing teams. In the *3rd Annual State of Agile Marketing Report,* 74 percent of Agile marketers

were satisfied with how their team was working and the results they achieved, compared to just 58 percent of traditional marketers and 34 percent of ad-hoc marketers.[1]

- *Attracting and retaining talent.* This is related to improved job satisfaction, of course. Top marketing talent can be difficult to find. Organizations that practice Agile are more likely to attract and retain this talent. Practicing Agile marketing also develops talent. It encourages marketers to get closer to customers, to align with business units and meet their needs, and to learn how to get their job done more effectively.

As valuable as you'll find this book, reading is no substitute for doing. You'll learn more by applying what you learn to your own situation than by careful study of the book without hands-on experience. Steven Blank, one of the foremost experts on successful startup practices, gives the following advice to startups, which applies equally to marketing, "Rule No. 1: There are no facts inside your building, so get outside."[2] Learn by doing, by experimenting, by trying things out. *See* what works, and what doesn't, for you and your organization.

Let's get started!

Part I

Overview

C hapter 1 begins by outlining many of the challenges that face marketers today. It answers the question "Why should I change?" Change is hard, and most people are reluctant to change just for change's sake. Perhaps you feel that your existing marketing is pretty good or even great, and that may well be the case. However, most non-Agile organizations that produce good marketing do so through hero mode—talented people working long hours—and when good people leave or burn out, the quality of marketing suffers.

Chapter 2 defines the values and principles of Agile marketing. The values I outline differ slightly from those expressed in the Agile Marketing Manifesto. Those of us who attended Sprint Zero, where the Agile Marketing Manifesto was written, acknowledged that we produced only a first draft. I've taken the liberty of revising that draft, and I've been teaching the six values to organizations throughout the world for many years.

These values and principles are the core of Agile marketing. Before embarking on an adoption of Agile marketing, it is critical that marketers understand and embrace these values and principles.

Chapter 1

Challenges Facing Marketers Today

You should never view your challenges as a disadvantage. Instead, it's important for you to understand that your experience facing and overcoming adversity is actually one of your biggest advantages.
　　　　　　—*Michelle Obama, former First Lady of the United States*

I t took 110 years for the telephone to be adopted by 1 billion users. It took 49 years for television to be adopted by 1 billion users, 22 years for mobile devices, 14 years for the Internet, and 8 years for Facebook. It took one year for the Internet of Things (IOT) to reach 1 billion devices.[1]

These new technologies and the accelerating rate of technological change present new opportunities to reach customers. Marketing must adapt.

According to the folks at Moz, an inbound marketing and search engine optimization firm,[2] Google releases between 5 and 35 major changes, and

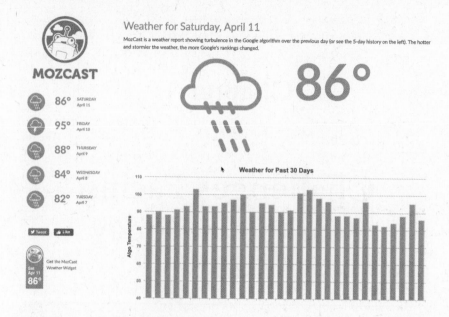

Figure 1.1 Moz's MozCast tool, image courtesy of Moz, Inc.
Source: Moz, Inc.

hundreds of minor ones, to its search algorithm each year. Its MozCast tool, shown in Figure 1.1, shows the turbulence in Google's ranking algorithm over time.

Google's own data (which Google stopped sharing in 2018) indicate that Google makes, in fact, more than 5,000 changes, major and minor, every year. That's 14 changes per day. No marketing plan can keep up with that pace of change.

In 2017 and 2018, marketers sprinkled artificial intelligence (AI) into their marketing copy, almost like fairy dust, and sometimes with nothing but dust behind the words. AI live chat, using tools like Intercom and Drift, was in every marketer's toolbox. Podcasts surged. Voice search, on Alexa and its competitors, became a way for consumers to find products and services, and hence became something else that marketing needed to address.

In 2019, marketers advertised on smart speakers like Amazon Echo or Google Home. Tools like YotPo and BazaarVoice helped marketers collect reviews and ratings for e-commerce sites and create referral programs. 360-degree videos offered more opportunities for interactivity and engagement.

How, in 2020, will marketers adapt to new uses of artificial intelligence? How will marketers adapt to newer social-media channels like TikTok, Caffeine.TV, Lasso, Vero, Kik, and Houseparty? And the largest question of 2020: How will marketers respond to the impact of the Covid-19 pandemic and the changes to our lives as we respond to that crisis?

If you wrote a marketing plan at the beginning of any of these years, you could not have anticipated the impact of new channels and new technologies, and in 2020, the impact of Covid-19. The requirements put on marketing, constantly changing, emerged at their own pace.

The "write a plan, work the plan, declare victory" method of operations is dead! Modern marketing must keep up with the pace of change and learn to address emergent requirements as they happen.

The Shift to Digital

Digital advertising and digital channels present new challenges and new opportunities to modern marketers. As Scott Brinker discusses in his book *Hacking Marketing*, digital channels have new dynamics:

- *Speed*. Digital campaigns can be rolled out, changed, and adapted at a speed unimaginable to marketers in channels like television or print. Marketers with the right scale of user interaction can modify campaigns in minutes or hours; almost anyone can achieve a rhythm of weekly change and experimentation. This presents a tremendous opportunity and a challenge. How do we build and manage the marketing processes to take advantage of this speed? How do we organize our teams to move at this speed? What tools do we use?
- *Adaptability*. If a digital campaign works in one channel (display advertising, say), it's not that difficult to adapt the campaign to work in another channel (Facebook). Compare this to adapting a television campaign to print. Opportunity and challenge: When a prospect sees a message in multiple digital channels, how do we measure the impact of spending in each channel? With each channel having its own ways of grouping audiences, how do we think about audiences holistically, across channels?
- *Adjacency*. In the physical world, where competitors rarely share a parking lot, consumers tend to value convenience over price. Few drive across town to save a few pennies. On the Internet, your competition is one click away. Opportunity and challenge: It's easier than ever to compete, and, if you're the incumbent, you compete on more than price or you risk the consumer clicking away.

- *Scale*. If a campaign works for 10,000 digital prospects, then in most channels, given sufficient budget, campaigns can be scaled up overnight for millions of users. But scaling digital campaigns comes with hidden challenges. Often, when we begin a campaign, we focus our message on the most receptive audience possible. Sometimes, we get a very good conversion rate and then, when we scale up the campaign to a more diluted, more representative audience (in terms of receptivity to our product or message), we fail to duplicate that conversion rate. And we often don't know when to scale—do we continue to refine and improve our message with small groups before we scale up? Do we scale up quickly to deliver revenue as quickly as possible?
- *Precision*. Digital campaigns can be measured with a precision unheard of in analog media. Challenge: Do we teach everyone to understand statistical significance and how to report on and understand the data? Do we leave that function to intermediary experts? What do we measure? How do we avoid the vanity metrics described by Eric Ries in his book *The Lean Startup*? (Vanity metrics feel good but do little to forward our business goals.)

The shift to digital, on balance, provides tremendous opportunities for the modern marketer, while presenting new challenges and requiring us to find new ways of operating.

The Impact of Technology

Technology changes how buyers shop, creates new and fragmented channels of communication, transforms how marketers manage marketing, and expands the information that marketers can access to personalize and direct marketing messages.

Technology—the Internet—provides more product information than what organizations typically provide. It changes how buyers access that information.

Increasingly, buyers access information through their phones. Since 2017, about half of Internet usage has been through mobile devices.[3] Marketers must therefore think mobile first. And the desktop still commands such a sizable minority of Internet use that marketers must create multiplatform experiences.

Technology, by providing new tools to meet the needs of marketers, transforms how marketers manage marketing. Every year, Scott Brinker publishes the Marketing Technology Landscape Supergraphic, shown in Figure 1.2. In 2011, its first year of publication, it listed approximately 150

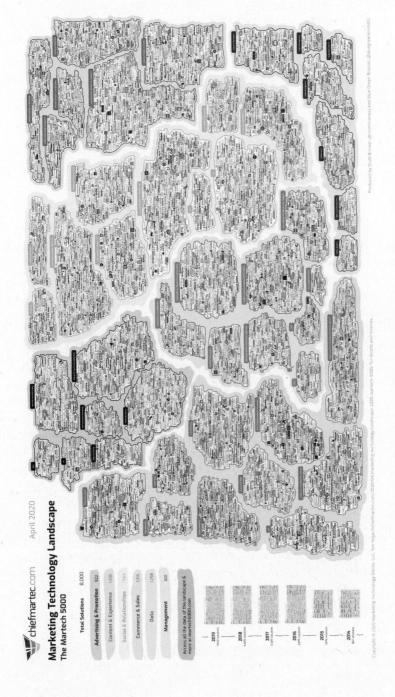

Figure 1.2 The 2020 Marketing Technology Landscape Supergraphic, courtesy of Scott Brinker

Source: Scott Brinker

marketing technology solutions. Nine years later, the marketing technology landscape has expanded to over 8,000 solutions.[4]

How do we deal with the complexity of thousands of marketing solutions? Many marketing organizations develop *marketing stacks*. The stack (or "stackie," as Scott calls it) describes the categories of marketing technology and how they relate, and it illustrates the choices that the organization has made in each category. Add this to the list of responsibilities of the modern marketer: They must not only figure out how to modify their marketing to adapt to the technologies that customers or potential customers use; they must develop and implement marketing stacks.

The Shift in Power to the Buyer

The Internet, and the increasing availability of mobile devices to access it from anywhere and at any time, powerfully impacts how products and services are bought and sold. Companies like Best Buy struggle with *showrooming*: consumers use Best Buy stores as a showroom to examine and learn about products and then buy the products, at a lower price, from Amazon or other online retailers.

According to data from Google's influential Zero Moment of Truth (ZMOT) study, "the average shopper used 10.4 sources of information to make a decision in 2011, up from 5.3 sources in 2010."[5] According to *Adweek*, 81 percent of shoppers conduct online research before buying.[6]

This phenomenon extends beyond consumer businesses. Business-to-business buyers also consult sources of information. This shifts the balance of power increasingly away from the supplier and to the buyer. *McKinsey Quarterly* describes this as "the consumerization of business buying."[7]

This ability of business-to-business buyers to shop around also shifts the balance in an organization between sales and marketing. According to data the market research firm Gartner customers progress nearly 60% of the way through the purchase process before engaging with sales[8] (see Figure 1.3). Marketing, not sales, must take responsibility for influencing this pre-engagement decision-making.

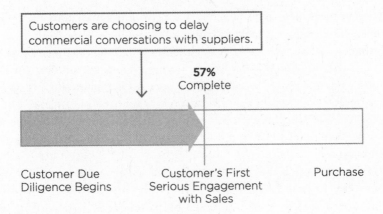

Figure 1.3 Customer progress through the purchase process before engaging sales (Gartner, Inc.)
Source: Gartner, Inc.

Competition

Businesses always have competition. Marketers must plan pricing, promotion, distribution, and positioning of their products and services with an eye to the competition. Three recent changes present even more challenges to the marketer:

1. *Concentration and consolidation.* In many markets, one or two competitors dominate the market. In digital advertising, for example, Google and Facebook own a collective 59 percent of the US market[9]–down from 73 percent in 2017.[10] Amazon's share of the US e-commerce market is 47 percent, or 5 percent of all retail spend.[11] In 1995, Geoffrey Moore wrote in his book *Inside the Tornado* that all markets consist of a gorilla (the player with the largest market share), a few chimps (players with combined market share equal to half of the gorilla's share), and many monkeys (everyone else).[12] Twenty-five years later, the chimps have disappeared; most US markets now consist of a gorilla or two and a lot of monkeys. Good luck to the marketer for one of those monkeys, who must avoid being crushed by the gorilla while striving to rise above the other monkeys.

2. *The speed of disruption.* In 2013, the value of a taxi medallion in New York City reached $1.3 million. Although Uber had launched in the city

two years earlier, its presence was yet to be fully felt. Five years later, medallions were available in bankruptcy auctions. New York City had stopped issuing new medallions indefinitely and the value of a medallion sat at around $160,000–an 88 percent drop due to the presence of Uber and its competitors. What does this portend for other markets such as, say, prescription eyeglasses? Today, online companies like Zenni Optical and Warby Parker own about 10 percent of that market.[13] As technology makes online eye exams possible, what will that market look like in a few years?

3. *Rising consumer expectations.* Amazon can deliver anything to your door in a day or two. Uber and Lyft make the process of hailing and paying for a ride seamless for both the passenger and the driver. Zappos accepts returns of unworn shoes, no questions asked, for a year after purchase. Consumers increasingly expect these experiences everywhere and always. Companies in all industries—in consumer sales and in B2B—face a rising tide of buyer expectations. Marketers must help their own companies meet these expectations or explain why they can't.

Limited Resources

In survey after survey, marketers list their number one or number two problem as "lack of resources."[14] To the modern marketer charged with performing all the duties of a traditional marketer while finding time for social media, content marketing, SEO, building marketing stacks, and real-time marketing, this comes as no surprise.

When you have limited resources, you need frequent prioritization; prioritizing twice a year does not work. You also need to spend less time planning and more time doing. Traditional marketing plans soak up time to write and time to communicate; and by the time those tasks are completed, the plans provide no guidance as to what's important now. To survive on limited resources, marketers need new ways to prioritize their work and reduce waste.

Meeting the Challenges

Marketers today are faced with an unprecedented set of challenges. This can be daunting—after all, CEOs aren't handing you more resources as they hand you more responsibilities.

We can take a lesson from medical professionals. When emergency-room staff are faced with an overwhelming number of patients, they triage: Lacking sufficient resources to care for everyone, they prioritize their patients based on the severity of their conditions and in doing so, maximize the number of survivors.

Marketers, lacking resources to do everything, must triage to maximize effectiveness. That's where Agile comes in. Agile, applied to marketing, empowers us to focus on and execute the actions most likely to have a positive business impact.

What is Agile marketing? How does it differ from traditional marketing? And how does Agile, developed for managing software, change as it is applied to marketing? Read on.

Chapter 2

What Is Agile Marketing?

It's not hard to make decisions when you know what your values are.
—Roy Disney, American businessman and
co-founder of The Walt Disney Company

O ver the years, I often attempted to define Agile marketing. I have explained it to thousands of people, over coffee, drinks, in large auditoriums, at conferences, and in classrooms. I generally start with an analogy:

Agile marketing is an operating system for marketing, like Windows or MacOS are operating systems for personal computers.

If they're interested and ask for more, I say something like the following:

Life for most marketers is chaos and frustration. Priorities change constantly; they sometimes don't know what customers want, and if they do, they can't provide it in time; they spend too much time in useless meetings; they get no respect; and while they like their jobs in theory, the day-to-day practice of marketing can be very frustrating. Agile marketing brings order to the chaos, reduces the number of meetings, brings them closer to customers, provides a productive way for them to interact with and get respect from the rest of the business, and over time reduces frustration.

And then there is my more formal definition:

> *Agile marketing is an approach to marketing that takes its inspiration from Agile software development and that values:*
>
> *Responding to change over following a plan*
> *Rapid iterations over big-bang campaigns*
> *Testing and data over opinions and conventions*
> *Many small experiments over a few large bets*
> *Individuals and interactions over one size fits all*
> *Collaboration over silos and hierarchy*
>
> *Agile marketing improves the productivity, effectiveness, transparency, and adaptability to change of the marketing function.*

What do these three definitions have in common? Clearly Agile marketing is an approach (or an "operating system") to marketing. It's also about bringing order to the chaos and responding to change. And it's about improving marketing.

Let's break the formal definition down into its component parts, starting with the phrase "an approach to marketing that takes its inspiration from Agile software development."

A Little History: Agile Software Development

In 2001, 17 developers gathered in Snowbird, Utah, to write a set of values and principles that later became known as the Agile Manifesto.[1] These developers were looking for solutions to problems that plagued development done using the standard software-development lifecycle model, known as the "waterfall" model.

The waterfall model has a number of disadvantages, including:

- Difficulty in responding quickly to changing business needs
- Difficulty in accommodating the ambiguity that is typical at the start of a project

- Working software that is delivered late in the process, making it difficult to get feedback early enough to make changes
- Lack of predictability in delivery schedules
- Rigid roles for analysts, developers, testers

The Agile Software Development Manifesto

The developers proposed the following four values of Agile software development.

Agile Software Development Values

1. Individuals and interactions over processes and tools
2. Working software over comprehensive documentation
3. Customer collaboration over contract negotiation
4. Responding to change over following a plan

It's important to note that the authors of the Agile Software Development Manifesto didn't totally dismiss the items on the right (the words in each value after the word "over"). As they put it, "while there is value in the items on the right, we value the items on the left more."

In addition to the values, Agile introduced processes for managing software development. These include Scrum, Kanban, Pairs programming, and Extreme programming.

Agile has completely transformed software development; over 97 percent of respondents to a recent survey[2] say that they have adopted Agile software-development practices in their organizations. When asked, "What was your number-one reason for adopting Agile?" they responded, "Accelerating time to market."

A Little History: Agile Marketing

A few pioneers have now begun adapting Agile values, principles, and processes to marketing. In June 2012, 35 marketers gathered in San Francisco for a meeting called "Sprint Zero." John Cass and I organized this meeting. At Sprint Zero, we drafted an initial set of values, and later issued an Agile

Marketing Manifesto.[3] The initial set of values, which were considered to be in draft form, included:

Agile Marketing Values

- Validated learning over opinions and conventions
- Customer-focused collaboration over silos and hierarchy
- Adaptive and iterative campaigns over big-bang campaigns
- The process of customer discovery over static prediction
- Flexible over rigid planning
- Responding to change over following a plan
- Many small experiments over a few large bets

Today, roughly 40 percent of marketers practice Agile, with 42 percent of the nonusers saying they plan to adopt Agile in the next year.[4]

The benefits of Agile marketing are similar to those of Agile development:

- Faster to market
- Increased ability to respond to change
- Greater transparency and measurement of the impact of marketing
- Improved collaboration

Agile marketing is also ideally suited to take advantage of digital marketing and the increasing impact of technology on marketing.

We did not nail the values at Sprint Zero. Until we meet again to revise them, I've been using a modified version of the values listed above in my teaching and writing. Let's take a look at the next part of the definition, the values, and what they mean for marketers.

Responding to Change over Following a Plan

Change is a constant. It requires continual adjustment on the part of marketers. Google changes its algorithms, new channels gain traction, and buyers increasingly use new devices to access information at critical junctions in the buying process. Companies that can quickly adjust to these changes gain competitive advantage in the marketplace.

Responding to change puts a premium on monitoring the market and paying attention to what works in the current environment, as opposed to blindly following a plan. Helmuth von Moltke the Elder, a Prussian general and disciple of Clausewitz, once wrote, "No plan of operations extends with any certainty beyond the first contact with the main hostile force," or as he is often paraphrased, "no plan survives contact with the enemy."

The same principle applies to marketing plans—no marketing plan survives contact with the reality of customers and their buying behavior. Agile marketing recognizes this truth and emphasizes responding to reality over following a plan that doesn't work.

It's not that Agile marketers don't plan. The plans they write, however, are short (one or two pages), oriented to delivering value rather than selling something, and they are subject to constant revision. If Agile marketing were music, it would be more like jazz than like classical music—just enough of a plan to ensure understanding among the band, with freedom to improvise based on what works in the moment.

Rapid Iterations over Big-Bang Campaigns

In 1959, industrialist Henry Kremer established a prize of £50,000 for the first human-powered flight around a figure-8 course demarcated by two markers a half-mile apart, starting and ending the course at least 10 feet above the ground. For more than 10 years, the prize went unclaimed, as teams struggled to create a human-powered airplane that could fly far enough and that could maneuver around the figure-8 course.

In the early 1970s, an American aeronautical engineer named Paul Mac-Cready took up the challenge. MacCready noticed that the early designs were all made of wood; they were heavy and fragile. Teams would build a design, fly it, and almost inevitably crash. It might take 6–12 months to rebuild the crashed plane. With time for only an iteration or two per year, they made slow progress.

MacCready built his plane, the *Gossamer Condor*, out of PVC tubing, wires, and a few aluminum struts covered in Mylar. When it crashed, he could quickly reassemble it; and he iterated in days, not months. Over the course of three years, he made three major redesigns and hundreds of small changes. This iterative approach (along with a large wing area inspired by hang-glider designs) netted MacCready's team the Kremer prize in 1977.

Many of our marketing campaigns still take the long-cycle, iterate-every-6-to-12-months approach used by MacCready's competitors for the

Kremer prize. The result is less innovation and less adaptation to the realities of the market.

Another factor is at work here. When marketers invest in a big-idea, big-campaign approach, they succumb to the human tendency to want to prove themselves right—to prove that the results are worth the investment. This frequently leads to "finding" data that validates the big idea. Contrast this with the experimental, iterative, metrics-driven approach advocated by Agile marketing, where marketers follow the data to a better outcome. By not investing large portions of the budget into something until after it has been proven to work, Agile marketers are more efficient with their marketing spend.

Testing and Data over Opinions and Conventions

In his brilliant book *The End of Marketing as We Know It*, Sergio Zyman tells a story about the value of data over opinions. As a matter of courtesy, when he first started working with the CEO of the Coca-Cola Company, Roberto Goizueta, Zyman took the latest Coca-Cola television ads to Goizueta and played them for him. Roberto didn't like the ads. As Zyman tells the story, he said, "Look, Roberto. If you're willing to buy a hundred percent of the volume out there worldwide, then I'm happy to do advertising that *you* like. Otherwise, I've got to keep doing it for those damn consumers."[5]

Goizueta got the point immediately, and asked Zyman to show him only the results, not the ads themselves, from then on. Sergio Zyman valued testing and data over opinions—even the opinion of the highest-paid person in the room.

For some areas of marketing, testing and data is the norm. Search-engine marketers creating pay-per-click ads routinely test headlines and offers to determine which have the highest click-through rates and conversions. In other areas, opinion still reigns. When presented with a new web design, many marketers begin by offering suggestions about the colors, layout, and overall design rather than conducting experiments to determine, "How well does it engage and convert?"

As Agile marketers, we follow the dictum often attributed to American engineer and management consultant W. Edwards Deming, "In God we trust. All others bring data." We also form a hypothesis as to which variant in a test will perform better; and then, rather than hope to see ourselves proven right, we determine through testing which variant delivers better outcomes.

Many Small Experiments over a Few Large Bets

Many organizations, including such titans as Google, Gillette, Disney, and Coca-Cola, take the 70-20-10 approach to budgeting for innovation.[6]
The 70-20-10 approach goes something like this:

- Spend 70 percent of the budget and 50 percent of your time on low-risk, known-to-work approaches. Distribute this marketing across all of our geographies and sectors.
- Spend 20 percent of the budget and 25 percent of your time innovating off these already known-to-work approaches. Again, broadly distribute this marketing.
- Spend 10 percent of the budget and the final 25 percent of your time on high-risk ideas, expecting that many will fail; and base the next generation of approaches on the few that work. Do not broadly distribute these high-risk tests; limit their scope, until they are proven, to select geographies or sectors or audiences.

Agile marketers experiment constantly. They begin with a series of small bets, investing small amounts of budget to figure out what works and what doesn't. Only when they prove to themselves and management that they have a working approach do they begin to make larger investments.

Individuals and Interactions over One Size Fits All

In 2017, software company Optimizely went from one homepage for all users to 26 versions of the homepage, each personalized for specific visitors.[7] Individuals and interactions over one-size-fits-all.

Amazon keeps track of your order history and your browsing behavior and shows you "more items to consider" on almost every page. Most marketing automation tools enable marketers to create custom calls to action (CTAs) based on past interactions and on where the buyer is in the buying cycle. Individuals and interactions over one-size-fits-all.

Marketers today create formal personas for their target segments and create personalized marketing for people based on either these personas or on customer behavior. As Agile marketers, we value individuals and interactive, two-way conversations over one-way, impersonal marketing.

Collaboration over Silos and Hierarchy

In 1998, Kellogg's launched Breakfast Mates. This convenience food combined a small box of one of Kellogg's most popular cereals with milk in aseptic containers (no refrigeration required) and a plastic spoon. This seemed like a sure-fire winner. However, it failed for several reasons: One, even though the milk didn't need refrigeration, it turns out that people don't like warm milk on their cereal; and two, no one in the marketing department told the guys in the packaging department that this product was aimed at children. The packaging was almost impossible to open without strong adult hands. Kids were either frustrated or ended up spilling the milk when they ripped open the package.

Similar examples of organizational silos leading to marketing and business failure occur every day. IT prepares for an upgrade and brings the system down just when marketing runs a promotion requiring not only that the system be up but that it also be able to handle heavy volume. An agency designs an advertising creative to drive viewership of college basketball games, but the media planners place the ads on the wrong sites and at the wrong time of day.

Agile marketing encourages collaboration by regularly bringing everyone on the project together for Scrums (brief communication meetings) to coordinate and align. Agile marketing also prescribes teams organized around delivery of value to the customer rather than around functional departments.

Agile Marketing Principles

As part of Sprint Zero, we listed (in addition to the values of Agile marketing) this series of principles that give more color and perspective to the values:

Agile Marketing Principles

- Our highest priority is to satisfy the customer through early and continuous delivery of marketing that solves problems.
- We welcome and plan for change. We believe that our ability to quickly respond to change is a source of competitive advantage.

(continued)

(Continued)

- Deliver marketing programs frequently, from a couple of weeks to a couple of months, with a preference for the shorter timescale.
- Great marketing requires close alignment with the business people, sales, and development.
- Build marketing programs around motivated individuals. Give them the environment and support they need and trust them to get the job done.
- Learning, through the build-measure-learn feedback loop, is the primary measure of progress.
- Sustainable marketing requires you to keep a constant pace and pipeline.
- Don't be afraid to fail; just don't fail the same way twice.
- Continuous attention to marketing fundamentals and good design enhances agility.
- Simplicity is essential!

These principles flesh out the values. They emphasize the importance of marketing fundamentals, design, and simplicity. Although most marketers nod in agreement when reading these statements, the principles are rarely put into practice. Take the principle, "Don't be afraid to fail; just don't fail the same way twice." I've observed many managers who pay lip service to this principle and then demote or fire the first individual who takes a chance and fails.

"Little a" agile vs. "Big A" Agile

Some argue that Agile marketing is nothing new. They have for years practiced marketing that is quick on its feet, responsive to change, and focused on the customer. That's fine. That is the world of "little a" agile marketing. It, does, after all, embody the dictionary-defined characteristics of the adjective *agile*.

How does "little a" differ from "Big A" Agile? In the specifics—the values, the principles, the approach to managing people, and above all, the process. Agile marketing is a method, the practice of which consistently yields those things that we associate with the adjective *agile*. You may feel that you are agile in your marketing, but until you replace your marketing plans with Sprints or the continuous flow of Kanban—until you identify the tasks to be done through an Agile planning process coordinated with the business and sales organizations—until you regularly communicate progress after assessing your marketing efforts through data-based metrics—until you're doing all of these all the time, you're not practicing "Big A" Agile marketing—and you're probably not achieving even "little a" agility most of the time.

Benefits of Agile Marketing

Let's take a look at the last part of the definition of Agile marketing: the benefits. Organizations that successfully adopt Agile improve their productivity, transparency, and adaptability to change of marketing. They also improve the job satisfaction of marketers and attract and retain top talent.

Beyond these benefits, Agile marketers improve the effectiveness of their marketing. The increased focus on customers, the validation of their approach through experimentation, the emphasis on measured improvements to business outcomes and the abolition of vanity metrics, the steady improvement of traffic and conversion rates through rapid iteration—these aspects of Agile improve what marketing is supposed to do in the first place: Get the word out, turn lookers into leads and then into happy customers, and blaze a trail for the rest of the organization to understand and respond to changing market needs.

This chapter answers two of the important questions about Agile marketing: *What* is it? *Why* should I adopt it?

In Part 2, we answer another question: *How* can organizations adopt Agile marketing in a way that leads to success? This is not a cookbook approach, but an approach based on mastery of appropriate disciplines and by a series of shifts in the way you think about and approach marketing.

Part II

The Six Disciplines

A gile marketing is neither a sprint nor a marathon. Agile marketing is a commitment to lifelong exercise. When you practice it every day, with commitment and consistency, the benefits accrue.

If you commit to exercise, you know that building a healthy body entails attention to all areas: cardiovascular, strength, and flexibility. Neglect one and your exercise program fails to deliver the full benefits.

Agile marketing also requires attention to various aspects, or disciplines. Each is essential. Neglect one and your Agile program fails to deliver the full benefits.

In Part 2, I describe each of the Six Disciplines and provide guidance and exercises for learning and applying them. For the process management discipline, I go into greater detail about each of the three major methodologies of Agile: Scrum, Kanban, and Scrumban.

Let's dive in by looking at each of the following Six Disciplines:

1. Alignment
2. Structure
3. Process management
4. Validated learning
5. Adapting to change
6. Creating remarkable customer experiences

Chapter 3

Introduction to the
Six Disciplines

Success is nothing more than a few simple disciplines, practiced every day.
—*Jim Rohn, American entrepreneur and motivational speaker*

When I first began coaching teams that were adopting Agile marketing, I thought it was enough to teach them the Scrum and Kanban methodologies used by software developers and show them how to adapt these methodologies to marketing. With experience, I realized that a successful Agile marketing implementation required more than adopting Scrum or Kanban. I saw that Agile marketing required the mastery of six skill sets, which I call the Six Disciplines, and a shift in the organization's beliefs and behaviors, which I call the Four Shifts.

The Six Disciplines provide a framework (not a roadmap) for adopting Agile marketing. They get marketers started in Agile marketing by emphasizing that, before doing Daily Standups or running Sprints, everyone must be aligned on what success looks like and you must have an organizational structure that enables Agile success. The Six Disciplines remind marketers

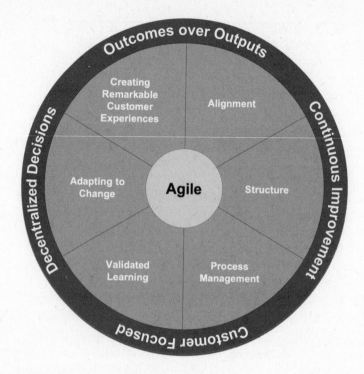

Figure 3.1   The six disciplines and four shifts of agile marketing

that implementing Scrum or Kanban as a process isn't enough—that the objective of the process is to meet customer needs, deliver remarkable customer experiences, and adapt quickly and effectively to change.

The Six Disciplines also help marketers in the middle of the journey, when they are struggling, by reminding them that a focus on core disciplines and the beliefs and behaviors that are part of the Four Shifts will put them back on track.

I represent these Six Disciplines and Four Shifts in Figure 3.1, which has become essential to my practice of Agile marketing. I'll discuss these topics in detail in upcoming chapters, but here is a brief introduction.

The Six Disciplines

If Agile marketing helps marketers be more efficient and get *more* done, alignment ensures that they are getting the *right things* done, things aligned with the needs of the customer and the goals of the business. *Alignment* is the first discipline to master; without it, nothing else works.

Structure, the second discipline, arose out of my conviction that most marketing organizations, particularly those in medium-to-large companies, are poorly structured to get the desired results. They are organized around skill sets: email marketing, digital advertising, SEO, analytics, creative, etc. I recommend organizing marketing around a portfolio of marketing initiatives that essentially answer the questions, "What does marketing need to do? What is critical for marketing to deliver?" Assign cross-functional teams to these initiatives, semi-permanent teams with the skills necessary to do their job.

I began my Agile marketing practice with the third discipline. *Process management* is the application of methodologies like Scrum and Kanban to the practice of marketing. Mastering this discipline helps reduce the chaos and allows teams to get more done while improving communication, both within the marketing team and to the customer and to other parts of the business.

The fourth discipline is *validated learning*. "Learning" because marketing requires that we learn how to satisfy customer needs and wants; "validated" because we validate that we have in fact learned this, not through opinions, guesses, and wishful thinking, but through testing and data analysis. I'd like to subtitle this discipline "Iterate Faster." Marketing organizations that iterate faster and learn faster are the most likely to succeed.

I used to tell my clients, without knowing precisely what I meant, that Agile marketing could help marketers with the fifth discipline, *adapting to change*. To some extent, that was okay; the processes of Scrum and Kanban and the rapid iterations of validated learning do help marketers adapt to change. I eventually saw, however, that adapting to change entails more than simply deploying Agile methodologies and building a culture of validated learning; I also saw that certain activities, including planning for the unthinkable, had to happen before marketers and their companies could best adapt to change.

Lastly, marketers must collaborate with everyone in the company to master the sixth discipline of *creating remarkable customer experiences*. Here, I use "remarkable" as author Seth Godin uses it: something that is extraordinary and amazing, and that people "remark upon."[1] We are no longer simply stewards of the brand; we are stewards of the customer experience. Mastery of this discipline, although it does not come easy, can have the largest impact.

The Four Shifts

Beyond mastering the Six Disciplines, organizations must make shifts in their beliefs and behaviors to become Agile. I've come to believe that they must make four critical shifts (see Figure 3.2).

Outcomes over outputs emphasizes the centrality of delivering results (outcomes) over the marketing approach of delivering outputs (marketing materials, campaigns, etc.). As marketers, we must change our mindset from "we're succeeding because we're delivering lots of content" to "we take responsibility for delivering business results." We're not Agile if we fail to deliver the right outcomes. If the result of all our Sprints, daily standups, and Kanban boards is more "stuff" shoved at customers but no improvement in business outcomes, we are just engaged in Agile for show or as some call it, Agile Theater.

Continuous improvement also applies to all of the disciplines. The wheel of the Six Disciplines doesn't imply that we implement from the top (alignment) and move once clockwise around the wheel. Given that all disciplines are avenues to continuous improvement, we must build in feedback mechanisms and opportunities to continuously improve in the application of all of the disciplines.

Each discipline benefits from a relentless focus on the needs and wants of the customer. Are we aligned on the needs and wants of the customer, and not solely on the business objectives? Do we have a common understanding of the profile of each customer we serve? Does our structure support meeting our customers' needs? Do our structures and processes facilitate quick and effective response to changes in customer behavior or in the customer base itself?

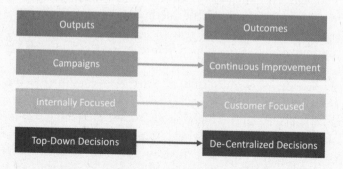

Figure 3.2   The four shifts of agile marketing

How are decisions taken when we're implementing the Six Disciplines? Are they distributed to the level of the organization most impacted and best suited to make each decision? Or are they made at the top and conveyed down and then back up the organization through tedious town halls and complex, time-wasting approval cycles?

When I teach Agile marketing to teams of individual contributors, they get it. They see Agile marketing as their opportunity to be empowered. Well, yes, and the flip side of empowerment is initiative and accountability. No one can empower you. People can get out of your way. People can help you by being what Robert Greenleaf, the founder of the modern servant leadership movement, calls a *servant leader,* but ultimately, everyone in the organization needs to take initiative and accept accountability. With the mentality, "I'm responsible for taking initiative and I take on accountability for my actions," marketers can produce great results and they can love their jobs.

Although the Six Disciplines and Four Shifts do not provide a one-size-fits-all roadmap for adopting Agile marketing, I've observed patterns as organizations adopt Agile marketing. What does a typical Agile marketing adoption look like? That's the subject of the next chapter.

Chapter 4

Overview of an Agile Marketing Adoption

Transformation is a process, and as life happens there are tons of ups and downs. It's a journey of discovery—there are moments on mountaintops and moments in deep valleys of despair.

—Rick Warren, American pastor and author

The transformation of a marketing organization—particularly a large one—into an Agile marketing organization usually gets its first push not from the top and not from the bottom, but from the middle.

A vice president or a director realizes that the organization can't sustain its current marketing practice. Things are getting done, but at the unacceptable cost of burnout—long hours and stress. It's all last-minute or late, quality is falling, and good people, to avoid burnout, are leaving.

Priorities are constantly shifting, due not to external pressures or the changing needs of customers but to the lack of internal communication and to re-work; and these, in turn, are the result of inadequate up-front communication and discussion of acceptance criteria.

This marketing organization is executing at the level of what I call "hero mode." It is only through the heroic efforts of individuals, not through teamwork and certainly not through a well-honed process, that anything gets done.

Somehow, one mid-level manager hears of Agile marketing. It sounds promising. Perhaps it can increase his team's productivity and help him deal with the seemingly crazy, constantly changing priorities. He hadn't initially thought that they were operating in silos or making decisions based on opinions rather than data, but as he heard about those things, he realized that they might apply to his organization and that they could use some improvement.

He reads some books and checks out some blogs. Maybe he even hires an Agile coach. They get started. He may or may not tell management that he is trying out Agile marketing. Sometimes this works. Often, it fails. Let's take a look at a successful effort.

A Successful Agile Marketing Transformation

Sharon (a fictional amalgam of leaders I've worked with) is a marketing vice president in a multibillion-dollar organization. She reports to the CMO; 130 people work in her group, and they collaborate with other marketers who report to Sharon's peers.

Sharon began by absorbing all she could about Agile marketing. She read books and blogs. She read the Agile Marketing Manifesto (https://agilemarketingmanifesto.org). She listened to podcasts.

She brought in a trainer who could teach Agile methodologies like Scrum and Kanban and who understood how these methodologies applied to marketing. The team attended a two-day course; at the end of the course, most were excited to apply what they had learned.

The team decided to apply a mix of Scrum and Kanban. They liked the idea of working in two-week Sprints and setting priorities in Sprint planning meetings. They also liked documenting the flow of work through their process and establishing process policies from Kanban. They picked and chose practices from each, and they planned their first Sprint.

The first Sprint went reasonably well. They didn't get everything done on their Sprint backlog—they had more interruptions than they expected, and they underestimated how long some things would take—particularly the process of approvals and reviews by people outside the team. Still, they got a lot done and they planned for their second Sprint.

Six months and 12 Sprints later, Sharon saw the benefits of their Agile practice. They had adjusted several things about the way they practiced Agile. They'd moved to a Scrumban approach, de-emphasizing Sprint planning and estimates and emphasizing the smooth and predictable flow of work. They kept their daily standups, as well as biweekly retrospectives.

Sharon reorganized to end the focus on skill sets (strategic marketing, creative, communications, analytics) and move the focus to mission (awareness, demand generation, customer retention). A few teams were still organized around skill sets, primarily because they couldn't afford to have someone with these specialized skills on every team.

She noticed that some people thrived under the Agile marketing approach while others seemed lost. Two of Sharon's first-line managers, who had always seen their jobs as telling their teams what to do, were struggling. "My team is self-managing. What's my role?" One of those first-line managers left, the other slowly began adopting a different approach to adding value to the team, coaching and hiring new people, as well as helping the team by removing obstacles.

After the reorg, Sharon focused on improvements in three areas:

1. *Reduce cycle time.* As a result of what they did in the first six months, they knew what it took to launch a promotion or generate content. They saw their process inefficiencies and focused on eliminating them.

2. *Emphasize results.* They focused on improving alignment with the sales team and with executive goals. They renewed their focus on results by holding *themselves* accountable for delivering outcomes, regardless of external trends and without blaming other groups (sales, the product, or whatever). They rigorously measured the impact of everything they did, and quickly eliminated or changed those things that didn't deliver results.

3. *Create a culture of experimentation, innovation, and continuous improvement.* They formed two teams, including people from products, sales, and marketing, to focus on two of the company's most pressing and long-standing issues. The first team focused on improving the online-to-retail experience and the second team focused on changing customer perceptions about a problem with their product that had long been solved: 25 percent of their time and 10 percent of their budget were diverted to experimenting with new approaches for reaching customers. Most of these experiments failed, and a few delivered spectacular results.

They experienced setbacks. Although efficiency improved, the work had also expanded; they still struggled to get everything done.

The previous CMO left. His replacement was skeptical about Agile marketing until one of their experiments delivered several new accounts and added millions to revenue. Many claimed credit (and it had required cross-function teamwork); data highlighted marketing's leadership in achieving this success.

They continued over the next few years to experiment with new ways of working. They established a quick-reaction team to respond to potential brand-damaging events and to take advantage of fleeting opportunities to generate positive PR. They collaborated with product management to bake marketing into the product and to create remarkable customer experiences.

Their industry changed. New technology threatened to nullify a major competitive advantage. A new competitor with a lower cost structure threatened to undercut their business model. Marketing, working with other departments, led the response to all of these threats and the company continued to thrive. Turnover dropped and marketing job satisfaction rose.

Agile spread beyond the software development and marketing organizations. Sales experimented with Agile techniques. So did finance.

Although Sharon's work life wasn't perfect, it was much better. She felt more in control. She met more regularly with her peers in other parts of the business and they were much more aware of marketing's contributions. Customer satisfaction and Net Promoter scores were trending up. Turnover had decreased and her employees encouraged others to join the company. Agile marketing had delivered!

Chapter 5

Alignment

Efficiency is doing things right. Effectiveness is doing the right things.
—Peter Drucker,
American management consultant, educator, and author

Many marketing organizations start their Agile journey by getting Agile training. Perhaps a few people attend Scrum master training and become certified; perhaps the entire team gets training on Scrum or Kanban. Learning the Agile methodologies is critical, but it is not the first discipline. Step one? Get alignment in three areas:

1. **Why are we adopting Agile?**
   - What problems do we intend to solve?
   - What must we keep (not lose) as we adopt Agile?
   - What does success look like? How will we measure our progress?
2. **Are we aligned with business?**
   - Are we meeting the needs of the rest of the business?
   - How are we contributing to the strategic goals of the business?
   - What are the most critical measures of marketing success?

3. Are we aligned with our customers?

- Who are we selling to?
- What problems are we solving for them?
- How do our customers buy?

Alignment on "Why Agile?"

When you begin your Agile journey, everyone in the marketing organization must be able to answer the questions, "Why are we adopting Agile? What do we intend to achieve?" If you're already practicing Agile, everyone must be able to answer the question, "Why do we practice Agile?" Leaders often fail to answer these questions for themselves, communicate the answers to their team, and get buy-in.

We often arrive at Agile marketing after experiencing the frustration and overwhelm brought about by traditional methods, or because upper management has told us that we're not meeting the needs of other parts of the organization; we grasp at Agile marketing as a drowning man might grasp at a life buoy. Agile marketing is not a life buoy, not a quick, simple fix for a long-unsolved problem. Rather, Agile marketing must be taken on as a commitment to an organizational and philosophical paradigm shift. The team must be realigned to solve issues and to know what success looks like and how it will be measured.

The Find Your Why exercise demonstrates one way to get alignment on these critical questions.

The Find Your Why exercise provides individuals and teams the opportunity to answer for themselves the questions "Why are we adopting or practicing Agile marketing?" and "What does success look like?"

It doesn't address how the organization will measure progress. That answer depends on why we're adopting Agile. If we're adopting Agile to improve productivity, then the team must measure productivity. If to improve communication, the team must measure communication. If to improve alignment with business and business goals, then the team must measure alignment and marketing's contribution to business goals.

While it's tempting to measure success on several fronts, choose instead a single measure or, at the most, two. And, given that we're committed to lasting change, we align the team, from the beginning, behind a metric that matters; we do not choose one later—a vanity metric—that conveniently demonstrates some improvement that makes no critical difference.

Exercise: Find Your Why

This exercise takes 30–45 minutes to complete; it is loosely based on Eli Goldratt's change matrix.[1] It builds on people's tendency to be more supportive of change if they are part of the change and if their experience is that their concerns are heard and responded to. It can be done solo or with the team and, if with a team, it is most effective when led by an independent moderator. The team leader might be present or not. If present, the team leader functions as a peer of all team members, without special status.

To facilitate change, it can help to articulate both your motivations for initiating the change and the limits of the intended change. As you fill out each quadrant of the following Find Your Why matrix, ask yourself these questions:

Keep: What elements of your current marketing practice work well? What do you want to make sure that you don't lose as you adopt Agile marketing? Another way to think about this: What are the limits of the intended change?

Improve: What can be improved? What isn't working well? Articulate your reasons for initiating the change.

Success: What does success look like? What will have changed when we successfully adopt Agile marketing? What are the benefits to the marketing organization and what are the benefits to the organization as a whole?

Concerns: What concerns do we have about the adoption of Agile marketing? What questions need answers?

Keep	Improve
Success	**Concerns**

Alignment with the Business

A complaint often made by the CEO to the CMO is that marketing does not speak the language of business. The CEO cares about increased revenue, lowered costs, and improved profitability; marketing talks brand, PR, and vanity metrics. If collaboration is about working well with others, alignment is about ensuring that marketing is contributing to the goals and objectives of the business while ensuring that the business is aligned with the needs of the customer.

Strategic Alignment

Marketing organizations do have ways to ensure alignment with organizational goals and objectives. Atlassian popularized the VTFM framework. Google, Amazon, and other tech giants use the OKR method. Either works; only effective execution matters, execution aligned on critical objectives and subject to relevant metrics.

VTFM Framework. **V**ision, **T**hemes, **F**ocus areas, **M**easurement

Vision: A singular statement, aspirational and unchanging; the reason for the organization's existence. Here's Bill Gates's 1980 vision for Microsoft: "A computer on every desk and in every home." Google's vision: "To provide access to the world's information in one click."

All of the organization's work, including the marketing function, must contribute to and reflect the vision.

Themes: A few actionable, inspirational, and durable statements, articulated by most-senior management, and known and understood by everyone in the organization. Themes tend to remain current for between one and three years. A T-Mobile theme: Radical simplicity—making it as simple as possible to do business with the company. Netflix themes: Embrace original content. Expand into international markets.

Effective themes engage our customers, motivate everyone in our organization, differentiate us from our competition, or drive change in our organization; and they tend to be measurable. They should not be "me too" statements that don't lead to productive change in the organization. You don't want themes like: "create a shopping experience that pleases our customers," "a workplace that creates opportunities and a great working environment for our associates," or "a business that achieves financial success."

Good themes involve risk. Radical simplicity led to T-Mobile doing away with contracts and data limits. Embracing original content converted Netflix from a distributor of Hollywood's output, something that people knew and liked, into a major producer of original (and unproven) movies and TV shows.

Focus areas: Focus areas are of shorter duration, typically changing from quarter to quarter. Companies recognize that they can't effectively and simultaneously satisfy all of the requirements of a theme, so management decides which requirements to focus on and in what order. T-Mobile, to realize radical simplicity, might focus for one quarter on simplifying contracts, for the next quarter on simplifying the bill, and for the next quarter on simplifying the process of switching a new customer from a competitive carrier. Netflix, to implement expansion into international markets, might focus first on Spanish-language content, second on French-language content, and so on.

Metrics: Do our themes and focus areas make any difference? Without metrics, we can't know. While articulating each theme and each focus area, we must simultaneously specify a metric relevant to the business: Does our theme or focus area increase revenue? Does it lower costs? Does it improve profitability? Does it generate a positive shift in customer behavior?

In his 2011 book *The Lean Startup*, Eric Ries decried the use of vanity metrics to measure the success of a startup.[2] He defined vanity metrics as those metrics that make us feel good but do nothing to move the startup forward. He noted that vanity metrics are often defined after the fact, as an attempt to cover up the lack of real progress in the business.

Marketers who brag on vanity metrics often disappoint the rest of the business. The following table shows some popular vanity metrics and some possible alternatives.

Vanity Metric	Metrics That Matter
Web impressions	Conversions
PR mentions	Additional traffic and leads attributable to PR
Social media followers	Additional traffic and leads attributable to social media
Net promoter score	Lower churn rate, additional repeat business
Brand awareness	Advanced multi-touch attribution data

OKR Method. OKRs—objectives and key results—were invented at Intel by Andy Grove and others. Investor John Doerr then popularized the method by requiring that all of his portfolio companies, which include Google, use it. It has since been adopted by LinkedIn, Zynga, Oracle, and Amazon.

Objectives are a hybrid of the VTFM framework themes and focus areas—typically of global scope, like themes, and of short duration, like focus areas. They can be as simple as answering the question, "What do you intend to achieve now?" Objectives are aspirational and more often qualitative than quantitative—although some companies specify the objective quantitatively, using the key results as milestones.

Key results measure the achievement of an objective by a specified time. If you can't attach a number to it, it's not a key result.

OKRs are specified at every level of the company. The company itself has OKRs, divisions have OKRs, groups have OKRs, and employees have OKRs. Part of the value of the OKR process is that employees see the OKRs of their company, their divisions, and their bosses.

OKRs must be challenging. Success is defined as achieving 60–70 percent, rather than 100 percent, of your OKRs in a given period. If you're consistently achieving 100 percent, you're probably not setting OKRs that are sufficiently challenging.

Which to Choose: VTFM or OKRs?. What matters is that you choose one. Then ensure that your marketing is aligned with the higher-level goals of the organization and that everyone understands their own goals and how they fit in with higher levels in the organization.

Tactical Alignment

In addition to alignment with the objectives and measurable results of the organization, to be effective, marketing must ensure tactical alignment. For example, if marketing executes promotions that bring many potential new customers to the website at the same time that IT is doing maintenance to the website, those potential new customers may have a bad experience. This is a case not of strategic misalignment, but of tactical misalignment.

Agile can help with tactical alignment through improved communication and the use of cross-functional teams. Let's take a look at each of these.

Improved Communication. Agile mechanisms improve communication within teams and with other parts of the organization. An important Agile practice is the Sprint review or demo. (Chapter 8 covers the demo in detail.) Essentially, it's a meeting where marketing demonstrates the work it has done, including the results and measurements of promotions or other marketing efforts.

The Sprint review improves communication between marketing and the rest of the business. This communication must be two-way: Marketing tells the company what marketing is up to; and the business provides feedback and alignment with what they're working on.

Teams that practice Kanban can also schedule reviews or demos; these meetings, however, don't correspond to a Sprint schedule.

Use of Cross-Functional Teams. Cross-functional teams, particularly those that include marketing and other departments to deliver business objectives, can also improve communication. The team knows what is going on, and non-marketing members of the team come to appreciate our skills and the challenges we face. We can likewise develop an understanding and appreciation of the skills and challenges of other groups, particularly development teams. All of this fosters teamwork, which in turn yields a great customer experience.

Alignment with Customers

As we align on our motivations for adopting Agile and align with both the strategic and tactical aspects of the business, it is also important that we align on our customer story and how we're going to tell it. Over the years, I've used a two-page model (or canvas), inspired by Alexander Osterwalder's business model canvases, for capturing that information as concisely as possible. I call it the Marketing Model Canvas (see Figure 5.1), and it consists of eight sections. A template for this canvas can be found at my website, www.agilemarketing.net/downloads.

Here's a look at each section on the Marketing Model Canvas and how to use it:

- *Who buys your products or services.* List all people and personas—decision makers and influencers—involved in your sale.
- *Customer problems and aspirations.* What problems does your customer look to you to solve? What aspirations can you put within your

The Marketing Model	Designed for: *your company*	Designed by: *your name*	Date: Iteration: 1

Who Buys Your Products or Services?	Customer Problems & Aspirations	Brand Promise	Proof Points	Brand Personality
List the various personas involved in your sale. You can fill out a persona profile for each of these personas, but in this column, just list the personas of the people you are selling to	What problems does the customer have that they're looking for you to solve? What aspirations do they aspire to that you can help them reach? What are the implications of solving these problems and fulfilling their aspirations? List both measurable, external impacts as well as internal, emotional impacts of solving problems/fulfilling aspirations.	Distill all the information about the impact of solving their problems/fulfilling their aspirations into a single sentence brand promise. Remember that brand promise is about them, not you. Read more at http://www.agilemarketing.net/stories-narratives-brand-promises/	What makes you the best guide or authority to solve their problems and help them reach their aspirations? Be very concrete on these supporting messages and proof points and check with your audience that these are believable. List only 3-4 of your strongest supporting messages/proof points.	Is your brand formal or informal? Fun or serious? Arrogant or humble? What does your brand voice sound like? Imagine that you are briefing an agency that's designing your logo or the look and feel of your primary website; what would you tell them about your brand?

How do your customers buy? (Buyers Journey)	What are the key metrics?
What stages do your buyers go through in deciding whether or not to buy, implement, and re-buy your product? Do you have multiple buyers journeys (are they different for different personas or different market segments)? You may need to illustrate the buyers journey in a separate document. Just list the major stages here.	How is marketing measured? What metrics indicate that the customer is moving from one stage of the buyers journey to the next? Which metrics are impacted primarily by marketing (as compared to metrics that are impacted by sales or product or other functions)?

The Marketing Model	Designed for: *your company*	Designed by: *your name*	Date: Iteration: 1

Competitors		
Company	What They Say About You	What You Say About Them
Company A	• Point 1 • Point 2 • Point 3	• Point 1 • Point 2 • Point 3
Company B	• Point 1 • Point 2 • Point 3	• Point 1 • Point 2 • Point 3
Company C	• Point 1 • Point 2 • Point 3	• Point 1 • Point 2 • Point 3

Figure 5.1 The marketing model canvas

customer's reach? What are the implications of solving these problems and fulfilling your customer's aspirations? List the impacts—measurable, emotional, external, internal—on your customer of having these problems solved and these aspirations fulfilled.

- *Brand promise.* Distill your "problems/aspirations" findings into a single-sentence brand promise—a promise not for you, but for your customers.
- *Proof points.* What qualifies you as the best to solve their problems and set them on the path to fulfilling on their aspirations? List three or four

of your strongest proof points, be clear and concrete on their value, and confirm with your audience that your story resonates.

- *Brand personality.* Is your brand formal or informal? Fun or serious? Arrogant or humble? What does your brand voice sound like? Imagine that you're briefing the agency designing your logo or designing the look and feel of your primary website. What would you tell them about your brand?
- *How do your customers buy? (buyer's journey).* What stages do your buyers go through in deciding whether to buy, implement, and re-buy your product? Do you have more than one buyer's journey?
- *Key metrics.* What action does your customer take to transition from one stage of the buyer's journey to the next? What core metric captures that transition? Which metrics does marketing primarily impact (vs. the metrics that sales or product primarily impact)?
- *Competitors.* Who are your key competitors? What story do they tell about you? What story will you tell about them?

Your team must eventually arrive at rough alignment around each of these eight items. Because you'll present your first attempt at the Marketing Model Canvas as a hypothesis rather than as a conclusion, plan on putting it together quickly—before you jump into Agile marketing. In a startup or smaller company, it should take no more than a day to create your first iteration of the marketing model. For a larger company, it may take a day or three; any time beyond that is better used testing and confirming a rough-draft model. In particular, if marketing teams have competing visions of one or more aspects of the model, don't gather in a conference room to resolve it. Figure out ways to test your marketing model, especially those sections in dispute.

Sustaining Alignment

Alignment, like all marketing disciplines, requires constant vigilance and practice. At least once a quarter, the marketing team re-examines its commitment to Agile, looking newly at the question, "Why do we practice Agile?" and determining whether we have new issues to resolve and better ways to measure Agile's success. Through quarterly business reviews or other regular meetings, we re-examine our alignment with the needs of the business and the needs of the customer. The Marketing Model Canvas should be re-examined and affirmed or changed on a regular basis.

Voices from the Field: Getting Alignment

When we met, Eric Schmidt was the vice president and Katie Lowell was the director of marketing and innovation at Spacesaver Corporation. They are now the co-founders of OneDayOne Marketing, an Agile marketing agency. They have practiced Agile marketing since 2016.

Jim: What prompted you to start practicing Agile marketing? What problems and challenges did you need to solve?

Eric: We were trying to drive a new mindset and, subsequently, new results with the same number of resources. We were in a reinvention at our company and needed to drive some significant results and just didn't see how that was possible with the traditional manner in which the group had worked. That traditional manner was really about spending long periods just churning and working (after getting agreement or alignment on initiatives) on building campaigns that, more often than not, missed the mark or didn't produce the needed results.

Although we had agreement, in theory, on the initiatives and the expected outcome, inevitably there was much room left for interpretation; and usually—once the team started to get into the tactics—too many variables and missing pieces were found. Historically marketing solved these issues on their own, using their experience and industry knowledge to make decisions. We also wanted/needed to get more input from those closer to the customer (Sales and Distribution) and actual customers themselves; so we looked at Agile and also adopted elements of design thinking.

Marketing also historically wasn't very data driven in our organization, and really didn't assume some of the burden of pipeline development and results. We wanted to take on some of the burden with our sales and distribution partners to strengthen the relationship and provide a more valuable service. We didn't want to be the group that just made stuff look pretty or could produce a sell sheet, when asked. We needed to start being transparent in our attempts to drive results and be ok with the accountability that comes with that.

Jim: What results did you see from adopting Agile marketing?

Katie: We began by focusing on just one of the vertical markets that Spacesaver addressed. This market had been in decline for us

(continued)

(*Continued*)

for a few straight years. Over the course of the first six months we managed to increase our qualified leads or opportunities by 70 percent for this particular market, while the other markets in this same time frame only increased by 25 percent. Accounting for a longer sales cycle, the actual sales increased by 93 percent over a six-month period compared to the same six months in the year prior. The key to creating this increase was in developing a strong partnership with the sales head of this market, creating alignment with him and his team.

Jim: How important do you think it is to get alignment before embarking on an agile marketing journey? Why?

Eric: Alignment is obviously huge; but how you have worded that question was a bit challenging for us. BEFORE embarking on the journey? Alignment for us was a constant effort that took several successful iterations to start getting light bulbs to turn on. Should there be alignment at the sales and marketing level? Of course! But our experience was that the alignment was superficial and truly not understood at the level needed to be successful. And honestly, that wasn't possible until we started and people learned together. What was critical for us, to start, was credibility and trust, at the executive and/or leadership level, and a commitment to a build-measure-learn approach. That was the crucial first step for us: to get over that hurdle and find resources that were truly willing to embark on the journey with us. And there is a difference in people saying yes, I'll support it and dig in with you, versus folks who are truly passionate about trying something new and achieving significant results. We created alignment with folks that we believed would dig in, support, and learn with us. We used those successes and stories to drive further alignment and organizational adoption. It was almost viewed or positioned amongst the organization as a pilot so as to manage expectations. Having (in our case) sales resources embedded and bought into the journey was hugely important and impactful for our organization.

Jim: You made the point that finding the right partner, in your case someone in sales, was critically important to your success. Can you elaborate on that?

Katie: We found that there was always some skepticism between sales and marketing. It was years and years of how marketing had previously operated and some perception of what marketing had always executed on that needed to be overcome. Going from a department that was looking to make things "look pretty" to leading with data to drive decisions are radically different positions. Since leading with data from a marketing perspective was "new" for the department and company, even with the facts and sources, it was a bit in question of, did you manipulate those? And what do those really mean?

Some of the data we brought forward was new to the organization and took time to help teach and get sales and others to understand. This would sometimes get lost in translation. It was important to find common terminology and educate two, three, four times to help folks understand why that data or metrics were important.

Jim: Are the challenges of getting alignment with other parts of the organization (sales, executive management) different than getting alignment within the marketing team? How are they different, and what are the challenges?

Katie: Very, very different. With marketing, we were introducing a new way of working and dealing with the inevitable issues of change and change management. We were a smaller department, so we had to figure out workload balance and flow, bottlenecks, etc.; but from a higher-level perspective, the team was brought into the Why and aligned on how this was going to make us more efficient, effective—make us a better partner to the organization. Most of the questions and issues were in the tactical level and the how of execution.

Outside the marketing department, it was a very different conversation on alignment. Again, at the highest level, people agreed on the need for alignment, but folks didn't understand how this new Agile approach was going to provide it. We went for a "prove it"-type approach—leveraging some political capital and trust to get a pilot up and running. We had a very willing resource from sales to partner with and drive early results. We leveraged these stories and results to get further awareness and understanding amongst

(continued)

(*Continued*)

the broader executive and sales team. This partner had credibility amongst his peers, so it helped when he told the story in his own words. Through a couple of sprints, we gained more and more traction and alignment with this new way of working.

One thing that we learned—and wished we had understood better going into this effort—was the need to truly embrace a growth mindset: build, measure, learn—or what you call validated learning. Too many years of launching something and then not touching it again—success being declared because you worked hard and launched the campaign. Making that transition was something that we found incredibly important.

Jim: How did you get the marketing team to get out of that campaign mindset and into the growth mindset?

Eric: What was eye-opening for me, and what I didn't realize at the time, was that people would fear putting down a specific hypothesis with a specific number about what I think is going to happen, because what if it doesn't? If I put it out there, what's going to be the recourse or ramifications if the hypothesis is wrong or I don't make the number?

We had to really work to create a safe environment for creating hypotheses. We had to help people understand that this wasn't about if we failed if the hypothesis wasn't true or we didn't make the number; this was about learning and getting better. We had to spend much more time in meetings and conversations reassuring people. We also had to set expectations with the broader business, so that they understood this as well, and they didn't look at an invalidated hypothesis as a failure. We spent a lot more time creating a safe environment than we had initially anticipated.

Jim: What methods or tools did you use to ensure ongoing alignment?

Katie: One thing that we learned right away: We wouldn't be able to follow Agile exactly as prescribed. We knew that because of our history and environment (team size, culture, history, maturity, buy-in, alignment, etc.) we would have to modify the approach. For us, we were concerned with the end game (or results) versus following or adopting a methodology to a T. This was huge for us—and I would assume for many.

We used our versions of the Sprint Planning meetings (invited key stakeholders) to provide transparency and alignment prior to a sprint. We used a hybrid Sprint review/retrospective with the stakeholders to showcase results of the sprint and talk about the process. We then shared the stories with a broader audience and welcomed dialogue. Another scary element of this for us was the notion of actually creating a hypothesis and putting some thought into the expected outcomes. That was a whole different level of scrutiny and accountability that we had to be open to. We had to make the team feel safe with this new approach. But the idea of putting out goals helped with the alignment, as it forced us to speak the same language on results and timeframes.

Jim: What do you mean by a "hybrid Sprint review/retrospective"? You included the stakeholders in both the Sprint review and the Sprint retrospective?

Eric: We thought there would be significant value for our partner in sales to get to know the marketing resources, the process we were following, and the conversations about what went well and what didn't go well. All of this helped us build credibility for marketing through that radical transparency.

There was also value in the relationships, for our sales contact to get to know the content writer and vice versa. If the content writer had questions, she could go directly to the sales contact. If he had questions, he could go directly to the content writer.

Jim: You and your partner now run a marketing agency. Are the challenges of getting alignment with the client any different? How do you ensure alignment with your clients?

Eric: This is a massive philosophical shift that is going to take time and patience (on our part). Working with a customer in an agency model, with an Agile approach, is incredibly challenging. (At least that's what we are finding.) The whole model isn't really set up to work in that manner—pricing, meetings, trust, tactics, measurements of success, etc. Many clients want to measure success in terms of deliverables and expect to pay for deliverables (time). We are shifting that model to work and deliver results. In our experience, as stated above, a big element was trust and credibility to get started. You don't necessarily have that with an agency to start with.

(continued)

(Continued)

The notion of building, measuring, and learning together is foreign for most of the clients that we have engaged with. There is a sense that you are the consultant and I am paying you to deliver results.

This notion of alignment with clients is a definite work in progress for us, and yes, has proven to be different in every case so far.

Once the team is aligned, the team must decide how to organize. This is not a simple question. Most marketing teams today are organized around marketing skill sets: digital, social media, email, print, creative, copywriting, etc. Agile proscribes cross-functional teams. What is a cross-functional team, and how do marketing organizations transition to this new way of working? That's the subject of our next chapter.

Chapter 6

Structure

Organizational structures that allow divisions and departments to own their turf and people with long tenure to take root creates the same hardened group distinctions as Congressional redistricting to produce homogeneous voting blocs—all of which makes it easier to resist compromise, let alone collaboration.

—Rosabeth Moss Kanter,
American author, educator, and management consultant

Structure, the second discipline, is as important as alignment. How you structure the marketing team impacts how the team works; it impacts how you execute, both strategically and tactically; it impacts your ability to respond to change and to deliver a remarkable customer experience.

It's not the boxes of the org chart or the lines that connect them that is important, it's how those boxes and lines impact the people, the people's propensity for collaboration, and, ultimately, the flow of work. Any process that requires crossing organizational boundaries, from idea to delivery of value to the customer, carries the potential for problems, out-of-sync priorities, and delays.

Let's illustrate this with a common example: producing a digital marketing campaign, one that potentially involves display ads, emails, the building of landing pages, and analytics.

Challenges of the typical Marketing Organization

In the typical marketing organization shown in Figure 6.1, strategic marketers are responsible for strategy and for approving copy, images, and many other campaign details. Other marketers residing in what I refer to as skill-set silos include the creative team, with graphic designers and copywriters (or an agency); the email infrastructure group that does targeting and the technical work required to get emails out the door; the web group that develops landing pages and other web deliverables; and the analytics group that sets up and publishes the campaign results.

The marketers in the strategy group compete for the resources of the skill-set silos. They call meetings to brief each group on the campaign and to prioritize the work. Priorities shift frequently, and the people in the skill-set silos, who often have no context for the shifting priorities, get frustrated. The priorities are set by the largest business units or by the leader with the loudest voice, leaving the smaller business units—those who often drive

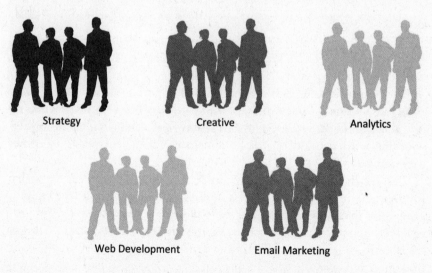

Strategy   Creative   Analytics

Web Development   Email Marketing

Figure 6.1   Typical marketing organization

company growth—starved for resources. Resources are wasted on work that isn't important to customers.

Organizational silos lead to the following problems:

- *A failure to communicate.* A campaign begins typically with a creative brief, written by the marketing strategy team. That brief is presented at a meeting to the creative team, who absorb some portion of what the marketing strategy team intends to convey. Web development and testing and measurement don't attend the meeting; they might, or might not, skim the creative brief. The result? A customer experience that does not meet the expectations of the strategy team and of the customer.
- *Too many meetings.* Each project requires meetings: meetings to share the creative brief, meetings to share the creative drafts, meetings to share the revised creative drafts, meetings to brief the web-development team, meetings to review wireframes of the customer experience, meetings to ensure that the right things are measured and the right tests run. Because members of each team work simultaneously on this and other projects, they attend daily or weekly status meetings to track the progress of each of their projects. If they work on 8–10 projects at any given time, they may attend anywhere from 8 to 50 status meetings a week.
- *Conflicting priorities.* Each employee in each silo is assigned to multiple projects, and each employee—or his or her boss—must prioritize each of those projects. Prioritizing at the level of the silo invariably produces inconsistencies and delays. For one silo, project 3 has top priority. For another, project 3 has lowest priority and project 5 has top priority. Project 3 either slows down or stops.

You can sometimes break down silos without organizational change; you can improve communication and implement virtual teams. Lasting gains, though, usually require a move from the traditional function-based structure to one built on how we add value for the customer and for the business. In this chapter, we look at working within the silo model, working within the value-based model, and effective transition from the old to the new.

Improving Collaboration Without Organizational Change

Sometimes it's not possible to change the organization. In these cases, Agile can still help improve collaboration among marketing teams.

Improving Collaboration Through Improved Communication

Improved communication is a natural byproduct of adopting and putting into practice any Agile methodology—Scrum, Kanban, or Scrumban. For example, if you build a physical Kanban board and you place that board in a prominent place in your work environment, communication improves within the team and outside the team. Everyone sees what everyone is working on. Everyone sees what's getting done and what is blocked.

Daily Scrums improve collaboration, particularly when members of multiple groups attend; issues stopping any campaign or project are uncovered and solutions generated.

Larger teams or projects requiring coordination across skill-set-silo teams can employ a technique known as "scrum of scrums." Each Scrum team designates an ambassador to meet, every day or two or three, with ambassadors from other Scrum teams. They use the standard Scrum reporting technique—covering what they've completed and what they're working on—with a focus on those blocking issues that can best be resolved through inter-team coordination.

Improved Collaboration Through Process Flows and Process Policies

Teams also collaborate by documenting the process flow for common or problematic work and by establishing and enforcing process policies for the handoff between groups. Service-level agreements (SLAs) help, particularly when working with internal service organizations (legal or finance, for example).

Chapter 9 covers how to create process flows, process policies, and SLAs.

Organizational Change to Improve Focus and Collaboration

In many cases, improving communication between groups, creating process flows, and establishing SLAs is not enough. A better approach? Cross-functional teams organized to deliver customer value or business value.

What Are Cross-Functional Teams?

Cross-functional teams are small teams of four to seven people who have all of the requisite skills necessary to deliver completed work. They may have a few dependencies: on legal to provide legal review or finance to review a promotional offer, but they should have as few dependencies as possible.

Cross-functional teams may have multiple people with the same skill set on the team, both to back up each other and to provide additional capacity. For example, if the typical Sprint requires enough work to keep three graphic designers busy, then there may be three graphic designers on the team.

Cross-functional teams are long lasting and semi-permanent. In other words, don't organize a cross-functional team around a critical one-time problem and then disband the team when the problem is solved.

The people who are members of the cross-functional team are dedicated to the team. Occasionally, if a limited amount of a certain skill set is needed, a person might provide services to multiple cross-functional teams. This should not be the most common practice, and don't split someone's time so much that it becomes a bottleneck.

Cross-functional teams can be formed solely within marketing, with multiple marketing disciplines as part of the team, or they may be formed across functional departments of the organization. For example, a cross-functional team could have one or two people from marketing, one from a business unit, one from finance, and one from operations.

Cross-functional teams are self-managing. They do not have a leader. Instead, they figure out how to get the work done among themselves. Often, people on the team have multiple skill sets or they are cross-trained, and they can help each other out. The team assumes accountability for finishing work and generating business outcomes.

Eliminate Conflicting Priorities. In organizations structured around skill-set silos, each silo has a different set of priorities. When work on a project is handed off from one skill-set silo to the next, it goes to the end of the queue. This delays the work. Cross-functional teams eliminate most, if not all, of the conflicting priorities. Everyone on the team has the same priority: the success of the project and the completion of the next iteration of work.

Improved Communication and Quality. Coordinating projects across multiple departments requires meetings. In many cases, lots of meetings. Documents and processes like creative briefs or development specifications introduce the possibility for miscommunication, with the attendant quality issues and rework implications.

Cross-functional teams improve communication and quality. A web developer, for example, develops a deeper understanding of the project if they're assigned to it from the beginning. It may seem inefficient to have a web developer or a creative sitting in on early meetings where scope, target audience, and other important considerations for the project are discussed. But these discussions provide important context, and the time "wasted" before the web developer writes code or the creative starts providing concepts is small, particularly if the team is working in an Agile, iterative fashion rather than a waterfall fashion.

Consistent Focus on the Customer Experience. Many cross-functional teams are organized around a particular customer intent, customer action, or value stream. This helps the team stay focused on the customer experience.

Faster Iteration. Organizations that seek to achieve agility should improve their ability to iterate quickly. Rapid iteration leads to testing out assumptions early on, getting direct feedback from customers, and delivering value in the marketplace before competitors.

Cross-functional teams can often iterate faster than skill-set silos. Cross-functional teams have all of the resources and the necessary skill sets available to rapidly prototype and deliver minimum viable products (MVPs).

Cross-Functional Teams Improve Conflict Resolution. This is one of the biggest and most overlooked benefits of cross-functional teams. Skill-set silo teams often spend many hours in meetings trying to reconcile conflict, each team taking a point of view that often relies heavily on the approach and biases of their formal training. Developers emphasize rigor and specificity and safety, often pushing back on approaches that postpone decisions until more is known and favoring a "right" solution. Creatives often take the opposite approach, delivering a variety of solutions and valuing the new or the different, even as some customers want the familiar. In almost all cases, teams with a full plate of work and tight schedules often have veto power over a project and there is little incentive to work with other teams.

With cross-functional teams, people with valuable skill sets are rewarded not just for exercising their skills but for the success of the project. If the schedule seems impossible or they disagree about a particular approach, rather than just throwing up their hands and going on to another project, they must find a way to resolve the conflict so that the project moves forward.

More Innovation. People with different formal training and different skill sets often look at a problem in different ways. Having multiple skill sets on the team can often lead to innovation in unexpected ways. For example, a developer working on a product whose audience is other developers may provide insight to creatives that wouldn't otherwise be available if the creative brief was written by the marketing strategy team. Someone who is experienced at testing code and finding underlying assumptions leading to unanticipated outcomes may contribute to the testing of assumptions in a marketing context. Multiple points of view may lead to unexpected insights.

There is some scientific research that confirms that cross-functional teams are more innovative. Rajeth Sethi, Daniel C. Smith, and C. Whan Park studied 141 cross-functional product development teams and found innovativeness was positively related to the strength of team member's identification with the team, encouragement to take risk, customer influence, and monitoring of the team by senior management.[1]

Cross-Functional Teams Improve Alignment and Use of Resources.
One of the common objections to cross-functional teams is that there aren't enough people in the organization to form cross-functional teams addressing all of the current problems that people are trying to solve. Rather than seeing this as a limitation, this should be seen as a strength. When forming cross-functional teams, management is forced to prioritize the problems to be solved and the most important customer processes to be improved. Teams can work rapidly to solve these problems and improve these customer processes, and then the teams can address other challenges.

Cross-Functional Teams Can Improve Employee Engagement.
A *Harvard Business Review* study that looked at the effectiveness of cross-functional teams found that 75 percent of them failed, mostly because employees were not engaged in the team, but retained loyalties to their skill-set silos. The 25 percent of teams with high levels of engagement to the project, rather than their former skill-set silos, were very successful. Does establishing cross-functional teams automatically lead to success? Clearly not. However, cross-functional teams that have strong employee

engagement to the project perform very well, better than comparable skill-set silo teams.

How to Organize into Cross-Functional Teams

You can build cross-functional teams around any of the following:

- Projects or programs aligned with business themes
- Customer challenges
- Business units
- Customer journeys

Let's take a look at each.

Business Theme Cross-Functional Teams. You provide mobile phone service. Your theme, "We make it easy for you to do business with us," has three projects:

1. Make it easy to compare the price you'd pay us against the price you pay now.
2. Make it easy to choose the right mobile phone for you.
3. Make the online-to-store process easy. (Many people research online, make their decision, and pick up in-store.)

You could form three cross-functional teams, each focused on one project. Figure 6.2 shows an example of a cross-functional team, arranged around a particular project. Note that they have a dependency on an email-marketing team, which is not cross-functional and not shown in Figure 6.2, but serves multiple cross-functional teams.

Each team has subject-matter experts (pricing, phone features, store operations), graphic designers, web developers, and analytics. The teams are long-lasting—we have many improvements that we could make for customers—and self-organizing.

Customer Challenge Cross-Functional Teams. Some marketing-specific customer challenges may be unrelated to business themes. You're with a company that is a challenger in your market space. The leader in the market space is the company that potential customers first research or talk with and is perceived to have a competitive advantage in one area. If that perceived advantage is based on old information and in fact no longer

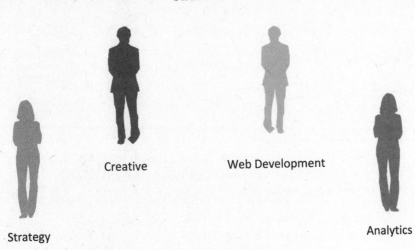

Creative   Web Development

Strategy   Analytics

Figure 6.2   Example of a cross-functional team

valid, it's marketing's job to change prospective customers' perceptions, so we organize a cross-functional team around this customer-perception issue.

Business Unit Cross-Functional Teams.   Although not usually the most powerful model, organizing a cross-functional team around business units can be the easiest way to go. It may be the best way to go if customers typically don't cross business-unit boundaries. Further, it can help align marketing with the business unit and ensure that marketing is responsive to the needs of the business unit.

If you adopt this model, then develop themes or projects for the team to tackle. The danger of not developing themes or projects is that the cross-functional marketing team may become a tactical service arm of the business unit, with no strategic focus.

Customer Journey Cross-Functional Teams.   A *customer journey* is the sequence of steps a customer takes to realize value from your product or service. Steps in the journey can take place before and after the sale. You may have a unique journey for each customer persona. (Resist the temptation to adopt someone else's customer journey or value stream. Research your actual customer's journey, through data and customer interviews.)

You've determined that your customer journey looks like what's shown in Figure 6.3.

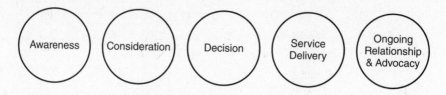

Figure 6.3   Sample customer journey

Now identify the critical marketing challenges of this journey. (If you have product or service issues, note them, but be aware that you, in marketing, probably can't solve them.)

- Are potential customers aware of your company or brand?
- Are they aware of your brand, but not that you offer a new product or service?
- Are they aware of your brand and your product, and are they eliminating you during the consideration phase because of a perceived deficiency rather than a real deficiency?
- Are you losing customers because of a mismatch between price and perceived value?

These examples of critical marketing challenges of the customer journey can be the basis for cross-functional teams.

Transitional Strategies

Should you immediately organize your entire marketing organization into cross-functional teams? In most cases, the answer is no.

If you have a small team, you are inherently cross-functional. Your decision is whether to continue doing everything at once, using Agile process methodologies to increase your productivity, or to operate like a business theme or customer challenge team, tackling the most important business theme or the biggest customer challenges first.

If your marketing team is larger than one team, transition gradually to cross-functional teams. Apply one of the following strategies:

- Implement Agile marketing only in parts of your marketing organization—starting in your content-marketing team, for example. Content production resembles software production; you can manage either with the same processes. Build a content-marketing team with all of the skill sets necessary to produce, deploy, and promote content.

- Form a cross-functional team to support a new business initiative, where the test-and-learn approach of Agile marketing is ideally suited. Build a cross-functional team with all the skills to support the new business, including people from the business unit.
- Form one or two Agile delivery teams focused on select marketing challenges or perhaps a stage or two of a customer journey. Once you realize some success from these teams, you can spread the joy to the remainder of the organization.

You may decide to have a mix of cross-functional teams and skill-set teams. For example, if you have a small team focused on video production, you may decide to leave that team alone (at least for now), and use process flows and SLAs to ensure that team effectively serves the cross-functional teams.

Voices from the Field: Cross-Functional Teams
Tara Wilkinson is the director of marketing, Best Buy Canada. They began practicing Agile marketing in 2018.

Jim: When you began your Agile marketing practice, how did you approach it?

Tara: There are two ways to get in a lake for a swim: a two-foot jump or inch by inch. We chose the latter approach to exploring and adopting Agile marketing, taking time to find the right operating model and build support.

We started with the WHY—why it's important for us to increase the metabolism of marketing. We see, firsthand, the pace of change that digital transformation and marketing technology is driving. What has been important for us to highlight is the gap between the rate of technological change and the rate at which teams typically adapt to change, as well as the exciting opportunity we have to be leaders in closing this gap. Throughout our journey, we've spent a lot of time talking about the why and creating a culture that embraces and thrives on change.

We then began introducing Agile concepts to our team members through workshops facilitated by experienced practitioners. After this, we dipped our toes in by teaching "easy and safe" Agile

(continued)

(Continued)

practices to team members keen to experiment inside their existing functional teams. Daily standups came first, then the adoption of Jira to make work more visible, and then other ceremonies like retrospectives.

Next, we set up a two-week, cross-functional team tasked with developing a proof-of-concept, go-to-market approach for a new digital-transformation business initiative. The team included marketers from various functional teams, along with someone from our Technology team who was used to working in an Agile environment, and an Agile coach. The pilot was very successful, both in terms of driving business value and in converting a few Agile skeptics to advocates. Today, we have a permanent cross-functional team dedicated to this business initiative.

Finally, we began to implement cross-functional marketing teams structured around the types of products we sell. We started by standing up an Appliances marketing team, and later expanded to other product categories. Each team includes a campaign specialist, a digital-marketing specialist, advertising coordinator(s), and designers. Specialists, like video producers and translators, remain easily accessible outside of the team. We call these teams "ARMS" teams: Agile Retail Marketing Streams.

Jim: Why did you have a mix of cross-functional and skill-set focused teams? How has that worked out?

Tara: A mix of the two team types has proven to be the best approach for us. We have teams that serve our entire company, like French translation, as well as individuals with unique skill sets, like broadcast production and PR, where it isn't feasible to have a person assigned to each business team. Instead, the cross-functional teams have real-time access to the specialists on the "support" teams whenever they need them. Fortunately, we have a collaborative and "let's make it happen" culture, so team members work fluidly with whomever they need to on a campaign-by-campaign basis.

Jim: What benefits did you see from using cross-functional teams?

Tara: The ARMS have been a huge success. The key benefits are:

1. We're doing some of our best work ever: Each team's client is the head merchant for their category. The merchants are thrilled to have a dedicated marketing team to support them, so they invest time in teaching the intricacies of their business to the marketers and designers. In turn, the marketers and designers have greater insight into the business and are more invested in the results they drive. The net result is a more engaged and knowledgeable team doing amazing work and driving better business outcomes.
2. The highest-impact work gets done first: Because the teams are focused on driving business value, they naturally do first whatever delivers the most value. Team members cross train (e.g. digital design and ad ops) so that they can swarm to help where they are needed most.
3. Things get done faster: Colocation has been key to this—team members don't brief, they talk. Instead of campaigns being worked on sequentially by functional teams, team members work collaboratively and in parallel.
4. The teams are built for testing and continuous improvement: These teams are ideally structured to test and iterate on creative audience targeting and process improvements. When they think of a better way to do something, they try it, and if it works well, we roll it out to other teams.
5. We can pivot when we need to: We've had several situations, such as a postal strike, where we've needed to pivot quickly, and our Agile teams are best equipped to do that.

Jim: How do you work with the business units? Have you formed cross-functional teams with people from the business units, finance, operations, etc. on the team?

Tara: We have done two truly cross-functional business team tests. We've had some early wins, but I think it's too soon to call them a success. Colocation has definite benefits, and there are challenges, too. In a large company, departments are like tribes; the key challenge we need to solve for is how to best keep team members connected to their community of practice and functional department.

(continued)

(*Continued*)

One initiative that has worked very well is our Creative CoP (community of practice)—designers and copywriters from all areas of the business (e-commerce, creative, print and digital production) belong to the CoP and meet regularly to exchange ideas and collaborate to ensure brand and creative consistency across all media.

Overall, we are really proud of what we've accomplished and where we're going. Our purpose is to help enrich lives through technology and we have a highly engaged marketing A-Team (Agile, Adaptable, and Amazing) committed to this purpose.

The next chapter covers what many people consider the heart of Agile marketing: the adoption of processes created by software developers to manage their work. Let's take a look at Scrum, Kanban, and Scrumban and how they can be used by marketers.

Chapter 7

Process Management

If you can't describe what you are doing as a process, you don't know what you're doing.
—*W. Edwards Deming, American engineer and management consultant*

Applying processes like Scrum and Kanban to manage marketing is what many think of as Agile. My focus when I began my Agile marketing practice was on translating the software-development methods of Scrum and Kanban into methods that work for marketers.

What are these methods? How and why were they developed? What benefits can we expect from adopting Scrum, Kanban, or some combination of the two?

Scrum

Scrum was first mentioned in conjunction with product development in a 1986 *Harvard Business Review* article called "The New New Product

Development Game."[1] That article did not fully flesh out the Scrum methodology, but it did contribute to some of its most important concepts, including nonlinear development and the use of self-organizing project teams. They borrowed the term *scrum* from the sport of rugby to emphasize the importance of working as a team, particularly during the daily huddle.

In 1993, one of the creators of Scrum, Jeff Sutherland, was the first to apply it to a software project. He developed the process with Ken Schwaber, who presented the first description of the methodology for software development at OOPSLA in 1995.[2] In 2001, both attended the meeting in Utah where the Agile Manifesto was written.

Scrum was born of a need to address emerging global issues in software development: increasing complexity, fast-changing customer requirements, time-to-market failures, declining quality, delays in delivery, and new risk-management challenges. All of these issues confront modern marketers.

Scrum delivers work every one to four weeks. During those periods, known as Sprints, if unplanned work is added, something of similar scope must be removed from the planned work. Scrum delivers work in packets at the end of the Sprint, not during the Sprint. Kanban, the other major Agile methodology, emphasizes the smooth, predictable flow and delivery of work. See Figure 7.1 for an overview of Scrum.

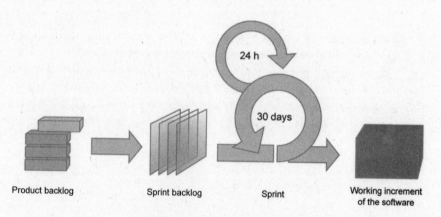

24 h

30 days

Product backlog   Sprint backlog   Sprint   Working increment
of the software

Figure 7.1   Scrum overview
Source: Scrum process; Wikimedia commons

Scrum has more predefined roles (scrum master, product owner) and meetings (Sprint planning session, daily standup, Sprint review, Sprint retrospective) than does Kanban. While Scrum is fairly straightforward to learn, it can be quite challenging to master.

Kanban

Kanban was created in the 1940s by Taiichi Ohno to increase manufacturing efficiency for Toyota, and was adapted decades later for software. Kanban's primary aims are to reduce the time to finish well-understood work by reducing bottlenecks; to ensure quality by applying process policies; and to provide flexibility, as work changes, through evolutionary adaptations of process flow.

Kanban—which literally means "a card that you can see"—emphasizes a visual approach to tracking the status of work items. Hence, its most well-known artifact is the Kanban board, a simple version of which is shown in Figure 7.2.

It can be easier to get started with Kanban than with Scrum, because Kanban entails less up-front learning of formal methodology and has fewer new terms and concepts. Beyond the early stages, however, Kanban can be challenging to master.

Figure 7.2 Simple kanban board
Source: Jeff lasovski, https://commons.wikimedia.org/wiki/File:Simple-kanban-board-.jpg. Licensed under CC BY-SA 3.0.

Scrum is the most popular of the Agile methods, but Kanban is gaining on it, particularly among more mature teams. Marketing teams use both methods.

Scrumban

Scrumban is a mash-up of the methods and practices of Scrum and Kanban, and is also now a recognized methodology in its own right. Corey Ladas first described Scrumban in his 2008 book *Scrumban: And Other Essays on Kanban System for Lean Software Development*; Ajay Reddy's 2015 Scrumban book for software developers, *The Scrumban [R]Evolution: Getting the Most out of Agile, Scrum, and Lean Kanban,* also works well for Agile marketers.

Begin new paragraph Reddy defines Scrumban as a framework within which each organization can evolve Scrum to a unique set of processes and practices. Scrumban uses Kanban as a lens to evolve Scrum to the organization's preferred and most productive way of working. Scrumban has longer duration than Scrum—rather than wiping the Kanban board clean at the end of each Sprint, Scrumban provides powerful methods for handling unfinished work. Because Scrumban recognizes that the time spent rigorously estimating each task and building a Sprint backlog rarely produces commensurate value to the customer, it uses lightweight estimating and only enough planning meetings to ensure a smooth flow of work.

Benefits

Marketing teams adopting Scrum, Kanban, or Scrumban can expect to reap improvements in at least three areas:

1. *Communication.* Daily standups increase communication among team members. Everyone, including management, can see the status of projects and progress through physical or digital Kanban boards. Meetings like Sprint planning sessions, Sprint reviews, and Sprint retrospectives increase communication in planning, demonstration of completed work, and process improvement. Many Agile teams also hold quarterly business reviews to further communication in large teams.

2. *Prioritization.* Low-producing marketing teams prioritize using the "loudest voice in the room" method. Scrum and Kanban, each in its own way, enforce more rational prioritization and shield the team from random interruptions. This increases team efficiency while raising morale.

3. *Discipline.* Building a backlog, deciding what work gets done in the next Sprint or how work flows through a Kanban process, holding daily standups to recognize blocking issues early on, establishing and enforcing process policies, reviewing work with shareholders early on to get feedback: Each practice enforces discipline on notoriously undisciplined marketing teams.

Which to Use: Kanban, Scrum, or Scrumban?

Adopt the method that works for your team. Try one for a time (at least 90 days) and evolve.

Many teams mix and match Kanban and Scrum without learning the formal approach of Scrumban. This often leaves them with little understanding of either methodology, no experience of the power of either one, and an inability to take their mix-and-match methodology to a level where it makes a serious difference. I don't recommend this mix-and-match approach.

Here are some recommendations as to which methodology to use for each marketing discipline:

- Content marketing, website development, sales tool development, and marketing-technology implementation lend themselves to Scrum. They can be planned in advance, with fewer interruptions as the norm. Incremental delivery once or twice a month is acceptable.
- Social media, PR, analyst relations, and marketing-technology support lend themselves to Kanban. They often cannot be planned and can't wait two to four weeks for a deliverable.
- Everything else can be delivered with Kanban, Scrum, or Scrumban.

	Scrum	Kanban	Scrumban
Iterative- or flow-based	Iterative	Flow	Flow, with planning and retrospective sessions as needed
Push- or pull-based	Mostly push; members can pull work after completing their first assignment	Pull	Pull
Estimation Prescribed meetings	Required Sprint planning, Sprint review, Sprint retrospective, daily standups	Optional None; teams may hold daily board reviews and retrospectives as needed	Optional or lightweight Planning on demand, daily standups, optional retrospective
Prescribed roles	Marketing owner, scrum master, team	Team	Team, optional scrum master
Unplanned items allowed during iteration	No	Yes, added to top of queue	Yes, added to top of queue
Kanban board	Reset after each Sprint	Persistent and continuous	Persistent and continuous
Best suited for	Content marketing, website development, sales tool development, Martech implementation, demand generation	Social media, Martech support, PR/AR, Creative teams and agencies, events	Startups, anyone who has practiced Scrum and wants to apply evolutionary improvement aspects of Kanban and reduce planning time

Figure 7.3   Comparison of Scrum, Kanban, and Scrumban

Voices from the Field: Scrum, Kanban, or Scrumban for Marketing?

Justin Zimmerman is the director of Content Development at REDX (Real Estate Data X-Change). He has practiced Agile marketing since 2018.

Jim: Did you start with Kanban or Scrum? Why?

Justin: Like a lot of companies, we started with Scrum. That was the low-hanging fruit for us. We started with Jeff Sutherland's *Twice the Work in Half the Time*. It addressed my pain points and problems. Just like building software, marketing experiences some of the same problems: waste, restart, frustration that the ratio between the amount of work and the output wasn't anywhere near optimal.

We started with two-week Sprints. We modified the language but kept the principles. We weren't dogmatic about following the precepts of Scrum, and there's a part of me that wishes we had been. We tended to blur the end of one Sprint with the beginning of the next. We scheduled regular Friday meetings, which we called kickoff meetings, every two weeks. Getting these on everyone's calendar was an important first step; it made it more real. The name was also important. I'm a writer by trade, and words matter, so we changed the name to Start Right meetings.

The two-week container of the Sprint had advantages that drove people to finishing a body of work, but without assigning due dates to each item. This was better than assigning a due date to each item, which would have resulted in us managing due dates rather than managing work.

Jim: What worked and what didn't in your use of Scrum?

Justin: We moved to a mix of Scrum and Kanban. If I were to modify our process, I'd switch us to 75 percent Kanban, 25 percent Scrum. We'd keep daily standups and Sprint meetings but make the Sprint planning mini-meetings. Instead of committing to everything in a two-week Sprint, we'd just create the next body of work to work on.

Jim: Sounds like you're headed to Scrumban.

Justin: Yeah, that's the direction we want to go. We need to get our WIP limits in place to get our flow right. We don't want to refactor or hold a Planning Poker session every Sprint planning session. There's a certain amount of predictability in a newsletter campaign, in a webinar, in a blog post. The amount of effort to get each of those out would become institutional or team knowledge. Then we have estimates without doing Planning Poker.

Jim: What did work as you adopted Scrum? What were the benefits?

Justin: The concept of the deadline of the two-week period gave the team a goal. The concept of a container of work. You could have a lot less management with team accountability. The

(continued)

(*Continued*)

manager didn't have to micro-manage everyone, asking the question: Is this done? We came up with the saying "visibility equals autonomy." The whiteboard helped us visualize the existing work. We let people pick and choose what they wanted to work on, based on priorities. Letting the teams self-organize around the Friday deadline.

I have this graphic in my office: storming, norming, performing, etc. There is this image that shows the manager in front of the team, the leader standing in the middle of the team, the leader standing in the ring of the team, the leader standing outside the team. Over the last 2½ years, it took me standing in front of the team, being a bit of a dictator, to set up the process; now that the process exists, it serves as a scaffolding for new projects. Instead of me having to manage every one of these projects, the team manages them. Each person's strengths show up. I get to step back and allow them to lead the process.

Jim: How have you coordinated your Agile methodologies with other departments (development, perhaps others) and your "clients" in the business units?

Justin: For a long time, funny enough, marketing was the leader in Agile for the company. Then the CMO got promoted to COO. What we pioneered was what the rest of the company started thinking. They're not quite there yet; they're getting there.

In particular, the product managers are coming to us and suggesting that we align the workflow process. That's our vision of how we'd like things to work.

Jim: What about for big projects, like your response to Covid-19? What are you doing? Do you coordinate with other departments? Do you have joint standups?

Justin: Yes. Let me explain the hierarchy of our meetings. Marketing has a daily standup. We have our bi-weekly planning meeting. Marketing—the entire department, not just my team—holds a leadership meeting before the company meeting, which is before the individual department level meetings. Therefore, anything that happens at those leadership-level meetings can influence the individual department-level meetings. We have a lot of top-down process, and a lot of information flowing up.

We also have a quarterly offsite, where the department heads meet with the executive team to talk about the initiatives for the quarter. The next level up is our annual goals, those that tie to our mission, etc.

Jim: What do you see as the difference between Scrum and Kanban, and which would you recommend for marketers?

Justin: The reality is that you can put a very structured, precise Scrum process with two-week Sprints in place, but unless you're working with a company whose culture would enforce that, it's not going to work. Most companies change priorities frequently, which pushes you toward a Kanban-like flow process.

There's a newly established chain-of-command where new priorities come to the product owner so the prioritization doesn't interrupt the work of the individual contributors. The biggest problem I see in most marketing organizations is the constant context-switching. Anything a team can do to reduce this is good. Protect the executers from interruption. The exceptions are what we call *leprechauns* or *fires*. Leprechauns are unique opportunities that need to be acted on now. Fires have to be acted on immediately to protect your reputation. Everything else needs to be prioritized without interrupting the individual contributors.

As far as contrasting them goes, most marketers drift toward the flow of Kanban, so perhaps marketing teams should start there.

Let's take a deeper look at each of these methodologies, starting with Scrum, and how it can be adapted to help marketing teams achieve greater levels of agility.

Chapter 8

Scrum

Multitasking Makes You Stupid. Doing more than one thing at a time makes you slower and worse at both tasks. Don't do it. If you think this doesn't apply to you, you're wrong—it does.

　　　　　　　　　　　　　—*Jeff Sutherland, author and co-creator of Scrum*

S crum is an iterative and lightweight project management methodology, best suited to complex problems with changing requirements. It was developed to manage software projects; *you* can use it, with a few tweaks, to manage your marketing projects.

Scrum Basics

Figure 8.1 illustrates the Scrum process.

Scrum begins with a *backlog*—a list of deliverables requested by stakeholders (customers, management, sales) or developed by the marketing team to achieve marketing goals. In standard Scrum, we describe those deliverables in terms of user stories to better understand the audience: Who are they? What do they want to accomplish? Why will doing so matter to them?

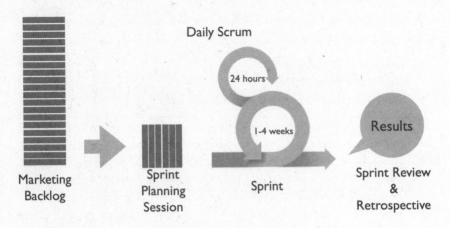

Figure 8.1 Scrum process

The Scrum methodology includes someone—a person or a team—responsible for managing the list of deliverables and writing user stories, clarifying them, and prioritizing them; and who represents the voice of the customer and ensures that the team delivers value to the customer and to the business. An individual who fills this role is called the marketing owner. If there is not an individual marketing owner, the team fulfills the role, with everyone responsible for delivering value and for writing, clarifying, and prioritizing user stories.

During the Sprint planning meeting, the team reviews the backlog and agrees upon the set of deliverables—the Sprint backlog—to deliver during the current Sprint. The scrum master—through a daily standup meeting and a tracking tool (an electronic tool or a whiteboard, usually a Kanban board)—tracks the completion of these deliverables and maintains the burndown chart, a visual representation of how the work is progressing.

A *Sprint* is a period during which the team works on and completes the work in the Sprint backlog. The team determines the period—usually one to four weeks. Most teams start out with two-week Sprints and lengthen or shorten the duration as needed.

A Sprint may or may not have an organizing theme, sometimes called the Sprint goal. A theme can be anything that helps the team focus; it's usually related to business priorities, projects, events, customer needs, or a portion of the customer journey. I encourage teams to follow the practice of having an explicit theme for each Sprint; this helps each Sprint have a larger impact than if each Sprint is simply a random collection of deliverables or tasks.

The *daily Scrum* is a short standup meeting, where each team member answers three questions:

- What did I do yesterday?
- What will I do today?
- Are there any obstacles that stand in my way?

The team does not attempt to remove the obstacles in the daily Scrum meeting. Instead, the scrum master either pulls people aside after the meeting, allowing the other members of the team to engage in productive work, or notes the obstacle and works to solve it before the next Scrum meeting.

Although it is called the daily Scrum, not every team holds these meetings daily. When you're new to Scrum, hold daily standups. Mature teams may decide to hold standups every two or three days; longer gaps between meetings increase the risk of obstacles not getting solved quickly and delaying the completion of work for the Sprint.

When the Sprint is finished, the results are reviewed with stakeholders at a one- or two-hour meeting called the Sprint review. The Sprint review provides opportunity for early feedback and encourages transparency and trust between the marketing team and the business units.

After each Sprint, the team holds a 30-minute to 1-hour Sprint retrospective meeting to discuss changes they want to make to their process to improve efficiency or effectiveness. Iteration applies not only to our marketing but also to the process by which we manage our marketing. The Sprint retrospective provides the opportunity to iterate on our process.

To summarize, Scrum has four key meetings or events:

- Sprint planning
- Daily Scrum (or standup)
- Sprint review
- Sprint retrospective

Scrum also has three key roles:

- Marketing owner (known as product owner for developers)
- Scrum master
- Team members

Lastly, Scrum has a number of artifacts or deliverables that help Scrum teams do their work. The most common of these are:

- Marketing backlog
- Sprint goal or theme

- Sprint backlog
- Burndown chart

Scrum also prescribes that the four- to seven-person team be cross-functional and self-organizing. Larger organizations, with multiple Scrum teams, have available a variety of methods to coordinate them. We'll look at scaling Scrum in Chapter 24.

Good books on Scrum include *Scrum: The Art of Doing Twice the Work in Half the Time* by Jeff Sutherland and J. J. Sutherland; *Agile Project Management with Scrum* by Ken Schwaber; and *Essential Scrum: A Practical Guide to the Most Popular Agile Process* by Kenneth S. Rubin. Some marketers take courses and seek certification as a Certified Scrum Master, although many of these courses focus on software development and ignore the unique challenges faced by marketers.

Let's take a look at how we can adapt Scrum to the needs of marketing.

The Marketing Backlog

I recommend that marketing backlogs consist of delivery increments and tasks, *not* user stories. This is different from standard Scrum, where each entry in the backlog is a user story. Each delivery increment and some tasks will have an associated user story, but the user story is not the unit of work. Why is this?

While developers typically have multiple ways of fulfilling a user story, they generally choose just one. They implement a new feature one way among all the different possibilities for implementing that feature. Marketers also have multiple ways of fulfilling a user story. They may write a blog post. They may film a video. They may create a webinar. They may write an Ultimate Guide. Unlike developers, who choose one of these possibilities, marketers typically choose several or all of these possibilities.

Delivery increments are marketing deliverables: a blog post, a video, a web page, a webinar. We say *delivery increments* rather than simply saying *deliverables* because some deliverables take more time to deliver than is available in a single Sprint. In this case, portions of the final deliverable are delivered in increments.

A delivery increment is a completed portion of work—it goes through the whole process used to deliver work to the customer. This applies even if the delivery increment is not delivered to the customer at the end of the Sprint. Let's say, for example, that your marketing team is producing a large document, the Ultimate Guide to whatever you sell, and that the Ultimate Guide runs 50 to 100 pages. You likely can't outline, write, edit, revise, and get approvals for that entire document in a two-week Sprint. Rather than outline the document in one Sprint, write it in the next, edit it in the next, and so forth—you deliver portions of the document in increments. In the first Sprint, you might deliver the introduction and Chapter 1. Then go through the entire process—outline, write, edit, revise, and approve—in a single Sprint. In future Sprints, the team works on other delivery increments—subsequent chapters. When all chapters are done, you publish the document; and you may decide to add a task to the Sprint Backlog: promote the Ultimate Guide.

This Ultimate Guide can be called an *epic*. An epic, in Scrum terminology, is any chunk of work that requires multiple Sprints to deliver.

We break up—or decompose, in developer jargon—projects or deliverables in a backlog into smaller chunks—delivery increments—to be delivered within the scope of one Sprint. Many teams break up work into delivery increments that take no longer than two or three days to complete. This encourages a regular flow of completed work and makes it easier to estimate the overall amount of work to be done.

Some marketing tasks are not end-user deliverables. You may decide, say, to audit your website to ensure that you have material for each stage of your customer journey. That audit is a not a delivery increment; it's a *task* in a marketing backlog.

Take care to have more deliverables than tasks in your marketing backlog. Tasks are often internally focused, whereas marketing deliverables are customer-focused and deliver value to the customer. Also make sure that you decompose large deliverables into smaller delivery increments that can be completed during a Sprint.

Writing Agile Marketing User Stories

Although in marketing backlogs the user story is not the unit of work, we still write associated user stories for all deliverables. A user story is a high-level description of what the user needs to do and why, where the user is a prospect, a customer, or an internal stakeholder. The standard way to write a user story for developers is as follows:

As a [type of user], I want [some goal] so that [some reason].

I recommend that marketers write user stories in a slightly different fashion:

As a [role or persona], I want to [list the task to be done or need to be fulfilled], so that I can [list the benefit of accomplishing that task or fulfilling that need].

The difference may be subtle, but I think it's important. Marketers are accustomed to understanding customer needs (or wants) and benefits. Write your user stories in terms of these needs (or wants) and benefits. Marketers will find the greater specificity of my recommended approach to be more helpful in satisfying a user story.

Here is an example of a marketing user story:

As a father of young children, I want to save money on a visit to Disney World so that I can take my kids on a vacation that they'll never forget and be a hero in their eyes.

User stories take us out of our head as marketers and help us understand what our audience wants to accomplish, and why. For that reason, always write them from the audience's perspective rather than from your marketing perspective.

Be as specific as possible in writing user stories. Notice how the user story above is much more effective than the general user story below:

As a customer, I want a discount coupon so that I can save money.

Writing user stories from the audience's perspective can be difficult at first for teams accustomed to working in skill-set silos. For example, let's say that delivering a promotion requires the skills of three different people, one to come up with the promotion, one to create the graphic design, and a third to write the copy or words of the advertisement. These three people should not write three different user stories:

As a customer, I want to take advantage of a promotion so that I can save money.

As a customer, I want an eye-catching graphic so that I will be attracted to this promotion and save money.

As a customer, I want to understand the terms of the promotion and get excited by the possibilities of taking my kids to Disney World.

User stories do not specify the delivery vehicle; they may be satisfied by multiple deliverables. For example, a user story about a user seeking information to make a better decision about your product could be satisfied by a blog post, a white paper, a webinar, or a video, and perhaps by all four.

You may break down some of the specific tasks to be done to satisfy the user story. Don't make those tasks too specific; rather, leave room for creativity and initiative by the marketer creating the content or the promotion to satisfy the user story. List only enough specifics to give a sense of the scope of the user story.

In describing the benefit of accomplishing the task, specify emotional reasons for doing so. Buyers buy for more than logical reasons; they often need a compelling emotional reason to buy. This aspect of the user story does not apply in the development world.

Every user story must have acceptance criteria described in advance; qualities that managers or marketing owners look for in the deliverable or delivery increment. The marketer doing the work can't read minds! When managers or marketing owners have assumed or hidden expectations, the deliverable inevitably goes through unnecessary rounds of review and revision.

Here's how *not* to write user stories:

As a marketer, I want to create and deliver a webinar so that I can generate leads for our salesforce.

What's wrong with this user story?

- It comes from the point of view of the marketer, not from that of the customer/prospect.
- It specifies the delivery vehicle (a webinar).

As a prospect, I want to watch a webinar so that I can understand the basics of marketing automation.

Although this revised user story comes from the point of view of the prospect, it still fails. Why?

- The prospect role or persona is not specific. What kind of prospect am I? What is my role in the buying process?
- It still specifies the delivery vehicle (a webinar).
- It states a vague goal (understand the basics of marketing automation) but no emotional benefit.

A better user story might be something like this:

As a manager of marketing automation, I want to understand the basics of marketing automation, so that I can select the best marketing automation tool for us, reduce the risk of making a bad choice, and feel good about improving the productivity of my team.

In the acceptance criteria, the marketing owner might expand on "the basics of marketing automation," ensuring that the deliverable in fact meets the criteria of "the basics."

Building and Grooming an Agile Marketing Backlog

Perhaps the simplest way to begin building an Agile marketing backlog is to list everything on the To Do list of everyone on the team, and then to create delivery increments and write user stories for these To Do items. As you do this, you may find that some of the items on your To Do list—attending meetings, reading and returning emails, writing marketing plans, attending training courses, updating status reports—aren't customer deliverables. You can't avoid overhead items but, as they do not add value for customers, you can exclude them from the marketing backlog.

In other cases, an individual To Do item may be a small part of a larger deliverable that needs only one user story. If you break a large deliverable into delivery increments, all of the delivery increments may share the same user story.

Some marketing, like social media, seemingly does not lend itself to the user story format. However, it always makes sense to keep the customer/ prospect point of view in mind, even when you're composing a tweet.

- Who is the audience for this tweet?
- What problem, need, or want am I solving or satisfying for the reader?
- What benefit does the reader get by reading or acting on this tweet?

Another approach to generating an Agile marketing backlog is to audit the buyer's journey and customer experience for all personas and channels, looking for gaps or weak marketing in each stage, in each persona, and in each channel. Because such an audit can add many items to the marketing backlog, it may make sense to audit one stage, persona, or channel at a time.

A third approach to generating a marketing backlog starts with key business themes, breaks them into major initiatives, breaks initiatives into projects, and breaks projects into deliverables and delivery increments. This approach ensures that everything in the marketing backlog supports a key business theme and that the relationship of each deliverable to the business is clear to everyone in marketing and to other departments and executives in the organization.

Format for Marketing Backlog Entries

I have a standard format for entries in the marketing backlog. Let's start with an example of an entry on a card that is part of a physical Kanban board (see Figure 8.2).

The title is the name of a deliverable or delivery increment. The *user story* is next, followed by acceptance criteria. Teams can add comments: the scope of the deliverable and assumptions to understand the size of the task. Somewhere on the card, specify the priority, any story points (the size of the task, as covered below), and the due date, if there is one. Leave a corner of the card open to affix a red dot to indicate a blocked item or to add hash marks to indicate the age of a card in a column. To learn more about how to handle blocked items or aging (tracking how long a card has been in a particular column without moving on to the next column), see the section "Daily Standup: Best Practices," later in this chapter.

Key Roles: Scrum Master and Marketing Owner

The role of the scrum master is unique to Scrum and one of Scrum's greatest contributions. A good scrum master can improve the efficiency and the job

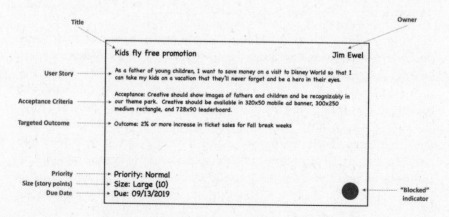

Figure 8.2   Sample marketing backlog card

satisfaction of the team. The scrum master is not the team lead; typically, no one on the team reports to the scrum master.

Some teams choose their scrum master and/or marketing owner, but it is more common that management chooses people to fill these roles. Scrum masters often attend training specific to their role and earn the designation Certified Scrum Master (CSM). Scrum masters need to have great organizational skills, both in terms of organizing and tracking work, as well as navigating the politics of an organization and exerting influence without authority.

Marketing owners need to have in-depth knowledge of the needs of customers and of the business's goals and objectives. They generally set the priorities of what gets done when and clarify requirements for user stories and deliverables. Marketing owners tend to see the big picture and take a strategic approach; scrum masters tend to be detail-oriented and take a tactical approach. This difference explains why it is difficult for one person to play both roles.

The scrum master helps the team stay on track by removing impediments and obstacles. For example, if getting approvals from one approver is consistently difficult, the scrum master works with the approver to eliminate the bottleneck. If the team lacks tools or resources to complete tasks in the Sprint, the scrum master ensures that this situation is addressed.

The scrum master also coaches the team in Scrum principles and ensures that the team neither over-commits nor under-commits during Sprint planning. The scrum master helps the marketing owner maintain the backlog, and the scrum master organizes meetings or ceremonies: Sprint planning session, daily Scrums, Sprint review, Sprint retrospective.

Is the role of the scrum master one thing for marketing teams and another for software development teams? The short answer is no.

Marketing teams tend to find it more difficult to justify the role of the scrum master than do development teams. Until Agile marketing becomes pervasive, and the need for a scrum master is self-evident, the best way for marketing teams to handle this might be to combine the role of scrum master with that of the marketing owner.

Having one person serve as scrum master and marketing owner can be a way to justify the position early on, but it is not ideal. It might make sense to separate these positions later, particularly if the person fulfilling both roles becomes overburdened. It can also help to justify the position by giving this position a name other than scrum master or marketing owner; perhaps marketing coordinator.

If you absolutely can't dedicate at least one person per team as the marketing owner/scrum master, ask one person on the team to serve as marketing owner/scrum master and rotate responsibility for the role every three months or so. This will give everyone a chance to learn the role and appreciate the challenges that come with fulfilling the role.

Sprint Planning Session: Best Practices

At the Sprint planning session, the marketing team selects which delivery increments to deliver in the upcoming Sprint. The inputs to the session are team capacity, marketing backlog, current business priorities, product status, and competition. The outputs are a Sprint goal or theme and the Sprint backlog.

A best practice for Sprint planning happens before the Sprint planning meeting: a backlog-grooming session in which the marketing owner and the scrum master add delivery increments, remove delivery increments unlikely to be completed, and prioritize a rough selection of the top delivery increments for consideration during Sprint planning. They also clarify scope and add acceptance criteria to the delivery increments.

Although the temptation may be to prioritize everything first, scope it, and estimate it, and finally select enough of the prioritized, scoped, and estimated tasks to fit within the team's capacity, this strays from best practice. As shown in Figure 8.3, teams select the first priority, scope it, estimate it, and then subtract the effort to complete the story from the team capacity. This process continues until the team capacity is exhausted, thus preventing scoping and estimating of tasks not selected for the Sprint.

Other best practices include:

- The team, not the manager, assigns the estimates.
- Team members select their delivery increments as late as possible—during execution. The team does not plan who executes which delivery increments during the Sprint planning session.
- Members can decide to collaborate on a delivery increment.
- Team capacity, also known as velocity, is measured and then used in subsequent Sprints in place of the initial velocity estimate.

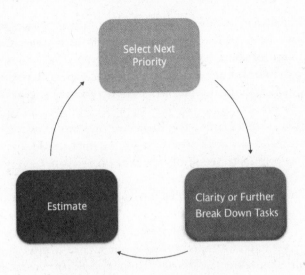

Figure 8.3   Sprint planning process

Teams may be tempted to assign Sprint tasks to team members based on skill sets, intending to ensure that no team member is overloaded. This approach is counter to the spirit of Agile, where the team, not individuals, takes responsibility for completing all work of the Sprint.

It follows that the team members have multiple skill sets and that the composition of the team includes enough members with specialized skill sets to complete the work. The number of graphic designers on the team, for example, should roughly match the amount of graphic design work in a typical Sprint. If one Sprint entails less graphic design work, then the graphic designers may be deployed to other tasks or they may be underutilized. Sacrificing 100 percent utilization is preferable to the inefficiencies of vertical silos and so called "virtual" teams, which are not teams at all.

Choosing the Length of Your Sprint

The official Scrum guide isn't much help in choosing the length of your Sprint. It defines a Sprint as "a time-box of one month or less during which a 'Done,' usable, and potentially releasable product Increment is created." Okay, that defines the maximum length, but should the team choose one-week, two-week, or four-week Sprints?

I favor Sprints of one or two weeks. These shorter Sprints provide more opportunities for feedback and course correction, whether that feedback comes from the marketing owner or from customers. Say you're working on a website redesign and the entire project is estimated to take three months. With month-long Sprints, you have only two opportunities for feedback (see Figure 8.4).

With two-week Sprints, you have five opportunities for feedback in three months, and with one-week Sprints, 12 opportunities.

Shorter Sprints also tend to keep the team focused. Construct delivery increments in chunks to be delivered within the scope of the Sprint. The team also has more opportunities to experiment with ways of working, as they review their effectiveness at each retrospective. This can make a difference with less mature teams, as the team figures out what works.

So why wouldn't every team choose one-week Sprints? More frequent Sprints require more frequent Sprint planning meetings, Sprint reviews, and Sprint retrospectives. These meetings add overhead.

Choose the shortest-length Sprint that works. If you believe that you can have short, focused, and effective Sprint ceremonies (planning, reviews, and Retrospectives), then go for it with one-week Sprints. Otherwise, begin with the two-week Sprints most commonly used by developers and marketers.

The marketing team does not have to choose the same Sprint length as the development group. This may seem counterintuitive, but most development teams don't ship at the end of every Sprint. Shipping a product release may result in work for the marketing team, but as long as you take this into account, you can choose a Sprint length that works best for the marketing team. It's more important that the marketing team choose something that works for them and that facilitates frequent feedback from the marketing owner and the marketplace.

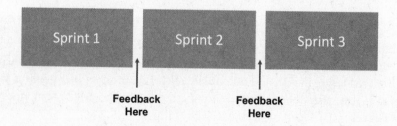

Figure 8.4 Month-long sprints provide fewer opportunities for feedback

Once you choose the length of your Sprint, stick with it for several months. Don't be tempted to change the Sprint length due to holidays and vacations; stay the course.

Calculating the Initial Capacity of Your Team

Working with Scrum gives you empirical data, measured in story points, on the capacity of your team to get work done. Story points are a better way to estimate than person days or person hours. Humans don't estimate well in terms of days or hours, but we are pretty good at relative estimating—we can look at a task and say that it's similar to, smaller than, or larger than another known task.

I recommend that marketing teams estimate tasks in terms of T-shirt sizes (x-small, small, medium, large) and assign story points according to Figure 8.5.

Develop your own reference stories, get empirical data about how long it takes members of your team to complete those stories, and then estimate based on grouping tasks into groups of similar size and scope. If something is larger than your largest T-shirt size, break it up into smaller chunks. No increment of work should take more than a week's worth of work for one person.

To calculate initial capacity of your team, I recommend the formula shown in Figure 8.6.

Here's a sample calculation. Let's say you've decided on two-week Sprints (10 working days) and you have 10 members of the team. To make this simple, there are no holidays, and no one is taking any vacation days. Here's the calculation:

10 team members $\times$ 10 days in Sprint = 100 team days
100 team days $\times$ 2 story points/day = 200 maximum story points

T-Shirt Size	Story Points	Reference Story
X-Small	1	Write a press release
Small	2	Write an 800+ word blog post
Medium	5	Create a product sales sheet
Large	10	Record and edit a podcast

Figure 8.5   T-shirt sizes and story points

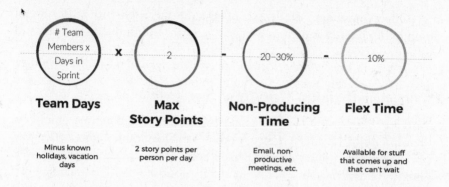

Figure 8.6 Formula for calculating initial team capacity

200 maximum story points − 30% nonproducing time (60 story points) = 140 story points

140 story points − 10% flex time (20 story points) = 120 story points initial capacity

Flex time is optional. If you think that you can eliminate work that comes up at the last minute and insist that you're only going to do planned work, then you can eliminate flex time; but this is rarely realistic. If you need to increase flex time to 20 percent, then do so. On the other hand, if more than 20 percent of your time each week must be put aside for unplanned work, then either you have a problem (someone else's lack of planning is causing you unplanned work), or you want to consider using Kanban, which better accommodates unplanned work.

Use this formula only to calculate initial capacity. As your team finds its rhythm and settles on a capacity, use that capacity while adjusting story points down for vacations and holidays.

Sprint Planning Session

- List of candidate delivery increments and tasks—check.
- Initial team capacity calculated—check.
- You can begin your Sprint planning session.

A Sprint planning session, according to the official Scrum Guide available at https://www.scrum.org, contains two sections:

Topic One: What can be done during this Sprint?
Topic Two: How will that work get done?

For topic one, define a theme or a large increment of work, rather than making each Sprint a random collection of marketing tasks. For example, your content marketing team has a theme relating to an aspect of your business, and you'll generate content deliverables on that theme. Everyone researches and writes about the same area and, by the end of the Sprint, you've greatly improved your content in that business area. The team gains a sense of accomplishment and collaboration increases with the business unit.

Or you're a marketing team working on customer experiences with your brand. Identify a testable change related to that experience. You can then test whether that change makes a difference in terms of conversions, customer satisfaction, or some other useful measure of the customer experience.

Continuing with topic one: To decide what can be done during this Sprint, the team selects delivery increments related to the theme or the testable change to be delivered. The team decides whether the delivery increments selected from the marketing backlog meet the needs of the theme or testable change; if they do not, the team writes more delivery increments.

Once a list of candidate delivery increments for the Sprint is compiled, determine what can be done, given the team's capacity, by iteratively following these four steps:

1. The marketing owner or the team selects the top-priority delivery increment from those that fit this Sprint's theme or testable change.
2. The team—not the marketing owner—estimates the number of story points required to complete this task. If necessary, decompose the work to be done into increments that you can accurately estimate. Use Planning Poker (covered in the following section) to increase the accuracy of your estimates.
3. Subtract the number of story points for this task from the story points available.
4. If team capacity remains, repeat from step 1.

You may be tempted to prioritize all the tasks, estimate all the tasks, and figure out which ones fit in the team capacity. This ends with you wasting time on estimating tasks that don't make it into the Sprint.

The team accomplishes topic two—deciding how the work will be done—throughout the course of the Sprint. In the Sprint planning session, the team assigns only enough work to keep everyone busy for the first three to five days.

If you assign work beyond the first three to five days, you'll discover that plans always change. Instead, once people finish their initial assignments, they come back and take on the next set of tasks. The team pulls together, deciding at daily Scrums which tasks are on track, which are behind, and how the whole team will work together to complete all the work committed to in topic one.

Once the team finishes with topic one and topic two, the team looks at the totality of the work and commits, verbally and consciously, to delivering everything in the Sprint backlog in the time allotted. It's important for the team to commit—to themselves—to delivering work in a predictable and sustainable fashion.

Planning Poker

Planning Poker enables teams to assign more accurate estimates by uncovering assumptions and getting agreement on the scope of a task. It works like this:

1. For each task, each team member comes up with a task-size estimate. Is it extra-small, small, medium, or large? They keep their estimates to themselves until step 2.
2. Each person reveals his or her estimate simultaneously (similar to turning over your cards in poker). If everyone chooses the same estimate, then you're done; assign that estimate to the task. More likely, some people estimate lower and some higher (the outliers), with most people choosing something in the middle.
3. Ask each outlier to discuss why they chose the estimate they chose. This often reveals hidden assumptions—by the outlier or by the rest of the team—or deeper understandings of the scope of the task. After all of the outliers have discussed their reasons, ask whether anyone wants to revise their estimate. This generally brings the group to consensus.
4. Sometimes the person doing the work gives a lower estimate than the rest of the group. The group then decides between accepting that estimate, assuming that the person doing the work knows most about the effort the task takes, or rejecting that person's estimate, assuming that we often underestimate our own work.

Daily Standup: Best Practices

While the daily standup can help teams improve communication, increase accountability, and identify obstacles, it is not the place to solve or remove obstacles. Some teams set aside time immediately after the daily standup for the scrum master to meet with those who have identified obstacles. You can use this additional time, which is optional for those whose work isn't blocked, to solve the problem or, more often, outline the next steps to take to solve the problem.

Best practices:

- Managers do not attend the daily standup, as their attendance changes the dynamic. We want the team to be self-managing.
- Vary the order in which team members present to prevent the creation of a sense of hierarchy. Some teams list all members on a whiteboard and move a magnet down the list, one member per day, to keep track of who begins daily standup reporting each day.
- Stick to the three questions: What did I do yesterday? What will I do today? What is preventing me from completing my work? If members of the team turn their attention to resolving the issues or to going down other rat holes, anyone can call this out and bring the team back to the three questions.
- Don't report status; report work done or work to be done. The emphasis is on getting things done.
- Some teams answer the first two questions by having everyone update the status of their work items in an electronic reporting tool, rather than reporting verbally at the standup. This can work for mature teams, but I recommend avoiding this at first. There is something helpful in everyone reporting to their peers what they did yesterday and what they will do today.
- The daily standup does not result in a report to the scrum master. It is peer-to-peer communication, without judgment, and with account-ability only within the team.
- Every team member commits to the team to improve their ability to forecast and deliver on daily work. In the beginning, team members tend to overestimate how much work they can do in a day. That doesn't help the team understand the flow of work and achieve accuracy in terms of completion dates.
- Limit the daily standup to 15 minutes. Because many organizations schedule meetings in half-hour increments, they schedule the daily

standup for a half-hour. This takes focus off of the three questions, and it creates opportunities for the team to shift into problem-solving mode. Less is more.

- If you are using a physical Kanban board with cards, put a hash mark on every card that stays at a stage in the process (a column), rather than moving on to the next stage in the process. This gives you a visual indicator of cards that are stuck.

- In some teams, no one reports obstacles. Members may see asking for help as a sign of weakness or ineffectiveness. The scrum master can empower the team by emphasizing that reporting obstacles is simply stating what's so and is critical to enabling the team to quickly identify and address issues. Pretending that obstacles don't exist simply makes the obstacles a bigger threat.

Sprint Review: Best Practices

The Sprint review communicates to the rest of the organization the work that the Sprint team has accomplished. It opens an effective channel for feedback.

Best practices:

- Make the Sprint review visual. Rather than tell attendees what work was accomplished, show the results. If the deliverable isn't finished (for example, during a major website redesign), show them the work in progress. The earlier you get feedback, the better. The later you get feedback, the more resources you'll put into work on a deliverable that will ultimately be rejected.

- Treat all feedback, particularly that from stakeholders, as welcome feedback. Record the feedback, where appropriate, as additions to the marketing backlog.

- Resist making commitments, particularly to deliverable dates, during the Sprint review. These decisions come out of Sprint planning meetings, where everyone has a say and where you get broad agreement.

The Sprint review often adds new items to the marketing backlog and influences what happens in the next Sprint. This is a good thing! Scrum is about getting feedback, early and often. This allows the team to learn and to deliver work that better meets the needs of customers and the rest of the business.

Sprint Retrospective: Best Practices

Successful Agile teams hold regular retrospectives to improve the way they work together. Although retrospectives are best known as a Scrum practice, teams practicing Kanban also hold retrospectives.

In either case, the focus is on the processes that produce the work, not on the work itself, with emphasis on improving efficiency and effectiveness.

The team meets biweekly, monthly, or at the end of each Sprint to ask key questions:

- What's working and what's not working?
- What parts of our process add little or no value? Can we eliminate them?
- What are teams in other areas of our organization or outside our organization doing? Can we adopt some of their practices?
- Are the tools we're using helping us do our jobs or getting in our way?
- If we didn't complete all of our stories (Scrum) or if we're not improving our throughput and cycle time (Kanban), why not? What are the root causes?

Reports from Retrospectives

Only team members attend retrospectives. No managers, no stakeholders, no outsiders. The retrospective must be a place of safety, where team members can freely bring up difficult issues without fear of retribution.

The outputs of the retrospective are reported as follows:

- *Learnings.* What did we implement recently? How is that working? What did we learn by adjusting our process?
- *Successes.* Let other teams and other parts of the organization know about your successes. If introducing a new element to your process improves productivity by 10 percent, document this and share it. You want to shout your successes from the rooftops; management often hears only about problems. Also, other teams may benefit by adopting your methods.
- *Trials and action items.* What new methods or practices—trials—will you start doing? What action items came out of the meeting? Who owns the follow-up? By when will the action items be complete?
- *Unresolved issues.* The number-one complaint about retrospectives is that the topics discussed cannot be solved by the team.[1] If that happens on your team, document the issues and assign someone to escalate them.

Learnings	Successes	Trials	Action Items	Unresolved Issues
Enforcing the 3-question rule in standups leads to shorter standups	We reduced the cycle time to create an 800 word blog post from a week to 3 days	Moving to hypotheses with ranges of improvement rather than exact numbers	Schedule recurring Sprint Planning sessions on Fridays at 2 pm	Approvals of front page banners still not happening within 2-day targets
Adding WIP limits to approval columns improves the flow of work	We're now averaging 3 tests per week compared to 1 test every other week previously	Moving Sprint Planning session to Friday afternoons from Monday mornings		
We're better at estimating the magnitude of lift for a given change than estimating an exact number.				

Figure 8.7   Sample retrospective report

Some teams send the retrospective report out through email or a tool like Slack, or perhaps they post it on a Wiki. Other teams create a poster board for each retrospective, with columns corresponding to each major area, and hang the poster in their team's area for other teams to see and learn from. See Figure 8.7 for an example.

Retrospectives support continuous improvement as long as they're done regularly and with a commitment to learning, experimentation, and discipline.

Sprint Retrospective: Best Practices

The Sprint retrospective provides the team an opportunity to examine what's working and what's not working in their process. Much of the power of Agile comes from its commitment to iterative improvement, and that commitment includes iterating on how the marketing team works together to improve their Agile practice.

Best practices:

- **Eliminate waste.** Ask, "What are we doing that isn't adding value?" and cease the activities that you identify as wasteful.
- **Experiment.** Empower the team to try new ways of working and new Agile practices. Avoid falling into a rut.
- **Make sure every voice is heard.** Identify those who tend to be reluctant to speak up and encourage them to contribute.

- **Make sure that the meeting doesn't look like your daily Scrum.** Hold it at another location or in conjunction with a meal or end-of-the-day refreshments.

Sprint Reporting and Measuring

Marketing teams, like software development teams, benefit from regular reporting and analytics about their work. Scrum masters measure and publish data about team throughput—aka velocity. Throughput is the number of story points completed per Sprint. Scrum masters can also publish a burndown chart, as shown in Figure 8.8. The burndown chart shows how the work is getting completed compared to an ideal. The X-axis represents the number of days left in the Sprint, and the Y-axis represents the number of story points left to complete. The burndown chart can show the team when it is running behind in completing work, and it can show whether the team is meeting the committed number of story points. A team consistently meeting its commitments indicates realistic work scheduling, and it builds confidence within and outside the team that Sprint work will be done on time.

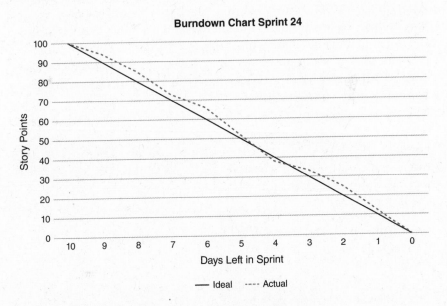

Figure 8.8 Sample burndown chart

Many Agile tools make it easy to collect and publish burndown charts and velocity. This data must be put in context; effectiveness of marketing is more than simple throughput or consistent delivery of outputs. Marketing teams should report foremost on outcomes. However, it's a rare marketing team that overreports or spends too much time looking at throughput data. The typical marketing team publishes no data about throughput or consistency of delivery.

The Power of Scrum

Scrum allows teams to identify the practices and habits that prevent them from achieving agility. If a team is constantly interrupted during a Sprint with new priorities, beyond the assigned flex time, they've identified an impediment to agility. If a team member reports out in daily standup a blocking issue day after day, they've identified an impediment to agility. If the Sprint review reveals that they're not building the right marketing for the business unit or for the customer; you got it, another impediment to agility.

Identifying an issue is not the same as fixing it. Many teams change or water down the Scrum process to adapt to the impediments, rather than fixing the issues. They stop reporting blocking issues in standup, because why bother? They expand the amount of flex time, rather than confronting the issue of constantly shifting priorities.

The power of Scrum comes from having hard conversations about what's limiting you from achieving agility. Scrum can expose the issues, but only you can fix them.

Chapter 9

Kanban

Of course, speed is most useful if it is in the correct direction.
    —*David J. Anderson, CEO at Mauvius Group and a leader of the*
                                                          Kanban movement

Scrum can be disruptive. Teams immediately start doing things in a different fashion: Sprint planning, daily standups, Sprint reviews, retrospectives. There are new roles to learn: marketing owner and scrum master. We begin to estimate tasks in story points with Planning Poker.

For some teams, it's better to start gradually. Kanban allows them to "Start with what you do now" and "Agree to pursue incremental, evolutionary change"; these are the first two principles of Kanban. The third principle, "Respect the current process, roles, responsibilities & titles," tells us that we don't need to create new roles or reorganize into cross-functional teams to practice Kanban. These three principles were "chosen specifically to avoid emotional resistance to change," according to David J. Anderson, one of the foremost proponents of Kanban.

Kanban—"a card you can see"—is a scheduling and work-management system developed by Taiichi Ohno, an industrial engineer at Toyota in the late 1940s. It is closely associated with the Lean Manufacturing philosophy that emphasizes eliminating waste and just-in-time inventory.

Kanban now shows up everywhere. If you've bought coffee at Starbucks, you've seen Kanban in action. The Starbucks cup provides a visual cue to the barista: how many shots of expresso, how many shots of which syrups, what kind of milk, etc. The barista sees at a glance what drink to make. The cup—the card you can see—specifies the work to be done. Figure 9.1 shows an example of a Starbucks cup, a form of Kanban.

In many Agile methodologies, a Kanban board tracks the work. Like the Starbucks cup, a Kanban board provides visual information—in this case,

Figure 9.1 A common form of Kanban
Source: Jim Ewel

about the status of work to be done, who is assigned to the work, when it is due, and more.

The simplest Kanban board, shown in Figure 9.2, has three columns: To Do, Doing, and Done. It could also have columns to represent multiple steps in a process. To describe the steps to produce marketing content, the board might have, between To Do and Done, columns for outlining, writing a draft, editing, and review, as shown in Figure 9.3.

The Kanban board provides other visual cues. For example, you could assign a card color to each kind of content: one color for blog posts, another for webinar scripts, and yet another for video scripts. The upper-right corner may have a photo or the initials of the person assigned to the work item. A calendar icon can represent the target finish date.

Colors and symbols can indicate priority levels or tasks that are stuck or blocked. An exclamation point can indicate urgent priority. A red X in a stop sign can indicate that the task is blocked: in other words, something outside the assigned person's control is preventing completion of the task.

Great Kanban books abound. My favorite is David J. Anderson's *Kanban: Successful Evolutionary Change in Your Technology Business*. Rather than duplicate what they say, I invite you to read one or two of them.

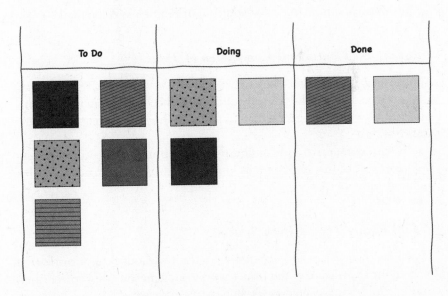

Figure 9.2 Sample Kanban board

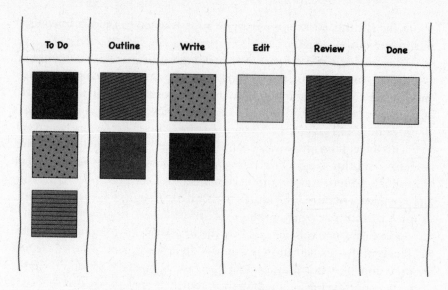

Figure 9.3   Simple content marketing board

Kanban Basics

Here, I'll review the basics of Kanban and then talk about how to get started with Kanban and how to evolve your use of Kanban in Agile marketing.

Frequent and Continuous Completion of Tasks

Kanban puts a premium on completing tasks in progress. This approach addresses the plight of the many marketing organizations juggling many priorities while completing few tasks—a scenario that includes endless updates and revisions.

To ensure frequent and continuous completion of tasks, Kanban teams implement work-in-progress limits, process policies, queues, and cycle-time and lead-time metrics.

A Pull Rather Than a Push System

Marketing managers who assign tasks to a team without clear prioritization or without knowledge of the team's workload, generate constant reprioritization and rework. The overwhelmed team experiences little control over its work, and burnout inevitably follows. Morale suffers. Good people leave.

Ironically, this push system carries a lot of communication overhead. A manager swoops in to speak to a marketer, asking for the status of a task or deliverable, and if the task is not done, the manager escalates that task to priority #1 with no thought to the impact on other priorities. Team members update each other and managers on the status of work in frequent, long, and unproductive meetings.

A pull system gives the team more control over the work. They pull work off of a prioritized queue when they are ready. Deliverables are bite-size tasks that can be completed quickly—in a few hours or a couple of days. To avoid generating unnecessary rework, managers provide clear scope and direction before adding tasks to the queue.

When priorities change, a new item moves to the top of the queue to be pulled through the system without interrupting the flow of other tasks being completed. Many marketers thrive in a properly implemented pull system, where throughput and morale rise together.

Work-in-Progress Limits

Marketers, often juggling priorities, benefit by establishing work-in-progress (WIP) limits, leading to a smoother and more predictable flow of work.

WIP limits the amount of work that can be taken on at any given process stage (as represented by a column in the Kanban board) or by individual team members. Limiting the amount of work or the number of items at any stage helps identify bottlenecks and encourages a culture of "done." It facilitates identifying and resolving the approval bottleneck, that place where work backs up, waiting on the attention of an all-too-busy manager.

Work-in-progress limits per team member help reduce multitasking. If you set it per team member, limit it to two or three items; few people can juggle more than three items at a time and be efficient. Both limits are helpful. Set these WIP limits as low as possible to ensure that all work is always moving toward done. Teams can always decide to raise the WIP limits if they're too low.

Process Policies

Process policies are one of the most useful and underutilized features of Kanban, particularly for marketers. A process policy converts often unstated "rules" for how things get done in a marketing organization into documented policies, and they provide common understanding among teams. For example, many creative teams require a creative brief, usually

Process Policy

**Work items can be pulled into this column that meet
the following conditions:**
- **Creative brief is completed**
- **Budget is set**
- **Creative director has assigned a resource**
- **Project deadline is set**

Figure 9.4   Sample column policy

conforming to a standard format, before launching a project to develop
new creative. Requiring a creative brief is a process policy.

You can also combine policies to document the requirements for pulling
an item into a new column. See Figure 9.4 for an example.

Making process policies explicit, and then enforcing them, has the following benefits:

- Everyone knows what's expected.
- Communication improves.
- Consistency and quality rise.
- New hires learn their roles quickly.
- Flow improves.
- Rework decreases.

Process policies take the following form:

- *Handoff policies.* Anyone who's watched a relay race or run in one knows
  the importance of the baton handoff. When a runner doesn't know
  how to execute a good handoff, the chances of his or her team winning are near zero. In marketing, between the time a final deliverable
  is created and when it's delivered to the market, handoffs from team
  to team are happening all the time. The creative brief, for example,
  is part of a handoff-process policy: work is handed off between the
  marketing-strategy team and the creative team.
- *What constitutes done policies.* What are the rules for finishing given
  tasks within marketing? When is a blog post "done," for example?
  Is it enough to write the blog post and publish it? Does finishing a
  blog post include promoting the post through specific social media
  channels? Is the blog post sent out in a newsletter? Is it cross-promoted

with partners? Perhaps a blog post is not "done" until a summary of the impact of the blog post is published. Some of these steps can be documented in the columns of a Kanban board. If a routine task entails many steps, a process policy or a checklist might best document what constitutes done.

- *Service-level agreements (SLAs).* Whenever one team hands off a portion of the work to another, and they're waiting to get it back, the inevitable and reasonable question is, "When will it be done?" The best teams establish expectations, commensurate with the size of the task, in regard to service. For example, for certain kinds of creatives that represent small tasks, the creative department may promise an SLA of one working day. Larger tasks require an agreement on more time. Exceptions occur, but establishing an expectation helps everyone. Legal review and web publishing are other areas that can benefit from establishing a standard SLA.

- *Workflow policies.* How will expedited tasks be handled? How many expedited tasks can be in the process at once? When a piece of creative or a piece of content is kicked back with review comments, does it go back into the same queue as new work, or is there a queue for revisions only? Who has to review a piece before it is complete? How does the team handle blocked items? Answer all these questions in process policies.

Process policies are not long documents hidden in a drawer, and they are not management imposed. The team decides which policies to create and enforce. Some Kanban tools document process policies. Others use legend cards or predefined task cards.

Legend cards sit permanently on a Kanban board, generally in the first column, and they document process policies. They are visible for everyone to see.

Predefined task cards also sit permanently on the board, generally in the first column. They are copied as new tasks are established. Custom fields are established as part of the card, and predefined task cards often have checklists to document process policies.

Queues

Another method to identify bottlenecks, and one that supports Kanban's pull system, involves adding a queue to each step. For example, in the Kanban board illustrated in Figure 9.5, we've divided each step in the process

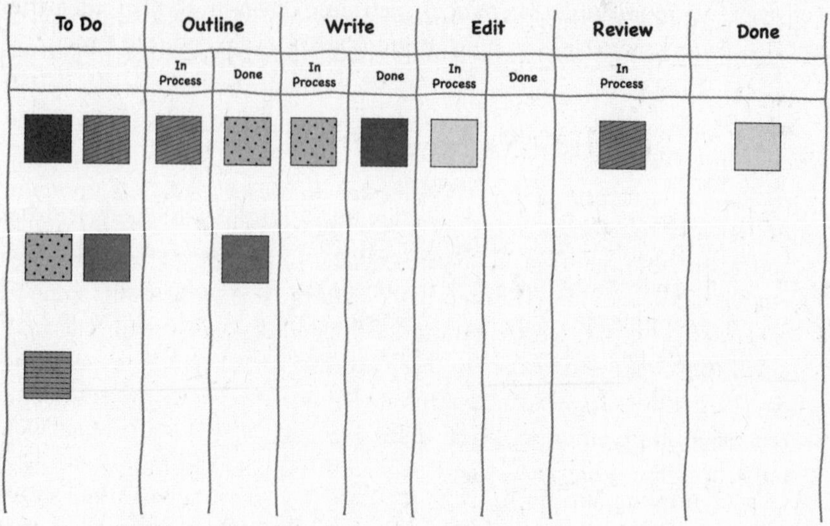

To Do	Outline		Write		Edit		Review	Done
	In Process	Done	In Process	Done	In Process	Done	In Process	

Figure 9.5   Kanban board with queues

except the last step into the columns In Process and Done. Each Done column is a queue where a card waits until it is pulled by a member of the team
into the next step in the process. To encourage the smooth flow of work
through the process, we can add WIP limits to the In-Process steps and the
Done queues. In the example board, each Done queue has a WIP limit of
three items, and each In-Process step has a WIP limit of one (essentially
saying that once you start working on something, you will finish it before
taking on another task).

Adding queues to a board has several advantages:

- Managers don't need to assign work to team members or balance out
  the assignment of workloads. Instead, team members pull work from
  the queues as they are available to do work.
- You can identify and correct bottlenecks caused by lack of resources if
  work builds up in a Done queue beyond the WIP limit.
- You can distinguish between value-added time, when work is In Process, and non-value-added time, when work is in a queue. You'll learn
  to minimize the amount of non-value-added time.

Kanban works particularly well in organizations suffering from approval
bottlenecks. Completed work sits dormant for days or weeks, awaiting
approval. Or the work goes repeatedly through the approval loop, with

each approver requiring new changes each time through. Kanban identifies these bottlenecks and their associated increases in cycle and lead times.

Getting Started with Kanban

I sometimes start marketing teams who are new to Agile with Kanban rather than Scrum. It can be easier for some teams to start with Kanban because they already have some kind of processes in place. We start their Kanban practice by mapping the categories of work performed by the team and the process they use to manage each category.

Mapping Your Categories of Work

Start by identifying and listing all categories of work with a unique flow. For example, the flow of work in producing a blog post differs from that involved in producing a video or from that involved in producing a display advertising campaign.

What outputs does your marketing team produce? Content? What kinds? Blog posts, guides, podcasts, videos, events? What kinds of regular projects does your team take on? Perhaps you regularly produce display advertising campaigns or social media campaigns. Try not to create too many different categories; if you can use the same workflow for blog posts and guides, create only one category.

Don't create categories for work that doesn't provide value for customers, external or internal. Don't create a category called "produce an annual budget," for example.

Map Your Existing Processes

For each category, identify the existing workflow that you use as things progress from To Do to Done. You might look at a few work items and ask the following questions: What is the status of this work item? Where did it come from? Where will it go next? Resist the urge to redesign your process. For now, just document it. And keep it simple. If you have more than nine steps in the process of creating a type of work, you probably have too many.

Divide a whiteboard or a virtual Kanban board into columns and write the title of each step of one of your workflows at the top of a column. If they're not already in your process, leave a bit of whiteboard on each side for a To Do column and a Done column.

Ask team members to post sticky notes, representing what they are currently working on, onto the physical or virtual whiteboard, in the column that corresponds with the work item's current status. If a sticky note doesn't fit, reconsider the process.

Document Your Process Policies

Document what constitutes "done" in order for an item to be pulled from one column to the next. Find balance here: Improve flow through the process without creating a rule book that slows it down. Process policies can also improve the quality of work by providing checklists of items to be done to ensure optimum quality. Refer to Figure 9.4 for a sample process policy.

If you are practicing a pure Kanban approach, you may also need a process policy for how work items are accepted into the To Do queue. Who accepts new work items, clarifying them and scoping them? Who prioritizes them? How (and how often) does this happen?

You don't have to get every policy documented at once and up front. As you begin your practice of Kanban, document only the most important process policies, and then add and modify policies as you go.

Document Your Classes of Service

Document your classes of service. These typically include Standard, Fixed-Date, and Expedited. How will you handle each class of service? For example, some teams limit the number of items in the Expedited class of service to one at a time. They put requirements in place, such as calculating the cost of delay, to ensure that this class of service doesn't get abused.

Evolving Your Use of Kanban

One of the key principles of Kanban is "Agree to pursue incremental, evolutionary change." I've always taken this to mean two things: Kanban, like all of Agile, should be approached with an iterative mindset, always trying to improve; and changes should be small and incremental, rather than large and disruptive. You may want to hold retrospective meetings every two weeks or so during the early stages of your adoption of Kanban, in order to discuss how you evolve your Kanban practice. (See Chapter 8 for more on retrospectives.)

Manage the Flow of Work

Kanban encourages the management of the flow of work, rather than micro-managing people. Rather than keeping each member of the team as busy as possible, how can we manage the flow of work so that we deliver value to customers, external and internal, quickly and efficiently?

The fourth and last principle of Kanban states, "Encourage acts of leadership at all levels." The responsibility for improving the flow of work doesn't rest with managers; it rests with everyone. Acts of leadership, whether they improve the efficiency or the quality of the work, can come from anyone.

Measuring and Improving Cycle Time and Lead Time

There's an old adage in business: You can't improve what you can't measure. To improve your process management, measure these two:

- Cycle time: The time it takes to complete work once it is started.
- Lead time: The time, on average, it takes for work to be delivered, once there is a commitment to do the work, including the time that it spends waiting in a queue for someone to start on it.

Figure 9.6 illustrates cycle time and lead time.

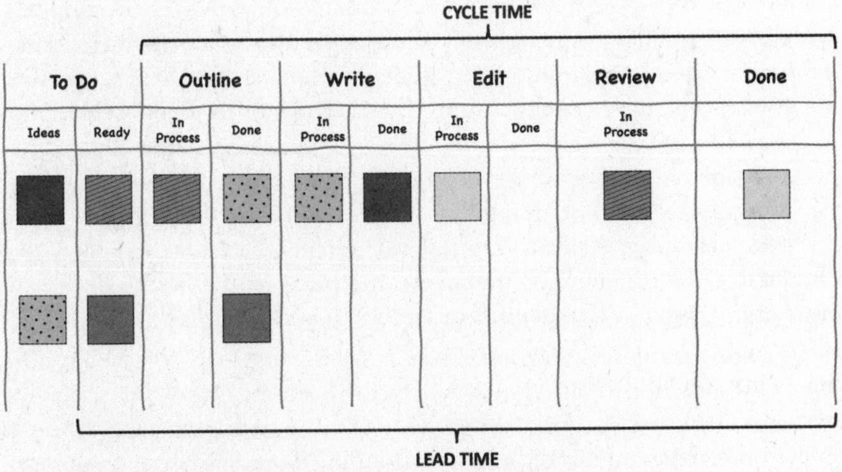

Figure 9.6 Cycle time and lead time

In marketing, you need to balance efficiency (shorter cycle and lead times) with effectiveness. It makes no sense, for example, to reduce the time to produce creative from five to two days if the resulting creative is ineffective and doesn't produce the desired marketing result. It's also true that creative that takes longer isn't necessarily the most effective. Find the balance: Measure efficiency and effectiveness for a complete view.

Eliminating Waste

After documenting the process in a visual Kanban board, marketers must look for ways to eliminate waste, particularly any work that doesn't contribute to customer value or business value. Here are places to look first for waste in marketing processes:

- *Excessive review cycles.* Limit review cycles to between one and two on average (or one higher if legal review is required). In other words, some items require only one review cycle and others require two. If most of marketing's work items require three review cycles or more, dig here! Either the person specifying the work isn't communicating exactly what they're looking for, the team doing the work isn't producing work that meets the specifications or the quality bar, or too many people are reviewing the work. When every piece of collateral requires review by several layers of management and legal, Agile is hard to achieve.
- *Excessive documentation.* The original manifesto for software development included the following value: working software over comprehensive documentation. Marketers must apply this value to their work. Replace long marketing plans, strategy briefs, creative briefs, internal PowerPoint presentations, Gantt charts, and postmortems with short communications—either visual, like Kanban boards with informative cards, or one- or two-page documents that capture the essence of the communication. For example, some teams replace the creative brief with a template Kanban card that documents the target audience, the goal for the creative, and the success metrics.
  - But what about marketing plans? Shouldn't we have a strategic marketing plan? Yes and no. It can help a marketing team to have a strategic direction and to do some strategic planning. However, strategies must be tested against the realities of customer acceptance. And no one reads long marketing plans; that time would be better spent marketing! Many teams limit quarterly marketing plans to two to three pages.

- *Excessive mandatory meetings.* Meetings are the bane of productivity. Scrum and Kanban eliminate useless meetings, replacing them with the short, daily standup and regular prioritization meetings. Check your calendar; which meetings can you eliminate (status meetings!) and which can you make optional?

Theory of Constraints Applied to Kanban

The Theory of Constraints, as described by Eli Goldratt in his book *The Goal,* says that the output or throughput of any process is limited by a small number of constraints or limitations within the process. It's easiest to visualize this as a bottleneck: The throughput of a six-lane highway is constrained if there is an accident, reducing the highway to one lane at the location of the accident. Key to the Theory of Constraints is the idea that there are a small number of constraints that greatly impact the overall throughput.

As we apply Kanban to marketing, where are our constraints that impact our throughput? Are they due to excessive multitasking? Add WIP limits. Are the people not trained to move work efficiently through their step in the process? Train them. Do we not have enough people at a certain step in the process? Add more people. Are approvals a bottleneck? Establish SLAs or reduce the number of approvals.

Portfolio Kanban

A risk inherent to adopting Kanban or Scrum is that teams executing effectively on individual tasks may lose sight of the bigger picture. Portfolio Kanban addresses this risk, allowing teams to see how their executables contribute to projects, programs, and top-level strategic themes.

For example, Figure 9.7 shows a hierarchy of projects, programs, and top-level strategic themes with their corresponding user stories/delivery increments.

Organizations can build Kanban boards to track their deliverables and how they contribute to the levels above. Figure 9.8 shows a series of deliverables, represented by the cards in the work breakdown row, and how they contribute to larger projects, listed above. As cards tied to a particular project are moved from To Do to Doing, the corresponding project card is also moved. As cards tied to a project are completed, a percent completion indicator is updated. When all the cards tied to a project are completed, the project itself is moved to the Done column.

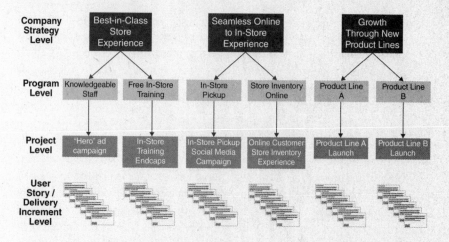

Figure 9.7 Hierarchy of strategies, programs, and projects for portfolio kanban

Projects		
To Do	**Doing**	**Done**
0% New Lead Magnet	25% Welcome Series	
	75% New Front Page	
Work Breakdown		
To Do	**Doing**	**Done**

Figure 9.8 Portfolio Kanban board

Portfolio Kanban boards are very useful, not only to allow the team to see their contributions to the bigger picture but also to allow management to see progress and status for various projects and programs. Project-level boards can be owned by project managers. In turn, program managers may have their own board, tracking multiple projects contributing to each program. The highest-level board would track the various programs and how they contribute to the key corporate strategies. This should eliminate some status meetings and reports.

Marketing teams can also use Portfolio Kanban to achieve a balanced portfolio of marketing investments. If the team wants to ensure that they are balancing their efforts between the marketing categories of awareness, demand generation, product marketing, and marketing operations, they might build a board like the one in Figure 9.9.

For teams that practice Kanban, Portfolio Kanban can be a powerful tool to manage the work of multiple teams and ensure the consistent flow of work, identifying bottlenecks and eliminating blocking factors before they delay entire projects and programs. With this approach, teams will need to establish WIP limits throughout the hierarchy of boards, measure cycle time and flow, and look at certain advanced Kanban metrics such as cumulative flow diagrams. This approach can replace Gantt charts and traditional backward-looking project management approaches, but it requires a high level of Kanban knowledge and team discipline. It also requires coordination across multiple departments and at different levels of the organization. While powerful, it is also quite complex.

Awareness				
To Do	Doing	Reviewing	Deploying	Done

Demand Generation				
To Do	Doing	Reviewing	Deploying	Done

Product Marketing				
To Do	Doing	Reviewing	Deploying	Done

Marketing Operations				
To Do	Doing	Reviewing	Deploying	Done

Figure 9.9 Marketing portfolio board

The Power of Kanban

The power of Kanban comes from its incremental, evolutionary approach to change. For some teams and organizations, it is less threatening than Scrum. It is also better suited for activities where it is impossible to plan several weeks out; the nature of the work requires constant reprioritization and a smooth flow of work.

The power of Kanban also comes from practices like WIP limits, process policies, queues, and Portfolio Kanban. These practices can be used, with data, to improve throughput and quality. Kanban practitioners call this incremental approach to improvement *Kaizen*. Kaizen is key to the effective use of Kanban.

Next, let's take a look at how you can use the incremental, evolutionary approach of Kanban to improve Scrum, the methodology known as Scrumban.

Chapter 10

Scrumban

No heroics. If you need a hero to get things done, you have a problem. Heroic effort should be viewed as a failure of planning.
  —*Jeff Sutherland, author and co-creator of Scrum*

No methodology works best in every situation. This holds true for marketing teams practicing Agile, where each team uses the methodology best suited for its needs. Deciding which to use may come down to personal preference, or it may reflect the nature of the work. Groups with control over their work and with work cycles of days or weeks tend to prefer Scrum. Groups with little control over priorities or timing and those with hourly or daily work cycles tend to prefer Kanban.

Many marketing teams choose to combine practices from each. You might adapt Kanban to include retrospective meetings to discuss what's working and what's not. You might adapt Scrum to implement work-in-progress (WIP) limits, to foster a culture of "done," rather than wait for everything to get done during the last few days of a Sprint.

Ideally, then, the methodology is an empirical choice. Experiment to determine which methodology or combination of methodologies yields the greatest throughput, effectiveness, and team satisfaction.

Which brings us to Scrumban. Scrumban may the best approach for many Agile marketing teams. But only if they are genuinely practicing Scrumban, rather than practicing what the developers derisively call "Scrumbut." Scrumbut gets its name from the phrase "We practice Scrum, but … " As in we practice Scrum, but:

We hold half-hour status updates rather than 15-minute daily Scrums.

We skip those pesky Sprint reviews and Sprint retrospectives, because what's the point?

We don't measure our velocity or bother with burndown charts.

We like Kanban boards because then everyone can see that we're Agile, but we don't implement WIP limits, state explicit process policies, measure cycle times, or do anything else to improve our throughput and quality.

Don't practice Scrumbut.

Scrumban as a Formal Methodology

While Scrumban often refers to any mash-up of practices from Scrum and Kanban, it is more than that. Scrumban combines the pull philosophy and WIP limits of Kanban, some of the formal ceremonies—daily standup and retrospectives—of Scrum, and a limited and efficient form of planning. Scrumban also applies the incremental, evolutionary approach of Kanban to improving Scrum.

But Scrumban is more than just the greatest hits of Scrum and Kanban. Scrumban applies Lean thinking and the theory of constraints to developing software or, in our case, managing marketing. Lean thinking focuses on waste in a specific way: What can we eliminate because it doesn't provide value to the customer? The theory of constraints identifies the most important limiting factors (constraints) slowing the flow of work. Rather than try to increase the speed of each step in a process, theory of constraints identifies critical bottlenecks and eliminates them, one by one.

In an important way, Scrumban is not a methodology at all; rather, it is a set of principles that "can be used to compose a process which will always be specific to the problem at hand and the resources available."[1]

Getting Started with Scrumban

Okay, if Scrumban is not a methodology, how do marketing teams get started with Scrumban? I recommend that they start by doing three things:

Take a different approach to Sprint planning; deliver fast by measuring flow; and optimize the whole. Let's take a look at each of these points.

A Different Approach to Sprint Planning

In Scrum, Sprint planning meetings can take half a day. Each delivery increment or task is prioritized and estimated, and these estimates might or might not be usefully accurate. More time goes into creating a Sprint backlog for each Sprint, and if the work doesn't get done in a Sprint then the team figures out what to do: Add it to the next Sprint backlog with a revised description of the work to be completed or try to complete it "off the books." All of the work put into Sprint planning is time away from doing productive work.

Sprints are sometimes planned out as far as three months, and adding anything—important or not—to the schedule can be difficult to impossible. This is counter to the spirit of Agile.

Scrumban, rather than estimating each task and creating a Sprint backlog, focuses on lightweight, just-in-time planning.

For example, let's say a team of five people completes on average of 10 tasks per week. Some of the tasks are small, some are large, some are medium. Forget all that; forget story points; forget Planning Poker. Instead, the team meets weekly to plan, for as little time as needed, but no more than 30 minutes. If this is the first week, or if everything got done last week, then they choose 10 items from the big backlog to move into this week's backlog queue, sometimes called the *approved* queue (see Figure 10.1).

If two items didn't get started last week, and there are only eight slots in the backlog queue, they add just eight new items. The goal is to fill the slots available and then get back to work. Work that is in progress continues to move smoothly through the process.

Occasionally, the backlog queue may get to zero before the next planning meeting. That's fine as long as there is WIP. If it happens repeatedly, you may want to increase the number of slots in the backlog queue.

The Scrumban board in Figure 10.1 has another property, the ready queue. The queue contains the highest priority items. Any team member who finishes a task pulls their next task from this ready queue, and the next highest priority item then moves from the backlog into the ready queue. This approach encourages just-in-time prioritization, a very useful concept for many marketing teams.

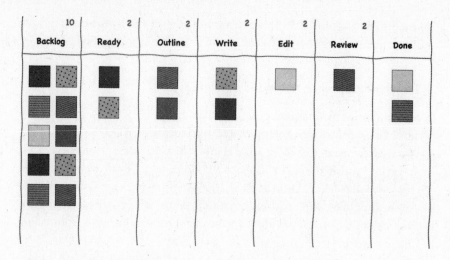

Figure 10.1   Sample Scrumban board

With experience, the team develops a sense of flow. Planning becomes an easy exercise in keeping the top of the funnel filled. If an important item comes up, the team promotes it to the ready queue with a high priority.

Optional Scrumban reviews (similar to Sprint reviews) gather feedback to confirm that the team is on the right track and to demonstrate to other departments the work of marketing.

Scrumban teams typically hold retrospectives—not necessarily at regular intervals but as needed to discuss and improve process.

Deliver Fast by Measuring Flow

A burndown chart tells you about your progress and whether you are on track versus an "ideal" completion rate. It doesn't tell you much about why you're not on track and where the problems might be in your workflow. For that, you need a cumulative flow diagram.

A cumulative flow diagram is a stacked area chart showing the number of tasks in each column of your workflow. It can show you whether work is smoothly flowing through your workflow, whether a particular stage is blocked or overloaded, and also where you may have too many resources. It can also give you a visual representation of cycle time.

Figure 10.2 is an example cumulative flow diagram. This diagram represents a simple Kanban board, with six columns: Backlog, Approved, Buffer,

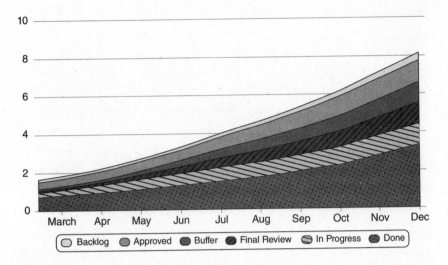

Figure 10.2 Example of a cumulative flow diagram
Source: Kanban Tool. Retrieved from: http://static.kanbantool.com/library/analytics-metrics/cumulative-flow-diagram.jpg.

Final Review, In Progress, and Done. The bottom area, which represents Done items, increases in size over time, as you would expect.

In an ideal cumulative flow diagram, the backlog and each of the areas represented by the various in-progress stages stay constant size, while the Done items steadily accumulate. This is seldom the case in reality. Here are some patterns to look for.

Slowdowns or Blockage. In Figure 10.3, the cumulative flow diagram shows two slowdowns, perhaps due to blocking factors. These slowdowns can be recognized by the flattening of the "Done" line. At the same time, notice the growth of work in progress shown by the increasing thickness of the middle or In Progress area. Review this during a daily standup to determine whether there are any blocking factors or other problems. To increase the flow, add WIP limits to the column that is building up or add resources at that point.

Cumulative flow diagrams can also help you visualize cycle times and whether they are increasing or decreasing. Visually, the cycle time is the distance between the start of the first in-progress queue and the done queue. Figure 10.4 shows the cycle time at two different points of the reporting period in the cumulative flow diagram. The lower double-headed arrow, ending in early March, shows a cycle time of three days or so. The upper

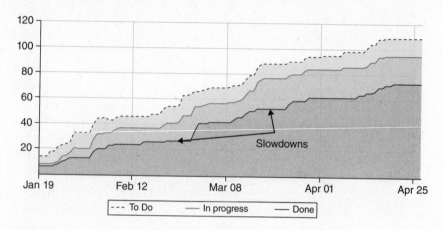

Figure 10.3   Cumulative flow diagram with flow slowing
Source: Wikimedia Commons; courtesy of Alhmodeus

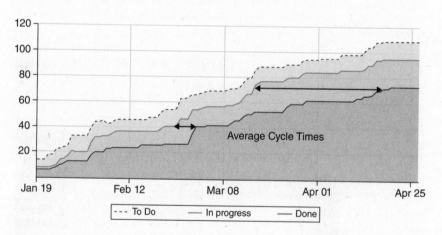

Figure 10.4   Visually inspecting cycle times with a cumulative flow diagram
Source: Wikimedia Commons; courtesy of Alhmodeus

double-headed arrow, ending around mid-April, shows a cycle time of 25–30 days. A report can give you the exact number, but for the moment, we're inspecting this visually using the flow diagram. This alerts us to a potential problem.

Kanban Daily Standups. Kanban daily standups place the emphasis on the work and the flow of work, rather than people. Rather than going around the room with each person answering the three questions of Scrum's daily standup, a leader reviews the Kanban board for any issues and to make sure that work is continuing to flow.

Kanban daily standups usually review the board from right to left, to emphasize the pull nature of Kanban and the team's commitment to getting work done.

Kanban daily standups can be done with much larger teams than the typical Scrum daily standup. While it would be impossible to conduct a 15-minute standup with 30 people, it is not unusual for Kanban daily standups to include up to 50 people. The usual rules apply: If the team identifies a blocking issue, take it offline. Don't try to solve it in the meeting.

Key Metrics to Track. If you want to go fast, track both throughput and cycle time, and seek to improve both over time. Throughput is the number of cards completed per unit of time. In Figure 10.5, the team's throughput varies between 7 and 10 cards completed per week.

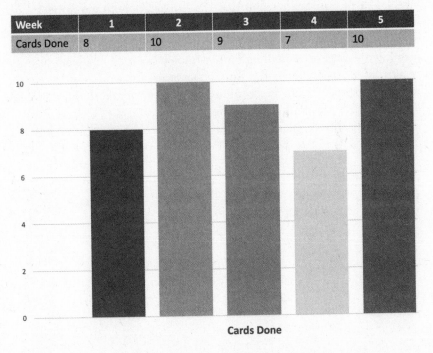

Week	1	2	3	4	5
Cards Done	8	10	9	7	10

Cards Done

Figure 10.5   Team throughput chart

Cycle time is simply the average time between when someone on the team starts on a work item and when it is done. You might want to calculate cycle times for different categories of work: blog posts versus video scripts. Most Kanban tools will calculate cycle times for you.

As we've mentioned many times, efficiency is not the same as effectiveness. While I encourage you to measure throughput and cycle time and improve it over time, remember that this must be balanced by an examination of the effectiveness of the work in generating business outcomes.

Optimize the Whole

Our job as marketers is to maximize the value we deliver to customers and to our colleagues in other departments. When we use methodologies like Scrum or Kanban to optimize the delivery of marketing, we sometimes lose track of the bigger picture. Unfortunately, this bigger picture can be painfully visible to prospects and customers.

Scrumban encourages practitioners to adopt *systems thinking*. Optimize not locally (the throughput of our content marketing group, for example) but globally. I encourage teams that want to be Agile to put a mechanism in place to optimize their marketing at the big-picture level.

This mechanism could be as simple as a discussion at your next quarterly planning meeting or something more complex like a value-stream mapping of all your marketing activities from a customer point of view. It's not the tool or the process you use to optimize at a big picture level; it's simply important that you don't forget to do so.

Now that we've taken a look at Scrum, Kanban, and Scrumban, let's take a look at the next discipline of Agile marketing, validated learning.

Chapter 11

Validated Learning

It ain't what you don't know that gets you into trouble. It's what you know for sure that just ain't so.
        —Usually attributed to Mark Twain, American writer and humorist

The Agile Marketing Manifesto includes three values that describe the importance of continuous improvement:

1. Rapid iterations over big-bang campaigns
2. Testing and data over opinions and conventions
3. Many small experiments over a few large bets

Rapid iterations. Testing and data. Experiments. Approaching marketing with these elements foremost in your mind is at the heart of the fourth discipline: validated learning.

The Importance of Iteration

In Chapter 2, we looked at American aeronautical engineer Paul Mac-Cready and how iteration earned him the Kremer prize in 1977 with the *Gossamer Condor*.

Agile marketers can take away several lessons from that story, and the importance of iteration is first among those. Many design features (the shape of the airfoil, the controls, the propeller) had to be tested and improved over hundreds of iterations to achieve success. The team could draw many of these designs on paper, but until each was tested, no one knew whether any would work.

Next is the importance of designing systems that enable ever faster iteration. If your approach limits you to three or four iterations per year, the team that iterates three or four times per week is eating your lunch. If finding the right solution takes hundreds of iterations, the team whose approach supports rapid iteration wins.

Build resilient systems that enable you to fail and recover. MacCready built the *Gossamer Condor* with materials that would withstand the inevitable crash. Marketing teams need to build systems to withstand the inevitable failure, enabling them to quickly get back on their feet and adjust their marketing to overcome whatever led to the crash.

The practice of iteration is more common in some aspects of marketing today than others. For example, most marketers who are executing search engine marketing (SEM) can expect to iterate many times to optimize the effectiveness of their ads.

When implementing landing pages, organizations often perform A/B testing or multivariate testing, iterating to create the landing page that produces the highest click-through rates (CTRs) and the most conversions.

But many other types of marketing are implemented in a classic one-and-done fashion: content is published once, with no modifications and no lessons learned. Campaigns are created, run with millions of impressions, and victory is declared. Offers are made to consumers based on the intuition of executives or experienced marketers, not based on data.

These one-and-done content campaigns and offers are created using marketing's equivalent of the waterfall methodology that created the need for Agile software development in the first place.

Figure 11.1 shows a classic waterfall approach to advertising campaigns. It is often used to produce television campaigns, print campaigns, and large digital campaigns.

The Waterfall Approach

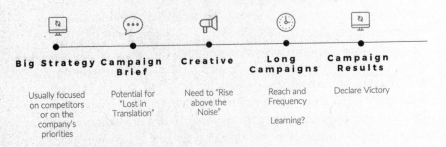

Big Strategy	Campaign Brief	Creative	Long Campaigns	Campaign Results
Usually focused on competitors or on the company's priorities	Potential for "Lost in Translation"	Need to "Rise above the Noise"	Reach and Frequency Learning?	Declare Victory

Figure 11.1   Waterfall approach in marketing

The marketing waterfall approach begins with a big strategy, focused on tweaking the competitors or on generating more sales—and not on the user's need for information or inspiration. Once the company settles on the big strategy after many meetings of senior people, the strategy is codified in a campaign brief. This brief, several pages long, intends to, but rarely does, capture the breadth and depth of the big strategy. Things get "lost in translation."

The creative agency, whether external or internal, then generates concepts or, sometimes, nearly finished work. They shoot for creativity and cleverness, hoping to rise above the flood of advertising and information that threatens to drown all of us today.

Once the campaign materials are finished and approved, they are distributed through channels appropriate to the medium—television or YouTube, digital advertising on websites or social media sites—the thousands of channels extant today. Companies often distribute their paid media on the most popular channels, giving scant thought to the cost-effectiveness and performance of these channels.

Many marketing organizations measure the success of traditional campaigns in ways meaningless to anyone outside of marketing. For example, digital campaigns may report site visits, bounce rates, and exit rates. To a CEO who is looking for a boost in sales, bounce rates and exit rates may be mostly meaningless.

In his book, *The Lean Startup*, Eric Ries described a concept he called vanity metrics.[1] *Vanity metrics* are the opposite of what he called *actionable metrics*. Here's how he describes the difference:

For a report to be considered actionable, it must demonstrate clear cause and effect. Otherwise, it is a vanity metric.

Too often we, as marketers, use vanity metrics such as reach, frequency, and site visits. They aren't actionable, as there is no clear cause-and-effect relationship between these measures and numbers such as sales, that the business cares about.

In the final step of marketing's waterfall, the team reviews the results of the campaign, typically with the strategists who came up with the big idea. Because of the time and money that went into the big campaign, and because it's in the best interest of the agency (internal or external) to flatter the client, the results are almost always positive. The marketing team declares victory and finds the metrics to support the claim.

Compare the marketing waterfall approach with the Agile approach shown in Figure 11.2.

The Agile approach begins with a small, customer-focused strategy aimed at learning how customers react to a promotion or whether the channel of distribution effectively reaches the right customers. The marketing organization forms a hypothesis, then builds a quick test and runs it until the data gathered are statistically significant. For large organizations with lots of traffic or lots of viewers, getting enough data for the test may happen in hours; for others, it may take a week or more.

If the hypothesis stands, great. Otherwise, the team learns something that may lead to strategies that work. The test costs less than a big campaign, so there is little incentive to declare victory when the hypothesis is invalidated.

The team then flows into a second iteration, with a revised strategy or hypothesis, and then a third, and so forth. Typically, an organization can do 10 iterations or more in the time it takes to do a large campaign—at less cost and with a higher success rate. Marketing teams that execute in this Agile, iterative way are more productive, faster to market, and more adaptable to change.

The Importance of Tempo

At the 2014 San Francisco Agile Marketing Meetup, Satya Patel, former VP of Product at Twitter, addressed the question "How many experiments would you run in any given month at Twitter?" His answer: "I would say we started with, honestly, one or two [a month] and by the end we were running, probably, 10 a week."[2]

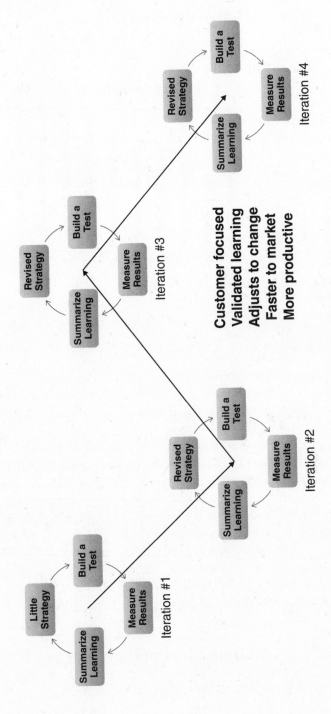

Figure 11.2 Agile approach to marketing

123

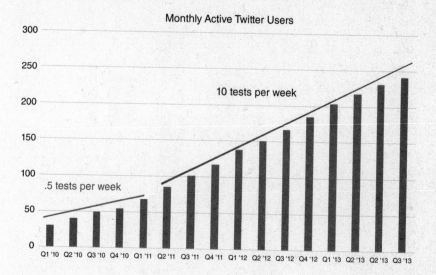

Figure 11.3   Impact of accelerated tempo in testing
Source: Courtesy of Sean Ellis, GrowthHackers

At a subsequent Meetup, Sean Ellis, one of the early adopters and promoters of growth hacking, compared Twitter's success in growing their user base before and after Satya Patel directed this increased frequency of testing.[3] The graph Sean showed looks like Figure 11.3.

The slope of the line describing active user growth improved dramatically after Satya Patel arrived. Sean attributed causal correlation between Satya's implementation of more and better testing at Twitter and the improvement in active user growth. In other words, by running more tests and by running tests that followed a scientific approach (as described in Satya's presentation), Twitter growth increased.

Sean describes this approach as high-tempo testing; I call it validated learning. The same growth improvements happen for my clients that adopt this approach. In short, a higher tempo of testing leads to a higher tempo of learning. And a higher tempo of learning leads to faster growth.

Best Practices

There are several keys to success with validated learning.

Understand the Problem You're Trying to Solve

Everyone in a business must understand the small set of metrics that drive growth, whether those be revenue, profitability, customer lifetime value, active users, or something else. This discourages teams from choosing other metrics for success and lets everyone in the business know the problem that you are trying to solve—a problem that depends not only on the business but also on the stage in the growth curve of the business. For example, in the early days of a business, active and engaged users might be more important than revenue or profitability.

Understanding the problem you're trying to solve and being specific about how you measure success also guides you in your testing. If your primary metrics are around customer lifetime value and profitability, running tests around new customer acquisition may not be as important as deepening relationships with existing customers and running tests to assess their impact on revenue and profitability.

Build a Team Dedicated to Validated Learning

Creating a process that enables you to run tens or hundreds of tests weekly requires dedicated resources. In my experience, this is best done by creating a cross-functional team dedicated to validated learning. The team includes members with expertise in, at a minimum, design, web programming, and product management. It may also include data scientists and experts in personalization and advanced analytics.

Brian Balfour, former VP of Growth at HubSpot, and Andrew Chen, a venture capitalist who coined the term "growth hacker," recommend that growth teams have at least five members with five roles:[4]

1. *Growth product manager*—responsible for the testing approach and the roadmap. May lead the team (if they're not self-organizing) or play the role of marketing owner.
2. *Growth engineer*—implements the experiments, either by making changes to the product or by building or modifying web properties.
3. *Growth marketer*—decides which marketing channels to use, how to approach using the channel, and, probably, writes most of the copy.
4. *Growth data analyst*—analyzes the data and provides data-based insights to the team.
5. *Growth designer*—designs either the user interface or the creatives used in the testing. The emphasis is on rapid design and modeling, not on perfection.

The business consulting firm McKinsey calls these "war-room teams" and recommends that they include between 8 and 15 people.[5] Smaller companies get by with teams of as few as three. Larger companies may have multiple validated learning teams.

Set Specific Goals for Testing Tempo

Rather than tell the team "we'd like you to run more tests," set specific, challenging goals for the tempo of testing. For example, if you're currently running only a test or two per month and you tell the team to run more tests, they will, through incremental improvements to their current process, increase the tempo to 3 or 4 tests per month.

If you tell the team that you'd like them to reach a tempo of 5 tests *per week* (or 20 tests per month), they'll rethink their entire testing process and all their tools, and they'll make much larger improvements. Once this results in an initial leap forward, they can then optimize incrementally to get to 7 and then 10 tests a week.

Develop Tools and Processes that Enable You to Test at Faster Tempos

A validated learning team is responsible for adopting tools and developing processes that enable them to test at ever-faster tempos. Google Analytics, Optimizely, and Visual Website Optimizer (VWO) are all popular tools, and many organizations develop their own tools. Validated learning teams must develop processes for ranking which tests to perform first, segmenting their audiences, establishing standards for how to measure certain customer actions, and minimizing the customer confusion caused by introducing too many changes.

Apply the Scientific Method

At some point in school, we learned the basic steps of the scientific method, as laid out in Figure 11.4.

The scientific method works for validated learning. The discipline of forming hypotheses and documenting and reporting the results guides your testing and improves how you communicate and justify changes to other groups.

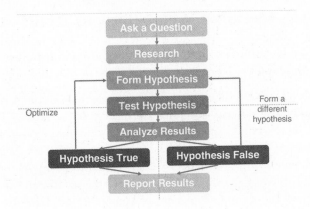

Figure 11.4   The basic steps of the scientific method

Research is also an important part of the validated learning process. Satya Patel tells the story of observing a high click-through rate on one tab during his time at Twitter. Research revealed that users were confused by the label on the tab and were clicking on it repeatedly, expecting each time to get a certain result only to be frustrated with a different result. Just analyzing the data would have led to the conclusion that the tab was successful in producing a high click-through rate; research uncovered that users were getting a frustrating experience.

Test Both for New Learning and for Optimization

As you construct tests, most fall into two categories: testing for new learning and testing for optimization. For example, you may test a new channel of distribution to determine whether it is effective in achieving your goals. If you determine that the new channel has some effectiveness, you may then run further tests to optimize that channel.

Understanding the difference between these two categories of tests is important. If you are executing a test for new learning, then your standard for the results—metrics like click-through rate or volume of new business—may be lower. Once you discover that a new channel has some effectiveness, you can then optimize to achieve the metrics that you are looking for. If you don't make the distinction between these two types of tests, you may prematurely eliminate a valid channel or approach.

Deciding Which Tests to Run

To decide which tests to run in a Sprint, teams must decide how to prioritize tests. I recommend the ICE method, used by Sean Ellis and others:

- *Impact*. What is the likely impact of the change on your key metrics? A hypothesis predicted to improve your conversion rate by 10 percent would, all else being equal, be run before a hypothesis predicted to generate a 1 percent improvement. Don't forget to take into account the reach of these improvements. A 1 percent improvement that reaches 50 percent of your customer base is better than a 10 percent improvement that reaches only 1 percent of your customer base. Rather than specify a specific percentage improvement, estimate impact on a scale from 1 to 5.
- *Confidence*. What confidence level does the team have that the data will support the hypothesis and have the predicted impact?
- *Ease of implementation*. An easily testable hypothesis would have a higher priority than one that requires large amounts of resources to test.

Teams can build a spreadsheet, or use some other tool, to manage their backlog of testable hypotheses. Each spreadsheet entry lists the hypothesis, a short description of the actions to be taken to test it, and the predicted impact as a change in a metric. Each entry also has scores, on a 1 to 5 scale, for Impact, Confidence, and Ease of implementation:

Impact: 1 is low, 5 is high
Confidence: 1 is low, 5 is high
Ease of implementation: 1 is easy, 5 is difficult

The final priority is calculated by the formula:

Priority = Impact + Confidence − Ease

The resulting priorities range from −3 to 9, where higher numbers indicate greater priority. See Figure 11.5 for an example.

Instinct Plays a Role as Well

When scientists construct experiments to test a hypothesis, they seek to gather enough data to ensure that their result is statistically significant. The most common practice is to set the significance level at 5 percent, meaning that there is a 5 percent chance that the results were due to chance. This is also described as a 95 percent confidence level that the data supports the hypothesis.

Hypothesis	Action	Metric	Impact	Confidence	Ease	Score	Result	Insights
Changing the color of the "Support Us" button will increase click-throughs by 10%	Change the button color at the top right of every page	Click-through rate	2	2	1	3	Click-through rate essentially the same; hypothesis invalid	
Changing the text of the "Support Us" button to "Donate Now" will increase click-throughs by 15%	Change the text of the button	Click-through rate	2	3	1	4		
Making the default gift a recurring gift will increase the percentage of recurring gifts by 50%	Change the default choice on the donation page	% of gifts that are recurring	4	2	1	5		

Figure 11.5 How to prioritize tests with the ICE method

If you have sufficient volume of interactions to test at high tempo and gather enough data to achieve a 95 percent confidence level, then do so.

Many organizations lack the interactions to achieve this level of certainty without letting their tests run longer than is consistent with their goal of high-tempo testing. In this case, I recommend following the 80 percent rule: If your instinct tells you that the data is consistent and you have enough testing for an 80 percent confidence level, move forward; future tests will likely detect any anomalies created by chance. Sometimes it is more important to move quickly, at a rapid pace, than to achieve scientific levels of certainty.

Instinct also plays a role in determining the tests you perform and the hypotheses you form. As a marketer, part of your value is your knowledge of the market and of the customer. That knowledge, commonly called *instinct,* is a valuable part of the testing process.

Building a Validated Learning Backlog

Validated learning backlogs may be tracked as cards on a Kanban board. In this case, a typical test card might look something like Figure 11.6.

There are many approaches to constructing a validated learning backlog. Here are three different approaches.

Examine Your Marketing Model

Back in Chapter 5, I asked you to construct a Marketing Model Canvas. With that marketing model in front of you, ask yourself the following questions:

- What assumptions have we made in the marketing model? What tests can we run to either confirm our assumptions or disprove them or clarify them?
- Which parts of our marketing model, if we changed them, could have the greatest positive impact on our business? How can we test the impact on our business by making changes in our marketing model?
- What are the biggest risks in our marketing model? What if one of the bedrock principles of our business, built into the marketing model, changes? How can we test new approaches based on potential future changes in our audience, new problems they need to solve, how they buy, or the actions of our competitors?

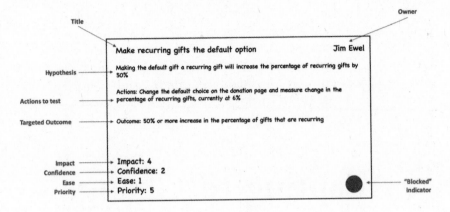

Figure 11.6   Typical entry in a validated learning backlog

Review Your Sales Funnel and Customer Journey

Examine your sales funnel or customer journey and then brainstorm ideas (hypotheses) for improving it. Start not at the top of the funnel but at the last step and work your way up. You want to optimize the bottom of the funnel before you begin increasing the number of new leads you pour into the funnel; otherwise, many of the leads you pour in will fail to convert, and you'll get no second chance with these leads. This is similar to plugging holes in a leaky bucket before you use it to carry water.

Perform a Content Audit

Which content is particularly effective? Which content is not very effective? How can you test your existing content? What content are you missing? What are new ways to distribute your content? How can you test these new channels?

There are probably many more ways to come up with ideas to build a validated learning backlog. The three above will get you started.

The next discipline, adapting to change, delivers on one of the key promises of Agile marketing: Agile makes marketers more agile as they respond to changes in the marketplace, changes in customer behavior, competitive challenges, potential brand damaging events, or fleeting opportunities. Let's take a look at how Agile marketing can help us adapt to change.

Chapter 12

Adapting to Change

Change is the law of life. And those who look only to the past or present are certain to miss the future.

—John F. Kennedy, American statesman

The Agile method includes some built-in adaptability to change:

- Agile teams don't write three-, four-, or five-year plans, or even yearly plans, so they have little chance of losing sight of the changing environment. Instead, they plan every quarter, with shifts in priority as often as the next Sprint (Scrum) or the next item in the backlog (Kanban).
- Agile teams don't run big campaigns, committing to year-long buys of advertising and continuing to run advertising and promotions despite changes in the market or the lack of success of those campaigns.
- Agile teams test regularly against customer perception and receptivity. If customers have new choices (new competitors enter the market) or customers stop spending in your category (the economy tightens), the impact of these changes shows up quickly to a team doing regular testing.

- Managers of Agile organizations who practice a balanced portfolio strategy, with at least 10 percent of their resources devoted to new, higher-risk projects, detect change more quickly than organizations that spend their marketing budget on "what's always worked." Agile organizations also tend to be the agents of change in their category, rather than the ones reacting to change.

Agile teams can implement other processes that increase their adaptability to change.

Reacting Rapidly

Webster defines *agile* as "marked by ready ability to move with quick and easy grace." Not surprisingly, this definition leads to the expectation that Agile marketers can react quickly and with "grace" to fast-moving events. But nothing in Scrum or Kanban prepares Agile marketers to handle a brand-damaging event or a PR opportunity window so small that it's measured not in days but in hours.

So how do Agile marketers react with grace to fast-moving events?

Disaster Preparedness

Just as your company has a plan for a natural disaster like an earthquake, your brand must have a plan for brand-damaging events and unexpected challenges like the worldwide downturn due to the Covid-19 virus.

1. *Form a disaster preparedness team.* Every brand is unique, but here's a starting list. The disaster preparedness team should include an executive leader, a marketing strategist, a copywriter, someone from creative, someone from HR, someone from PR (internal or agency), someone from investor relations if you're a public company, someone from analyst relations if you're followed by industry analysts, and an events coordinator. These roles might all be filled by a handful of people or by a dozen.
2. *Make sure that expectations are understood before the threat or the unexpected challenge occurs.* The team must discuss potential threats and must know senior management's expectations of the nature and the timeliness of the response. You can't precisely anticipate the threat, but a discussion while heads are cool reduces or eliminates the need for the same discussion in the heat of the event.

3. *Decide in advance how decisions are made.* Emphasize the ability to make decisions quickly; fight to require no more than two levels of executive buy-in. The executive on the brand-damage team must have the authority to make most decisions. Although you can't assess in advance all of the possibilities or make firm "rules" on decision-making authority, you must know the limits of your team's decision-making power. When disaster looms, no critical decision can wait more than 24 hours.

Membership in the disaster-preparedness team isn't a full-time role. All members have their day jobs. Unless responding to an event, the team meets quarterly to ensure that the preparedness plan is up to date, that no changes have taken place in membership, and to discuss any necessary changes in process or decision-making.

There is one special case of disaster preparedness that every company should plan for: a security breach. This can happen to almost any company, and it is happening with increasing frequency. The disaster preparedness team should have a PR plan in place for responding to a security or privacy breach, including who communicates to the press, guidelines for communications (honest, direct, short), and guidelines for communicating to the affected parties.

Opportunity Preparedness

Just as you have a plan to respond to brand-damaging events, you must have a plan to respond to brand-enhancing opportunities. In his excellent book *Newsjacking: How to Inject Your Ideas into a Breaking News Story and Generate Tons of Media Coverage*, David Meerman Scott calls this newsjacking: inserting yourself or your brand into the news cycle to gain favorable coverage.

How do Agile marketing teams prepare for these brand-enhancing opportunities? As with disaster preparedness, Agile marketing teams prepare by following these steps:

1. *Decide in advance who is on the team.* Typically, the opportunity-preparedness team is smaller than the brand-disaster-preparedness team, with perhaps as few as two people. One monitors the news for opportunities. One crafts the response.
2. *Know how decisions will be made.* Have as few levels of decision-making authority as possible so that decisions can be made quickly.
3. *Choose someone to monitor current events, current memes, upcoming events, and current social trends to identify opportunities.* This person—possibly the

lone full- or nearly full-time team member—nominates opportunities and the team must be prepared to decide, within hours, whether to take action.

4. *Determine the expectations of a well-executed brand-opportunity response.* What are the rules for what not to do in taking advantage of news events? For example, do not *newsjack* around tragedies. Obvious? Yes. And yet marketers have violated this rule.

There are many examples of poorly done newsjacking. A Texas mattress company tied a promotion to the September 11, 2001, terrorist attack in the United States. Kenneth Cole ads tried to leverage the Arab Spring. A few years after the Boston Marathon bombing, Adidas tweeted "Congratulations, you survived the Boston Marathon." On the other side, Italian fruit cooperative Melinda received positive press and positive comments on social media when it digitally printed two million boxes of apples with personalized messages of support to the victims of the 2016 earthquake in central Italy. Melinda then donated one euro to the relief effort for each message it received via social media.[1]

Newsjacking can be overdone. Brands that overdo newsjacking risk being seen as shameless promoters. It must also be done with humor and with an authentic voice. In their first attempts at newsjacking, the team discusses what authentic means for them, and monitors customers' reactions to its foray into newsjacking.

Adapting to Changes in the Marketplace

Agile marketers respond to fast-moving events, whether brand-damaging threats or brand-enhancing opportunities. They also respond to longer-term trends, including changes in the marketplace, recognizing the need to adapt to these changes before their competitors do. How can this be done?

Many organizations believe that responding to long-term trends is the responsibility of the CEO and other senior managers. That is true—and managers can be assisted by a person or a team dedicated to recognizing and proposing strategies for adapting to long-term trends and risks from changes in the marketplace.

This team pulls from many disciplines in the organization; experts tend to view the world through their own lenses, and they have access to a variety of trends and information sources. Joining the marketing strategist on the team are people from research, development, production, customer service, and finance.

The team identifies the critical assumptions inherent in the business model and examines whether the organization is prepared to adapt to changes to those assumptions.

The team may also examine the environment in terms of Porter's Five Forces model or Clayton Christiansen's Disruptive Forces model. With either, the team must be thorough, particularly in looking at risks posed by changes in critical underlying assumptions and technologies.

It can be useful to apply the ROAM model, part of the Scaled Agile Framework (SAFe), to risks identified through this examination of hidden assumptions and of risks presented by long-term trends.[2] In the ROAM model, teams examine and then categorize each risk as follows:

- _Resolved_—The team agrees that the risk is no longer a concern.
- _Owned_—A team member owns resolving the risk, mitigating the risk, or convincing the team that the risk is acceptable.
- _Accepted_—The team concludes that the risk cannot be resolved or mitigated, and that it is an acceptable risk.
- _Mitigated_—The team comes up with a plan to mitigate the risk.

Adapting to these long-term trends positions an organization to improve its competitive position, particularly if it isn't the number-one brand in a market. The team looks for opportunities to improve its competitive position by adapting to longer-term trends faster or better than the competition.

Responding to Competitive Challenges

Marketing teams often fail to respond to competitive challenges quickly or appropriately. The keys to success? Daily monitoring of competitors and rapid, customer-focused response.

Monitor Competitors

- _Google alerts._ At minimum, every competitive analyst sets up Google alerts on the main competitors, including their product names and names of their executives. These alerts provide news and mentions.
- _Investor relations._ If your competitors are public companies, frequently check the investor relations portion of their website, sign up for alerts if possible, and talk regularly with the analysts following the company. Everything that your competitor tells a financial analyst is public, and

it's surprisingly common for executives to reveal important information to these financial analysts. When I ran marketing for Microsoft SQL Server, I spoke regularly with one of the financial analysts that covered Oracle. My competitive reports were studded with information gleaned from his public reports and from my private conversations with him.

- *Social listening tools.* Tools like Hootsuite, Awario, Keyhole, Mention, and Brandwatch monitor social media channels and tell you what your competitors are saying and what people are saying about them.
- *SEO and AdWords spending.* Tools like SEMrush, Ahrefs, and SpyFu tell you where you rank compared to your competitors for keywords. Some also tell you approximately what your customers are bidding and spending on AdWords.
- *Display advertising spend.* Tools like Adbeat and What Runs Where provide limited information on what your competitors are spending—and which way they're trending—on display ads.
- *Industry analysts.* If you and your competitors are covered by industry analysts like Gartner, Forrester, or IDC, talking with the analysts that cover your competitors and reading their reports can uncover competitive strategies and information.

Respond Quickly to Competitive Challenges

In the 1990s, responding to competitors' threats in a week or two was acceptable. Marketers are now expected to respond within days, and sometimes within hours.

Keep your balance here, of course. Confirm that you have the information you need and a quality response before responding. A quick response that is inaccurate and weak could cost you more than no response.

Keep It Customer-Focused

Companies can become obsessed with competitors and lose sight of the customer. When I was at Microsoft, we competed with Novell in the networking business. Novell, obsessed with beating us and having lost sight of their own customers, failed to focus on why customers and dealers were switching to us.

In particular, Novell took many of its dealers for granted and failed to give them a reason to continue to sell Netware. When we announced our first dealer program, I was a sales representative for Microsoft in the

Midwest. I signed up one of Novell's dealers in Indianapolis as possibly the first dealer in this new Microsoft program. Later, the dealer told me that when he told the Novell rep that he had become a Microsoft dealer, the Novell rep kicked him out of his car, leaving the dealer stranded on the side of the road. Customer focus?

Voices from the Field: Adapting to Change

Roland Smart, author of The Agile Marketer, *is CMO/COO of the DBT Center of Marin, an evidence-based therapy practice in Northern California. He was VP of marketing at Pantheon and VP of social and community marketing at Oracle.*

Jim: How has Agile marketing prepared you for change? How were you set up? What did you do before the change?

Roland: Change is scary, especially when it's unexpected and coming on fast. After many years of putting Agile to use, I've become less afraid of change. I can't overstate how this has prepared me and set up my teams for change.

I've had opportunities to lead through such times. While at Involver, a social technology company, our business changed overnight once Facebook stopped supporting branded applications and custom pages. Recently, I've helped the DBT Center of Marin—a provider of mental health care—quickly transition to a fully online offering to support clients during the Covid-19 pandemic.

Though fairly extreme cases, these exemplify what we'd prepared for. At Involver, relationships with Facebook leadership alerted us to potential change. In general, we diversified to become less reliant on one platform. At the DBT Center, we'd noted a movement to bring therapy online and were investing in a foundation to bring such a model within reach. We did not expect online delivery to become our top priority.

The takeaway: integrate your Agile practice with your strategic planning practice—and specifically with scenario planning. This gives your teams a chance to build high-level backlogs for potential (and unexpected) changes. This may seem to conflict with "responding to change over following a plan," but in fact it occurs at the intersection of Agile and strategic planning. Give your teams a chance to role-play, responding to a crisis in an Agile fashion before they have to; they'll come away with greater confidence in their ability to self-organize and experiment in the face of an oncoming freight train.

Jim: How has Agile marketing helped you once an unexpected change occurs?

Roland: In the best-case scenario, Agile teams that have worked together—durable teams—know how to self-organize, prioritize work, and deliver without wasted time. This emerges from the inherent transparency of the Agile approach, the adoption and evolution of a shared method (via regular retrospectives), and shared social norms that gel over multiple projects.

At Oracle, I managed such a team, one focused on driving demand through the self-publishing platform, which we made available to all business units. About nine months after the initial rollout, we'd had enough success that leaders across the company started asking about novel applications of the platform. One such leader looked after the traditional publishing group that published print versions of *Oracle Magazine, Java Magazine,* and *Profit Magazine.* These sites were not within our remit or target customer set, although we had aspirations of eventually serving them. That opportunity arose sooner than expected.

Their legacy business model was at the end of its lifecycle. The online/offline experience was out of date. It came to a head quickly when their planned technology partner failed to deliver a workable solution. The technology provider approached solution development using waterfall and, fairly late in the process, it became clear that their solution would not work. We stepped in to work with the magazines to get a minimum-viable-product (MVP) site up and running in weeks.

This was possible because we brought an Agile mindset to the work and because we routinely delivered work in an incremental and modular fashion. We built solutions from component parts rather than from scratch. Beyond that, we enabled the magazine teams to break down and validate their vision through a backlog of work released biweekly—a revelation for a team once locked into waterfall with outsourced development.

(continued)

(*Continued*)

Not all firms have durable teams; in fact, it's more common to form a team in response to a change. Here, too, the fundamentals apply: The team members must be practiced at Agile; they must know how to quickly align on a method and establish the social norms that enable them to communicate and collaborate effectively; they must embrace an Agile mindset so that they invest only the bare minimum to validate that they're on the right track.

Jim: How has Agile marketing helped you take advantage of a fleeting opportunity, one that, if you don't act quickly, vanishes within a day or a week?

Roland: I've seen two key practices facilitate the ability to respond to fleeting opportunities (e.g., newsjacking). The first is resource allocation. The second is developing the capacity to quickly generate ideas and experiment.

Capacity allocation: Teams expected to respond regularly to unexpected work are candidates for burnout. Thus, it pays to bake in this capacity when Sprint planning or allocating work. Smaller firms reserve at least 10 percent of the team's bandwidth for unexpected or unplanned work. Bigger firms put dedicated teams on call to respond to unexpected or unplanned work. Companies large and small rely on external agencies and partners to supply the capacity to respond quickly; this works best when such firms are on retainer and working alongside the internal teams.

High-tempo testing: Teams that respond effectively to fleeting opportunities know how to develop creative solutions and break them down into the smallest releases that have value. Testing teams (and growth teams), who do this every day are well suited to respond to opportunities. They know that few experiments deliver positive results and that big wins come from running many experiments—as is true with fleeting opportunities. Consider investing in such a team and expect many small failures before you get a win.

The final discipline, creating remarkable customer experiences, builds on the other five. It requires alignment, cross-functional teams, the use of processes like Scrum and Kanban, lots of validated learning, and the ability to respond to changing customer needs. Let's take a look at this final, critical discipline.

Chapter 13

Creating Remarkable Customer Experiences

This is what customers pay us for—to sweat all these details so it's easy and pleasant for them to use our computers. We're supposed to be really good at this. That doesn't mean we don't listen to customers, but it's hard for them to tell you what they want when they've never seen anything remotely like it.
— Steve Jobs, American entrepreneur and co-founder of Apple Computer

Creating remarkable customer experiences lies at the heart of Agile marketing. It is the ultimate outcome.

If marketers use Agile simply to produce more content, more advertising, more social media shares—more unwanted copy that never gets read—then we've failed. The ultimate test of Agile marketing is this: Can it be used to create an engaging, differentiated customer experience that draws new customers and engages them powerfully with the brand, and in remarkable ways?

Marketing Is About Experiences

In their book, *Experiences: The 7th Era of Marketing*, Robert Rose and Carla Johnson argue convincingly that we are in a new era of marketing—an era based on *experiences*. Figure 13.1 outlines Rose and Johnson's seven eras of marketing. Although not everyone would describe the history of marketing in terms of these specific seven eras, there is general agreement among marketers that there is a difference between marketing products alone; marketing products plus services; and marketing products, services and a brand relationship.

This seventh era of marketing goes beyond marketing based on products or services or customer relationships. The seventh era is characterized by *compelling customer experiences*. Rose and Johnson describe the challenge of modern marketing thus:

It's not just HOW consumers are changing—researching, reviewing, and buying. It's also WHAT THEY VALUE MOST. This is also changing. And guess what? It's not your product any longer. They value experiences. If you don't offer compelling, differentiated experiences, your current customers will research, look, purchase, and become loyal elsewhere (emphasis in the original).[1]

Customers don't want products or services. Customers want to see their expectations met and their problems solved—and all on *their* terms.

Customers don't explicitly want relationships. Brands want relationships with customers, because they want to generate evermore revenue from that relationship.

Customers don't want brands. Increasingly, a customer's perception of a brand is about the experience: the experience of buying a product or service, the initial use of the product or service, the long-term value of the product or service, the experience of getting help with the product or service, etc.

Customer expectations are increasing for every brand in every industry. If you want to improve your shopping cart and checkout experiences, you're competing not only against companies in your industry but also against Amazon and the expectations set by their one-click checkout. When you look to differentiate by improving the friendliness and consistency of your service staff, you're competing not just against your direct competitors but against the customer experiences offered by Starbucks and by Chick-fil-A.

Companies that provide superior customer experiences cash in on greater customer satisfaction and reduced customer churn.[2] Great customer experiences build premium brands and greater profits. Research by American Express shows that more than two-thirds of consumers are

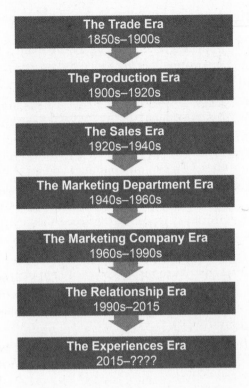

Figure 13.1   The seven eras of marketing
Source: courtesy of Carla Johnson

willing to pay more—17 percent more, on average—for better customer service.[3]

Chief marketing officers, in addition to their longtime role as stewards of the brand, are now stewards of the customer experience. Let me repeat that: CMOs are stewards of the customer experience. This requires new approaches to marketing; marketing that lends itself well to the Agile approach.

The Agile Approach to Creating Remarkable Customer Experiences

Let's take a look, through the lens of Agile marketing's six key values, at how Agile can be used to create remarkable customer experiences.

Collaborate and Create Cross-Functional Teams

The sixth principle of Agile marketing, collaboration over silos and hierarchy, is central to creating remarkable customer experiences. Creating remarkable customer experiences requires deep collaboration with other departments and cross-functional teams.

This is where marketing must take the lead and step outside its comfort zone. Too many marketers today see their role as explaining the product rather than creating the experience. Too many product-development organizations see their role as creating the product and then throwing it over the wall to marketers, to "market" the product, whatever that means. Marketers need to collaborate with product development and assume the role of the voice of the customer, accepting the accountability that comes with the role, and product development needs to be receptive to marketing's input.

Creating remarkable customer experiences requires cross-functional teams. Although the makeup of that team varies with the organization's objectives and the intended type of experience, the team generally includes the following skills:

- *Marketing*. Marketing must …
  - Identify the audiences for the experience.
  - Be the voice of the customer.
  - Ensure that the experience activates emotional connections, as opposed to presenting a list of features or services.
  - Tell the story of the experience.

  We'll look more at the role of marketing later in this chapter.

- *Design*. Remarkable customer experiences follow great design principles: simplicity, attention to detail, and consistency. Design thinking—research, generating ideas, testing ideas with prototypes, refining ideas, and telling stories—can help in developing remarkable customer experiences.
- *Product management*. A good product manager keeps the team on track and ensures that the experience delivers on its goals.
- *Development and operations*. Someone—through software, through hardware, or by orchestrating a series of human actions—develops the experience.

- *Testing and analytics.* Someone with skills in testing and analysis assesses whether the experience hits its goals and whether customers find the experience remarkable.
- *Executive leadership.* The CMO takes the lead and stays intimately involved in creating remarkable customer experiences, with day-to-day leadership delegated to the team or someone on the team.

Start Small and Rapidly Iterate

Remarkable customer experiences don't come out of nowhere. Your first attempt almost certainly won't suffice. The team realizes success by iterating to a great solution, not by creating the perfect solution on the first try.

As demonstrated earlier, rapid iteration translates to being first-to-market with a superior customer experience. Monthly or quarterly iteration? A thing of the past. Increase your metabolism. Turn the crank faster. Pick up the pace. Whatever the metaphor, iterate rapidly to create great customer experiences.

Validate Your Learning

How do you know that you've created a remarkable experience? Rave reviews from customers? Rave reviews from yourselves? Hardly. The metric is customer engagement with your brand and positive business outcomes. Decide up front how you'll measure remarkable, and experiment and adjust until the business outcomes demonstrate that customers, because of their experience, are engaging and buying.

Personalize the Experience

You can't design one experience that fits everyone. Instead, personalize the experience based on user actions and on customers' individual needs—a challenging task and almost always necessary. One-size-fits-all has little appeal. Customers expect experiences differentiated to their values, not yours.

Personalization may also entail risk. Brands that play it safe, trying to create an experience that appeals to everyone, usually end up creating an experience that appeals to no one. Brands like Red Bull don't appeal to everyone. I admire their marketing, but the product doesn't appeal to me or my baby-boomer generation. Red Bull's marketing is personalized to engage my millennial students; their experience is that Red Bull speaks directly to them.

Hedge Your Bets

The fourth principle of Agile marketing, "many small experiments over a few large bets," applies to creating remarkable customer experiences. Don't start by making a large bet or two on customer experiences. Start small and run many experiments. Make a lot of small bets. Figure out what works and expand after you get evidence that customers respond to your offering.

Starbucks did this with its Roastery, originally intended to be a Seattle one-off (see Figure 13.2). Although it was not cheap to build, especially when compared to the typical Starbucks store, it was a small bet within the

Figure 13.2   Starbucks roastery
Source: Jim Ewel

context of Starbucks' yearly spending. It turned out to be a hit at its original location, where it soon became a must-see for locals and tourists. Starbucks then opened additional Roasteries in New York, Chicago, Shanghai, Milan, and Tokyo.

Respond to Change (Quickly)

The experience that customers find remarkable today may not thrill for long if it doesn't grow and change as your competitors catch up and as your customers' needs and wants shift. Agile marketing, putting rapid response to change ahead of following a plan, can keep you ahead of your competition and relevant to your customers.

Once you've introduced a remarkable experience, continuously iterating on that experience and continuously validating its "remarkableness" enables teams to adapt to match any pace of change. And don't disband the team that creates the remarkable customer experience; instead, challenge it to continuously improve the experience and to adapt it to changing times and changing customer needs.

Case Study: Creating a Remarkable Customer Experience

Vail Ski Resorts and its creation of the EpicMix experience illustrates the importance of creating remarkable customer experiences. In 2009, the economy was in freefall. The collapse in housing prices led to foreclosures, to the demise of financial giants like Lehman Brothers, and to a global recession. Families looking to cut their expenses stopped scheduling expensive ski vacations.

Faced with this potential decline in bookings, Vail Ski Resorts could have applied the levers of the traditional marketing mix. It could have lowered prices, run expensive promotional campaigns, or marketed in new places. Instead it redesigned the customer experience to dramatically exceed customer expectations.

Vail created a new experience by taking advantage of new infrastructure based on RF-ID tags embedded in guests' lift tickets. Vail read these tags with RF-ID readers, installed at critical

(continued)

(*Continued*)

locations on the slope, to track customers and provide a new, information-rich experience. It applied many of the techniques for engagement used in games, a process known as *gamification*. For example, customers could earn "Pins," or awards on the ski slope, by descending a certain distance during their first hour of skiing or during their first day on the slope. They could earn pins for mastering more difficult ski runs. They could compete in real time with their friends and family, while competing virtually with everyone who ever did or ever would ski the slope.

Vail built "leader boards" into their mobile and online applications and made it very easy for people to share their success with others. Vail sent photographers out on the slope, who took pictures and then matched the digital images with the guests by swiping the RF-ID tags in the guests' lift tickets. Guests shared those images, containing an embedded watermark for Vail and EpicMix, on Facebook.

Vail also used the data gathered on guests to customize communications with them. Adventure skiers, for example, got one kind of communication from Vail; families skiing with young kids got another.

The results speak for themselves: "In its first season, EpicMix was a huge success. Nearly 100,000 guests activated their EpicMix accounts. Forty percent downloaded the mobile apps and nearly 6 million digital ski pins were given out. On top of that, 45 percent of the users chose to share their accomplishments on Facebook and Twitter—resulting in more than 35 million social impressions."[4]

In short, in the face of a crashing economy, customers told their friends about their remarkable Vail experience, and bookings *increased*.

We've covered the six Agile marketing disciplines that individual marketers and marketing teams need to master. We turn next to the Four Shifts that organizations must adopt for Agile to take root and flourish.

Part III

The Four Shifts

As I helped organizations adopt Agile marketing, I saw that they needed to do more than master the Six Disciplines. They needed also to shift their organizational culture, beliefs, and behaviors. Although each organization encountered its own challenges during this culture transformation, all came down ultimately to a commitment to make these Four Shifts:

- From a focus on outputs to a focus on outcomes
- From a campaign mentality to a mentality of continuous improvement
- From an internal focus to a customer focus
- From top-down decision-making to decentralized decision-making

The Four Shifts cover each of these shifts and provide some guidance on implementing them. Many people would argue that making the Four Shifts is more important than mastering the Six Disciplines. They may be right. I can certainly attest to the fact that making the Four Shifts can be very difficult for many organizations. If you are a senior executive or you prefer to start with the strategic, this next section is for you.

Chapter 14

Introduction to the Four Shifts

All serious daring starts from within.
—Eudora Welty, American author and essayist

In helping organizations implement Agile in their marketing organizations, I find that it's not enough for them to learn certain skills and adopt certain disciplines. The organization must also shift in terms of thinking and cultural norms. Otherwise, Agile gets used as a process-management methodology, with small improvements in communication and productivity, and without the transformational gains that can happen with a shift to an Agile mindset.

I've found Four Shifts to be critical to an Agile mindset:

The Four Shifts

A shift from a focus on outputs to a focus on outcomes

A shift from a campaign mentality to a mentality of continuous improvement

A shift from an internal focus to a customer focus

A shift from top-down decision-making to decentralized decision-making

These shifts are represented on the outside of the Six Disciplines circle (see Figure 14.1).

The first shift, from a focus on outputs to a focus on outcomes, requires that marketers shift their attention from producing content or advertising or social media campaigns or any other kind of marketing materials, and focus instead on how to achieve business outcomes as measured by customer

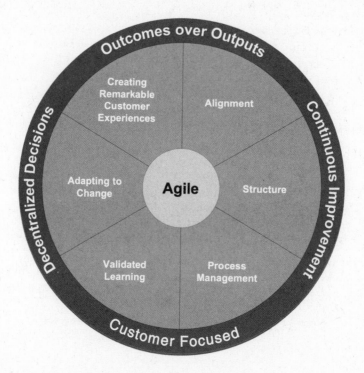

Figure 14.1   The four shifts and six disciplines of agile marketing

behaviors. This is a shift in mindset, requiring that marketing collaborate with business units to determine which business outcomes are important and how to achieve these in terms of customer actions.

The second shift, from a campaign mentality to one of continuous improvement, gives marketing departments trouble. We are so accustomed to thinking in terms of marketing campaigns. We plan for marketing campaigns. We budget for marketing campaigns. We report our success in terms of marketing campaigns. We fill our resumes with the results of marketing campaigns.

Agile marketers move away from the campaign mentality. Instead, we focus on two things: continuous, incremental improvements and disruptive marketing innovation. Campaigns may still exist to deliver brand awareness, sales leads, and core revenue, but the focus is not on the always-on campaign mentality and instead on continuous improvement and disruptive innovation.

The third shift, from an internal focus to a customer focus, receives much lip service. I've never met the marketer or marketing organization that doesn't claim to be customer focused. But customer focus is in the eye of the beholder. Customers don't necessarily find most companies customer focused. According to research from the consulting firm Forrester,[1] only 31 percent of companies are customer-experience-led businesses. Marketing organizations that hope to achieve an Agile transformation must help their company make the shift, for real, from an internal focus to a customer focus.

The fourth shift, from top-down to decentralized decision-making, may be the hardest for most organizations. Marketing executives don't want to give up examining and opining about almost every piece of customer-facing content. And give up they must, to free themselves to focus on leadership: translating big corporate themes into the programs and projects that execute on these themes, deciding where to deploy resources to have the greatest impact, removing obstacles to success for their team, and hiring and developing the leaders of tomorrow. Shifting from top-down to decentralized decision-making puts decision-making closer to the customer, where front-line employees tend to have the best information to satisfy and delight that customer. This shift, which makes frontline employees more accountable, also develops their decision-making skills.

The chapters that follow look closely at each of these shifts.

Chapter 15

From Outputs to Outcomes

Realists do not fear the results of their study.
—*Fyodor Dostoevsky, Russian novelist*

When I first began practicing Agile, a colleague said to me: "I'm impressed by all of the work that your team is producing. But is it producing business results? Or are we just generating a lot of advertising and content without generating more leads and revenue?" In other words, were we focused on the outputs of marketing, and not delivering the customer and business outcomes that were the reason for doing all of the work?

He had a point. I researched the issue and learned that the software developers had also run into this problem. Their solution, which fit well with Agile marketing, was to focus on outcomes over outputs.

The Value of Focusing on Outcomes over Outputs

Teams that focus on customer and business outcomes and are rewarded for achieving those outcomes produce better results than teams producing more outputs (advertising campaigns, content, events, etc.) and who are measured on throughput.

More marketing output does not translate into better business outcomes. A study by Amplero Research and Globsys confirmed this. After implementing a new targeting strategy—personalizing emails to customers—the average customer received just two emails per month, down from 17. The lift in average revenue per user attributable to the campaign, however, grew from 0.32 percent to 2.8 percent, a 9× increase! In a three-month period, this resulted in $3.2 million in increased revenue from fewer, higher-quality emails.[1]

The focus on outcomes also transforms marketing from a content factory and a cost center to a contributing member of the revenue and profitability team. It changes the relationship of marketing to the business units, aligning the two on common goals.

A focus on outcomes motivates the marketing team. No one wants to be part of a marketing factory, taking orders for collateral and spitting it out at an increasingly frenetic pace. A focus on outcomes empowers marketers to strategize with the business units, to take responsibility for poor outcomes, and to reap the rewards of great outcomes.

How to Shift from Outputs to Outcomes

Begin a shift from outputs to outcomes by establishing agreement with the various business units on the most important outcomes to be measured. Although sometimes these outcomes may be end goals of the business, such as revenue and profitability, often they are intermediate goals that marketing can directly impact. Marketing should be measured by the customer actions that lead to the end goals of revenue and profitability.

In a business that sells products or services to other businesses using a direct-sales force, marketing may be responsible primarily for producing sales-qualified leads (SQLs)—an intermediate outcome that becomes a primary measure of marketing's success. As shown in Figure 15.1, other examples of intermediate outcomes include same-store foot traffic (retailers), cart starts (online retailers), applications (colleges and universities), and members (membership organizations).

Outcomes	Outputs
Sales-qualified leads (SQLs)	Downloadable white paper
Conversions to membership	Ads and impressions
Average revenue per user (ARPU)	Webinars
Customer lifetime value (CLV)	Blog posts
Same-store foot traffic	Email flyers
Cart starts	Google Adwords campaigns
Student applications	Brochures

Figure 15.1   Example outcomes vs. outputs

Note that outcomes represent customer behavior, not your actions. A prospect signs up to become a member. A customer increases spending with you, resulting in higher average revenue. A customer walks into a store or adds an item to the online cart. Identifying the customer behavior associated with a metric ensures that you measure outcomes and not outputs. Identifying the critical behavior and what prompts that behavior also puts you in the mind of the customer and delivers higher quality and more relevant outputs.

The shift from outputs to outcomes also requires that the marketing team move from a production mentality to a learning mentality (see Chapter 11 on validated learning). Outputs are no longer one and done, but are multiple experiments to determine what generates the best outcomes. Which content generates the best results with which customers? How often and with what timing do we deliver the content? Marketers who shift from outputs to outcomes begin to ask interesting questions and learn more about their customers, producing better customer experiences.

Moving from a production mentality to a learning mentality gives marketers more flexibility and more accountability. In the old paradigm, marketing takes orders from the business units. Produce this brochure. It should be six pages long and have 12 images. The business unit is accountable for the outcomes; marketing just takes orders. In the new paradigm, marketing co-owns accountability for outcomes with the business unit.

There are some drawbacks to focusing on outcomes over outputs:

- *Impacting outcomes and measuring marketing's contribution is hard.* Did the customer not convert because of activities and content under marketing's control or because of product issues? Did those leads fail to convert into customers because of the quality of the leads or because sales didn't close the leads? Impacting outcomes and measuring marketing's contribution is much tougher than producing a glossy brochure.

- *Choosing the right outcome may be difficult.* A business that focuses on profitability may lose out over the long term to a business that focuses on revenue and customer growth. A focus on sales-qualified leads (SQLs) may turn the marketing department into a lead factory rather than the creators of remarkable customer experiences.
- *Impacting outcomes takes time.* You've launched a new promotion and the initial results are lackluster. Is this a problem with the promotion, or does it simply take time for the market to absorb and react to the promotion? Marketing effects almost always take more time than expected.

Despite these drawbacks, focusing on outcomes over outputs is a critical shift for most marketing organizations to take.

In his brilliant article in *Hackernoon,* John Cutler says that the discussion of outcomes over outputs is much more nuanced than the simple "everyone needs to focus on customer and business outcomes versus busy work or a check the box mentality."[2] We need to think about short-, medium-, and long-term business outcomes and put them into the context of what the organization intends to achieve and what is happening in the market.

We need to recognize the impact of uncertainty on our business decisions and realize that not every risk will pan out. If we focus only on sure bets, we miss out on the potential rewards of building a portfolio of safe bets, low-risk bets, and high-risk bets.

Mapping outcomes to short-, medium-, and long-term business priorities for the organization helps teams and individuals understand the importance of their work. Measurements like objectives and key results (OKRs) tend to focus on short-term outcomes, without putting them into a context that teams and individuals can understand.

Case in point: Everyone at Apple understands that the long-term goal of the organization is revenue and profitability, not market share at any cost to revenue or profitability (that would be Google's strategy with Android). Revenue and profitability are the context that leads to marketing that emphasizes lifestyle, design, quality—everything but price. You'll never see an Apple ad, except perhaps from the carriers, that emphasizes price.

Agile marketers also need to recognize the importance of uncertainty in business decisions and build a portfolio that includes both safe and risky bets. Risky bets are not the same as stretch goals. Many companies force managers to forecast and accept stretch goals for outcomes. In most cases, these stretch goals are unrealistic. They also don't serve as a catalyst for innovation.

Instead, marketers focusing on outcomes embrace the 70-20-10 approach, as described in Chapter 2. They create a portfolio of marketing activities. Most deliver on the core business outcomes in well understood ways that have been proven to work. Some improve on existing approaches through experiments and A/B testing. And a few are risky, innovative, and potentially disruptive approaches, many of which will fail; those that succeed form the basis of exceptional growth and customer satisfaction in the future.

When we focus on customer and business outcomes, we need to do four things:

1. Have a mix of marketing activities focused on short-, medium-, and long-term customer and business outcomes.
2. Have a mix of marketing activities reflecting different levels of risk: low risk, medium risk, and higher risk but potentially disruptive.
3. Put these customer and business outcomes into a context, defined by the organization's mission and values and by the needs of a changing market.
4. Make room for individual innovation and initiative.

Critical Outcomes

Part One: Identify Critical Outcomes
Through internal discussions in the marketing group and discussions with the sales or business groups that you work with, determine the critical business outcomes. There might be only one—sales-qualified leads (SQLs), for example. There might be as many as five.

Choose business outcomes that you can measure and on which marketing can have an impact. For example, profitability of a product line may be critical to the business, but can you measure marketing's impact on the profitability of a product line? Probably not.

You may also want to have a mix of short-term, medium-term, and longer-term measures. For example, you can measure and improve SQLs in the short-term, while measures like customer lifetime value (CLV) take longer to measure and improve.

Part Two: Tie Critical Outcomes to Deliverables

On each card in your marketing backlog, write the critical out-come(s) likely to be affected by this delivery increment. Where possible, put a goal for improving this outcome. Each resulting card looks something like Figure 15.2.

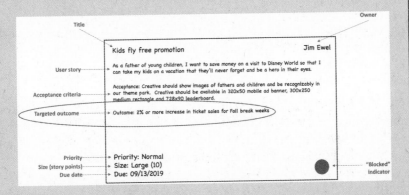

Figure 15.2   Backlog card with critical outcome

If a card cannot be tied to a critical outcome, consider whether the delivery increment or task belongs in the marketing backlog.

Part Three: Examine the Risk Profile of Your Portfolio

Put each card in your marketing backlog into one of these three categories:

1. *Low risk.* This is a well understood marketing activity, aimed at our core metrics. We've done this before, and we know that most marketing activities of this type work with little risk.
2. *Medium risk.* This is an experiment built off our core, low-risk marketing activities. It attempts to incrementally improve the effectiveness of our marketing.
3. *Innovation.* We have not tried this before. We don't know whether it will work. If it does, it could greatly affect our outcomes.

(continued)

(Continued)

After assigning a risk rating to each card, calculate the percentage of cards in each category. Look for about 50 percent of your activities to be well known and low-risk, 25 percent to be medium-risk experiments, and 25 percent to be innovation. Does the risk profile of your existing marketing backlog match these suggested percentages? If the percentage in the medium and innovation categories is lower than the suggested percentages, what will you do about it?

The next shift, from a campaign mentality to one of continuous improvement, is a change in culture—a change that doesn't come easily to marketers who have spent most of their careers creating, deploying, and celebrating campaigns. That's the topic of the next chapter.

Chapter 16

From Campaigns to Continuous Improvement

There is always room for improvement in our game.
—Virgil van Dijk, Dutch professional footballer

Most marketers think in terms of campaigns. The language is embedded in many of the tools used most commonly by marketers. Facebook Ad Manager and AdWords are organized around campaigns. And this works, if some of the campaigns are seen as experiments, some are continually tuned and improved, and others grow out of this experimentation and tuning. Too often, though, campaigns are run as "advertising" and declared as successful based on vanity metrics.

Marketers are like anyone else; we hate to report failure. And, typically, we are trained to weave stories. So rather than report that a campaign

161

failed to achieve the desired business outcomes, we tell a story using vanity metrics to demonstrate that the campaign was successful. Which of us has ever run a multimillion-dollar campaign and reported that it didn't deliver great results?

That is why, in Agile marketing, we recommend continuous improvement over big-bang campaigns. Before spending lots of money, Agile marketers test: They create and record a hypothesis about what might work, and then seek to prove or disprove that hypothesis. If the hypothesis is true, and the promotion or interaction delivers desirable business outcomes, the Agile marketer then tunes the promotion or interaction to produce the best business outcomes. Only when we have evidence of the efficacy of an approach do we spend the big money, and we continue to measure effectiveness as we scale up the campaign—knowing that some great ideas don't scale.

Continuous improvement lies at the heart of Agile. Agile requires that we put aside our attempts to ensure that something is perfect before we show it to a client or put it in front of customers. Agile requires that we build something quickly, get feedback through validated learning, and then have another go at it. Continuous improvement.

This shift, from a mentality of one-and-done campaigns to a mentality of continuous improvement, is critical to the successful adoption of Agile in marketing. So how do organizations accomplish this shift? I recommend four key areas of focus.

Build a Culture of Data-Driven Decision-Making

Many marketing organizations are anything but data-driven in their decision-making. Decisions are made instead according to the highest paid person's opinion, also known as the HIPPO method of decision-making. Even when decisions are distributed, opinions, rather than data, drive decision-making.

Organizations that make the shift from campaigns to continuous improvement build a culture of data-driven decision-making. Before embarking on a larger marketing spend, they confirm that the chosen approach works and is optimized.

This cultural shift starts, like almost all cultural shifts, at the top. Decision makers must demand data and then follow the data. Overriding the data by relying on instinct or experience sends the wrong message. If instinct suggests a different approach, then, rather than overruling the data, ask questions about the underlying assumptions and the sources of the data. Train people to meet your expectations on the quality and sources of the data.

Build an Infrastructure for Testing

Building effective tests requires process, people, and tools, so budget for people and tools. While commercial offerings for A/B testing may meet many of your needs, many organizations find that they have to build their own infrastructure by building their own tools or by putting together a stack of tools and integrating them effectively.

The infrastructure must address the following requirements:

- *Scalability*. The infrastructure must scale in terms of the number of tests and the volume of customer interactions. Some tools track up to 10 tests per week and then fail when tracking hundreds per week. Plan for growth.
- *Segmentation and personalization*. The infrastructure must support slicing and dicing your web traffic, mailing lists, and advertising audiences along many dimensions. It must support personalization based not only on segments but also on actions.
- *Cross channel*. Your testing infrastructure must support all of your important channels and be able to answer questions about cross-channel influences. Do users who arrive at a landing page from an email respond exactly like users who arrive there from a display ad?
- *Flexibility*. The needs of one team don't match those of another. A/B testing may be enough for one team when another requires multivariate testing. Teams that emphasize email don't have requirements identical to those testing your website, your social media, or your display ads.
- *Best practices*. You can't have a statistician design every test. Establish and enforce best practices to yield statistically valid results and to enable comparison of results. Build these best practices into the infrastructure. For example, calculate the confidence level of a test based on historical average traffic numbers.
- *Ease of use*. Some who run tests are skilled at doing so. Others are not. An easy-to-use testing platform encourages marketers to test their assumptions, invites scaling up the number of tests run weekly, and does so without turning expert testers into a bottleneck. Make sure that the analytics produced by the tests are easily understandable and readily accessed. Because more people examine the test analytics than are involved in designing the tests, be certain that the metrics-presentation dashboard adheres to sound design principles.

Hire people versed in the statistics of testing and people versed in creative test design. Growing a culture of relevant testing and continuous improvement matters at least as much as building out your toolbox.

Set Testing Goals

Rather than asking your team to test more, set goals for the number of tests run each week or each month. Base the number on the maturity of your testing organization, the number of interactions available from which to get statistically significant results, and your need for testing.

If the team is not regularly testing now, start with one test every two weeks. When they achieve that, increase the tempo to three tests per week. If this sounds like a large jump, it is. The team will have to make some big changes to handle that jump in the number of tests, which is what you want them to do. If you have the volume of interactions, continually increase the frequency toward your goal (X tests/period) until you have a culture and an effective infrastructure for testing.

Run Exploratory and Optimization Tests

Sean Ellis, entrepreneur and CEO of GrowthHackers, likens running exploratory and optimization tests to the 1960s board game Battleship. You have to locate the battleships before you can destroy them. You explore channels or new promotions before you optimize them. You run exploratory tests and optimization tests. Your marketing portfolio has a mix of optimized, well understood approaches and innovative approaches.

Many teams fiddle with existing channels and approaches to optimize them; the best teams also experiment with new channels and new approaches to reach new customers or existing customers in new ways.

Continuous improvement applies to our practice of Agile marketing and to all of the disciplines. The wheel of the Six Disciplines doesn't imply that we implement from the top (alignment) and move once, clockwise, around the wheel. All of the disciplines are subject to continuous improvement; we build in feedback mechanisms and opportunities to repeatedly improve our application of all of the disciplines.

Implementing Agile is not a campaign; not one and done, with success communicated by the citing of vanity metrics. It is a journey of continuous improvement, measured by metrics that matter.

The next major shift requires organizations to move from an internal focus to a focus on the customer. That is the subject of our next chapter.

Chapter 17

From Internal Focus to Customer Focus

Be not afraid of discomfort. If you can't put yourself in a situation where you are uncomfortable, then you will never grow. You will never change. You will never learn.

—*Jason Reynolds, American author*

The third major shift for many marketing organizations is from an internal focus to a customer focus. This is not just cosmetic. Teams that make this shift produce more relevant content, increase conversion rates, and ultimately increase customer satisfaction and loyalty.

The shift to a customer focus can have profound impacts on the business. *Forrester* found that the more customer-focused companies achieved compound annual growth rates 7 to 30 percentage points higher than peers in their industry who were less so.[1] According to the most recent Deloitte study of Enterprise Customer Success (CS), fully 49 percent of companies with strong customer-success programs see double-digit year-over-year revenue growth.[2]

Agile marketing teams have many ways to improve their customer focus. I'll cover a few, such as user stories, robust user personas, customer journeys, and marketing technology to gather user data. I'll also cover how the Six Disciplines improve a marketing team's customer focus.

User Stories

User stories, which we described in Chapter 8 as part of the Scrum methodology, provide a powerful tool for understanding customers' objectives and motivations. Here are some examples.

As a potential carrier switcher, I want to lower my monthly bill for mobile phone service so that I can have money to spend on other things that I enjoy.

The role described in the first clause of a typical user story ("As a potential carrier switcher") identifies the customer. The user story encourages the marketer to get inside the head of the customer and to take his or her perspective. In my experience, many marketing teams find it difficult to write user stories from the customer perspective. Instead, they tend to write user stories like the following:

As a marketer at XYZ Company, I want to deliver a piece of content so that I can meet the needs of whatever department is asking for this content.

Or they may write most of their user stories from the perspective of their internal customers:

As a salesperson, I need a presentation that causes all of my customers to buy today so that I can make a bunch of commissions.

These user stories exaggerate only slightly. Wherever possible, and it is almost always possible, marketers must write user stories from the perspective of the end customer. Only then can marketers shift from an internal focus to a customer focus.

The shift from an internal focus to a customer focus also requires that marketers spend more time with customers and less in internal meetings. Marketers often write user stories based on received wisdom or from their best guess of customer needs and wants, rather than on primary research or experiences with customers.

To be effective, modern marketers need to gather primary research, not only about what customers say they want but what customers actually do when presented with choices. This requires getting on the front line with customers, something that can be encouraged, measured, and rewarded by managers of marketing teams.

More Robust User Personas

Too often, marketers build user personas based on their intuition or their general knowledge about customers, without doing sufficient primary research and talking directly to an adequate number of customers to build robust user personas. Carry out primary research and talk to customers to build a persona that includes, at a minimum, addressing the following questions:

- What are the key pain points?
- What does success look like for this person?
- What triggers this customer to look for a solution?
- Where does this customer get her information?
- What are her real or perceived barriers to a solution?
- Who influences her?
- What early buying signals does she exhibit?
- What product features are important to her?

Figure 17.1 shows an example of a robust user persona.

A template for a user persona is available on my website: http://agilemarketing.net/download/2037. I also recommend checking out the work of Adele Revella and the Buyer Persona Institute.[3]

There is a special persona that many teams neglect to profile but that may be the most important buyer persona to dig into: the brand advocate. This is the person who not only buys almost anything that your brand sells but also tells others about his positive experience with your brand. What does that person look like? What motivates him? Why does your brand appeal to him? Defining this persona is the first step to creating more brand advocates.

Creating Customer Journeys

Customers take various journeys, with various touchpoints, as they decide whether to make a purchase from you and your brand. Sometimes marketers base these customer journeys on customer personas; if the personas have specific buying intent, that can work. More often, teams build customer journeys based on their understanding of how and why customers buy: What does the customer want to accomplish? What is his intent as he considers and purchases a product or service? A thorough customer journey includes what customers want to accomplish at each stage in the customer journey and what they think and feel. Teams can then map the stages of

Persona

Fictional name

Key Pain Points
- Under appreciated, any problems turn into major complaints from more powerful doctors and nurses
- Interpreting viewed as a cost, not an advantage; budget is always an issue
- New immigrant groups present new challenges with new languages, cultural issues
- In some states, new legislation and licensing requirements are a pain point

Triggering Event
- Her manager is questioning the size and growth of her budget
- Her internal customers are complaining about insufficient services
- She is seeing growth in demand
- Her onsite vendors are not meeting her needs

Early Buying Signals
- Reaching out to colleagues at similar companies
- Internet search
- Filling out a contact form
- Reaching out to existing onsite and telephonic vendors

Influencers
- Other similar managers
- Finance/CFO (sometimes)
- Nursing and clinical leadership

What Does Success Look Like?
- A reduction in cost per patient encounter of at least 10%
- Ability to handle more clients without proportional growth in budget
- Internal customers like the new system
- Complaints to her office go down

Real or Perceived Barriers
- You're going to replace all my people and they'll be fired
- Video can't possibly provide as good an experience as in-person interpreters
- We had a bad experience with VRI in the past
- I don't want to train people to use a new system

Key Product Features
- No scheduling—eliminates a major headache within her organization
- Language selection
- Minimal IT involvement
- Quickly access service
- Reporting

Information Sources
- National groups and conferences:
- Local groups:
- Newsgroups, listserves
- Sales presentations, emails, direct mail

Figure 17.1 Example of a robust user persona
Source: Jim Ewel

the customer journey to touchpoints (retail in-person, online, search, social media, etc.) and discover the gaps or opportunities for improving their customer journey.

Although most customer journeys are represented as a linear buying process, this is seldom the case. Customers skip a step or circle back. Our marketing needs to take this into account.

Building a Customer Journey
Using the matrix below, either by yourself or with your team, fill in the details of at least one customer journey. Define each customer journey by one customer intent: buying a used car, selecting a new service provider, joining a health club, and so on.

	Learn	Weigh Alternatives	Shop	Post-Purchase
Doing				
Thinking				
Feeling				
Touchpoints				
Opportunities				

Figure 17.2   Customer Journey worksheet

First, modify, if necessary, the number of stages (columns) and the name of each stage in the customer journey. Second, map what the customer wants to accomplish (do), what she's thinking, and what she's feeling at each stage. Then map the possible touchpoints for each stage and, based on the touchpoint mapping and a sense of your current marketing content, list a few opportunities for improvement. Either on your own or with the input of sales and management, prioritize the opportunities. Add graphics as in Figure 17.3 if you like.

	Learn	Alternatives	Buy	Post-Purchase
Doing	Review our website See an ad on Facebook Ask questions on forums Read reviews Ask friends and family	Review competitive websites Read comparison reviews Ask friends and family Test drive alternatives Build matrix comparing alternatives	Choose model and options Get price quotes, terms Decide lease vs. buy Negotiate price, trade-in Fill out paperwork	Driving vehicle Repair vehicle Maintenance Interacting with dealer's service dept Making warranty claims
Thinking	Should I keep my current car? Sure would be nice . . . . Is this better than what I have right now? Can I afford this? What's the best deal?	Should / can I finance the car? Which options do I want / need? Should I wait for a sale? Which dealer should I go to?	How much will I pay today? Am I getting a good deal? Am I doing the right thing? Am I getting a fair price for my trade-in?	Did I make the right decision? Can I make the payments? How do I look in this new car?
Feeling	Overwhelmed with information	Confused — What are the different option packages? Frustrated — can't find exact fit	Anxiety — credit Hassle	Mad — repair bills
Touch points	Ads (online/print/tv) Facebook / social Reviews Other online sites Search	Facebook / social Reviews Consumer guides Awards Auto trader, etc	Dealership Car buying services KBB/Edmunds	Car Dealer service center
Opportunities	Improve website navigation Build and price widget What can I afford widget	Prescreen credit Compare options and pricing Highlight awards	Trade-in, transparency Lease vs. buy comparator	Improve dealer service evaluations Improve warranty process

Figure 17.3   Sample Customer Journey

Using Marketing Technology to Improve Customer Focus

Marketing technology now offers more opportunities to gather information about customer intent and behavior than I can list here. And the technology is constantly changing. Let's look at a few of the ways to gather information to improve our customer focus.

Single Source of Truth Customer Data Repository

You can't clearly focus on your customers if your data on their end-to-end customer experiences is fragmented, inconsistent, and scattered.

Agile marketing teams need single source-of-truth customer-data repositories. This requires marketing to collaborate with IT, and perhaps an external vendor, to get consistent data definitions and presentation of data. This is not an overnight exercise. Jeff Rasp, director, US Consumer Health Digital Strategy for Bayer, says that their first attempt to bring a portion of their data in-house to a single platform took over a year to roll out for a limited set of brands. The results were worth the trouble: Bayer reduced wasteful spending by 30 percent while increasing sales through real-time data on the effectiveness of its promotions.[4]

Website Interactions

If your customers go online to research your product or service, or to buy, you have a choice of tools to help you understand customer intent and behaviors. Starting with Google Analytics, make sure you understand your sources of acquisition, both for pre-purchase and purchase behaviors. Which pages are the most popular? Determine why customers are going to those pages. If they spend a lot of time on a popular page, you've likely provided valuable content. If they don't, assume you're not meeting their expectations.

Also look at heat-mapping tools like Optimizely or session-recording tools like Inspectlet to get a deeper understanding of customer behavior with regard to mobile and desktop versions of your site.

Chat and Chatbots

Chat enables you to interact with prospective customers to understand what they want to do or where your current marketing fails them. Once you're past the discovery phase and have begun to understand some of the common questions people have, chatbots like Drift can automate conversations. Because this takes place in real-time, this can be more effective than sending out automated emails.

Surveys

Whether you include a survey as part of your email drip or ask questions online using tools like Qualaroo, surveys can gather important customer information. Make your surveys short. Ask open-ended questions, or, in areas where you need to focus, ask short-answer questions: "Did you find what you were looking for?" "What could we have done better?" "Why did you visit our website today?"

Marketing as the Voice of the Customer

Just as it is important to align with the goals and objectives of the organization, it is also important for marketing to champion the voice of the customer to the rest of the organization. Here are eight best practices for improving your voice-of-the-customer activities.

Get Out of the Building

Steve Blank, one of the foremost gurus on successful startup practices, preaches the importance of "getting out of the building." By this he means getting real customer feedback as soon and as often as possible. Blank's exhortation to entrepreneurs applies equally to marketers.

Don't assume that you know your customer's needs. Get out of the building and talk to customers, in person when possible, and over the phone or via teleconference when not. Marketers too often have strong opinions about "what our customers want," having had no conversations to support that assertion.

Formalize Voice-of-the-Customer Feedback

Do you have a formal voice-of-the-customer (VOC) program? What resources have you dedicated to VOC? Companies that have strong customer-success programs spend upwards of 5 percent of their revenues on customer success.[5] How often is VOC information collected—regularly, or only around planning cycles? Is it collected in a formal way (every kind of customer, multiple touchpoints, data summarized, and tracked over time) or informally (executives listening in to customer service calls, for example)?

Collect VOC from All Personas and Touchpoints

Consider the personas, segments, and touchpoints involved in your buying decision, and confirm that you have VOC data from each. By touchpoints, I mean those of the customer journey and those across channels—digital, retail, call centers, social media.

Gather Qualitative and Quantitative Data

It can be interesting to see quantitative data about the percentage of customers using a feature, or the percentage of prospects using a given section of your website. It can be equally illuminating to hear firsthand customer quotes about a new promotion or a feature that you just introduced. Gather qualitative *and* quantitative data and use one to inform the other: Customer stories bring the data to life and inform new measurements. Data—particularly for those executives who want to see data—bolsters and validates experiences.

Remember Internal Sources of Customer Data

Frontline employees can provide valuable VOC data. It might at times be skewed, but employees are often the most aware of common customer issues.

It can also be illuminating to see how other areas of the organization impact frontline employees, thus in turn impacting customers. Gather voice of the frontline data. Which departments are most helpful as they work with customers? Which departments are least? Which policies and processes create barriers to doing business with your organization? Many organizations start a customer-success program by focusing on frontline employees. But don't overlook back-office processes and policies. These may be the very thing that is ruining the customer experience. No amount of frontline training can offset a terrible back-office experience.

Distribute Feedback Throughout the Organization

Gathering and compiling VOC data, in and of itself, isn't useful. The information must get to people who can do something about it.

The way in which you distribute VOC data can also impact its effectiveness. A huge attachment sent out in a dense email is unlikely to get read. A meeting, starting with the major insights, with time for questions, followed by sending out more detailed data, is more likely to have an impact.

Act on the Feedback

Do you honor the customers who provide feedback? How long, on average, does it take you to respond to feedback provided by Twitter, Facebook, your helpdesk, and email to your contact address? Many companies set a goal of responding to every complaint within 24 or 48 hours. If you set and meet this goal, you're among the best. A mere 16 percent of customers using social media to report problems get their issues resolved.[6]

Close the Loop

Where possible, let customers know how you acted on their feedback. If you can't let them know individually, publicize the changes that you've made in response to VOC data.

The Role of Agile Marketing in Customer Focus

How can Agile marketing help you improve your customer focus? Let's answer this question through the prism of the Six Disciplines.

Alignment

You begin your Agile journey by asking "Why Agile?" and "How do I measure my progress?" Now ask yourself what you hope to accomplish by shifting from an internal to a customer focus, and how you measure that progress. Will you use customer satisfaction scores (CSAT)? Net promoter scores (NPS)? Customer lifetime value (CLV)? Customer effort score for particular customer experiences? Decide up front.

The shift from an internal focus to a customer focus involves more than the marketing organization. Align with business units, customer-facing areas of the organization, and critical back-office functions to ensure that everyone is committed to the shift.

Structure

Forming a cross-functional team around a pressing customer issue or around critical stages of the customer journey can immediately encourage a customer-focused mindset. Team members with little understanding of how their work makes a difference with customers tend to thrive when they find themselves working with others on a customer priority. The team's success is aligned with success for the customer. Executives who organize, supervise, and support cross-functional teams discover themselves to be customer-focused.

Process Management

Agile teams delivering work every one to four weeks through Scrum or at regular cycles in the continuous flow of Kanban don't automatically become more customer focused. They can find themselves simply delivering more stuff rather than delivering better customer outcomes. This transformation requires effective prioritization. As teams make their Sprint plans or prioritize work into Kanban's ready queue, they must prioritize their work with a focus on the customer: How does this work impact the customer? What work in our backlog is most important to the customer?

Validated Learning

No other discipline has the *potential* to transform a team from an internal focus to a customer focus. By validating how customers respond to our promotions, our offerings, and our experiences, we learn from and focus on the customer. As with the process-management discipline, customer focus does not occur automatically, but again calls for prioritization. Do we prioritize tests to wring the last little bit of conversion out of a promotion, or do we test to learn how we can improve the customer experience?

Adapting to Change

Customers change. Their needs and wants change. To be customer focused, we must adapt to their changing needs. We monitor their changing needs. We make ourselves aware of the alternatives that they have to our products or services to meet those wants or needs. Adapting to change doesn't always involve responding to customers; sometimes, we need to lead our customers and support their adaptation to external changes. How can we help our customers adapt to new technologies, climate change, pandemics like Covid-19, or financial shocks? With customer focus and leadership.

Creating Remarkable Customer Experiences

While validated learning may be the most important of the Six Disciplines in transitioning a team from an internal focus to a customer focus, creating remarkable experiences is the pinnacle of customer focus. Teams that create remarkable customer experiences are by their very nature customer focused. Again, the appropriate mindset and prioritization of work is necessary. Teams without a customer focus can create customer experiences, but they rarely create *remarkable* customer experiences.

Voices from the Field: Customer Focus

Justin Schroepfer is senior director of marketing at Deseret Digital Media. Its brands include KSL-TV, an NBC affiliate in Salt Lake City, Utah .com, and TheMemories.Com. The company has practiced Agile marketing since 2017.

Jim: How did adopting Agile marketing help you keep or improve your focus on customers?

Justin: I think that's the whole point of Agile marketing. The way that we would do things prior was to gather as much data as possible toward the end of each year: try to understand customer behavior, trends in the marketplace, what our competition was doing—and then we would build out an annual plan based off of that. We would lay it all out, identify the channels we wanted to hit, the messaging that we thought was appropriate, and then we would execute that plan throughout the year.

With Agile marketing, we transitioned to approaching this on a quarterly basis so that we could be more in tune with changes in the marketplace, especially with consumer behavior. We've got so much data coming in from the website, analytics, research, feedback from the customer service group. Things are changing not only externally but internally as well. We've had to pivot from a products standpoint and understanding how that new product might meet the needs of our customers. The Agile mentality has allowed us to focus on a plan that can be adapted and changed. We can see large shifts like we're now experiencing (with the Covid-19 pandemic), where we had to completely change what we are doing. If we had an annual planning process, it would have made things a whole lot more difficult to shift and change the direction of the ship, whereas now we know exactly what we can do and how to better accommodate what's happening with our customers.

Jim: You mentioned Google analytics and all this data that is coming in from the website. Were there particular tools or processes that you found helpful in maintaining customer focus or responding to changing customer needs?

Justin: We have all these data points that come in from analytics. We analyze them on a regular basis and then we meet to discuss what those data points are showing us. It may be that we'll see different search terms happening on our own site. These are indicators for us to ask, "I wonder why there is more interest (for example) in RVs than there was before?" And then we'll gather additional data points to help confirm what we're seeing with our own analytics. There is so much data coming in; the key is to be disciplined enough to have a process to harvest that data, analyze it, and then act on it.

Jim: What about marketing technology tools like marketing automation or personalization tools?

Justin: One of the big things we learned when you taught us Agile marketing was that there was going to be a lot of movement in behavior; for scalability in personalization you need a platform like a marketing automation tool. We didn't have one at the time. I put together a proposal to adopt a platform, but what we found was that we still had a lot to learn about our customers that

(continued)

(Continued)

would help guide us in the marketing automation and creating customer journeys. This year, we're gathering that information about customers to understand what our clients are doing, what needs they have in different parts of that customer journey. In what formats do they want to receive information or communication from us? We felt like more investigation into customer needs and the customer journey would help us to use that technology more effectively and also help us to identify the right platform. Marketing automation as a technology will be key to us because we're so diversified: we have nine brands. To address all of the needs of those brands, to choose a platform that is scalable and able to personalize messaging to all those different customers, is going to take a marketing automation tool. You can't be Agile without it.

When I was presenting the options for selecting a marketing automation tool, questions came up like "What kind of impact are you talking about? How can we justify the expense of this technology?" I would point out case studies available from the vendors saying that your conversion rates are going to go up by 15 percent or whatever. And then everyone asked "What does that mean for us? What does 15 percent mean for us?" As we started to look, we didn't have our funnel metrics nailed down. As I said, we have nine brands, so we have more than nine distinct audiences. We didn't have the metrics nailed down for each of those audiences. We had to go back and define each funnel and make sure we had the base metrics for each of them, so that, if we do implement a marketing automation platform, we'll know where the impact is likely to happen and to what degree, and then how that translates into dollars for us, so that the leadership feels comfortable with the money we put into it.

Jim: Last question. We're in the middle of the Covid-19 pandemic; how has Agile marketing helped you respond to something this unexpected and impactful?

Justin: We're now better prepared to make those type of shifts. We don't have massive programs that we invested in, where to change those would be a lot of cost, both in terms of media buys and time. We set ourselves up to put things into market, test them for a short time, analyze the data, and then see how we need to shift. Instead of a big, massive cruise ship that we established before Agile, where to make any changes would take a while and a lot of effort, we're now in a smaller ship; if something happens we can maneuver a whole lot easier. We're now gathering new data about our customers and not just assuming that what we gathered before still applies. Our customer behavior has changed dramatically. An example: we have an obituary product called Memories; it allows funeral directors to give an option—as opposed to the newspaper, where they get a very small space—to the family who might want to tell the full story of their passed loved one. I was researching how the funeral industry is being impacted by Covid. I found out that there are families that can't have a funeral or a viewing. There are studies that show that those two events are ways for families to come together and say goodbye; it helps with the mourning process, and now that's stripped away. Our product can play a role in that mourning process to help families say goodbye to their loved ones in the absence of a funeral. I'm now rethinking the marketing and messaging strategy to that audience. We better understand the consumer's behavior and are able to adapt. We also have similar situations with other products: our homes product, our jobs product, our cars product. We're seeing their needs change dramatically, and Agile is helping us figure out how our products fit in with those changing needs and behaviors. Our marketing team, our design team, our media team is now set up for that with Agile.

Moving from an internal focus to a strong customer focus is a marathon, not a sprint. It requires investment and perseverance. The rewards are substantial, and the requirements are for real change, not lip service.

The final shift, from top-down decision-making to decentralized decision-making, can be a major challenge for many executives and managers. They are trained and often very skilled in making decisions, and it can be very difficult to let go. How does an organization, and the individuals within the organization, make this shift? That's the topic of the next chapter.

Chapter 18

From Top-Down to Decentralized Decision-Making

Don't tell people how to do things, tell them what to do and let them surprise you with their results.

—*General George Patton, American military leader*

I n traditional organizations, all decisions are approved at the highest levels. Literally every piece of content, every campaign, and every internal email must be signed off by the highest-level marketing person. This is inefficient. Customer-ready material sits in the approval cycle for days, sometimes weeks.

The centralized model reflects a lack of trust in the people doing the work, and it robs those people of accountability. It can demoralize the team, particularly in the early days of adopting Agile, when individual contributors expect change. If Agile results in the same approval delays and the same burden of rework, morale suffers, people leave, and the change cynics are proven right.

Agile organizations must shift their decision-making in several ways: *who* makes decisions, *how* they are made, and *how quickly* they are made. Let's take a look at each.

Who Makes Decisions?

Who should make a given decision? Is the call made at the highest level of the organization or at lower levels? Here are some guidelines.

Strategic vs. Tactical

Effective management understands the difference:

- Strategic decisions—the goal and the unique approach we'll use to achieve that goal—belong to those highest in the organization.
- Tactical decisions—the intermediate objectives and specifics of how we'll get there—belong as low in the organization as appropriate and possible.

Great managers spend their time clarifying goals—providing teams with crisp descriptions of the goal and clarity on why it matters—what's within scope and what's out of scope. They have the wisdom to leave the how (along with the plan, which, as they know, will inevitably change) up to their teams.

Management maximizes team efficiency by pushing all tactical decisions down to the team level. When marketing managers find themselves signing off on ads, press releases, and any of the hundreds of other tactical components, that's their cue to change course, to get out of the way.

The exception: When two equally plausible approaches to achieving a goal come with two very different consequences, the decision to choose one over another is strategic. A business looking to compete in the mobile-handset market could take either the high-value, high-profitability route, as epitomized by Apple iPhone, or the low-margin, high-market-share-at-any-cost approach, as epitomized by Google's Android. Each is plausible; the decision is clearly strategic.

Tactical decisions sometimes lead to different consequences. Many managers convince themselves that they must make many tactical decisions because, they reason, what if someone makes a mistake? People will make mistakes. That's how they learn. As the parent of any toddler learning to walk knows, if they are protected from ever falling or making a mistake, they won't learn. Unless the consequences of a decision are catastrophic and irreversible, push the decision down to the lowest level possible.

Accountability

Many top managers insist on reviewing critical work because they feel a sense of accountability if something goes wrong. There is nothing wrong with feeling that sense of accountability; the right way to act on that sense of accountability is not to second guess your team, or review every piece of work, but to train them to think like a top manager (or better than a top manager, because they're closer to the customer and to the work).

For managers who worry that quality will suffer if they don't examine all work, I encourage them to adopt American engineer and management consultant W. Edwards Deming's definition of quality. Deming said that quality is whatever the customer says it is; that producing quality work is a matter of meeting and exceeding customer expectations. Deming also said that you must "cease dependence on inspection to achieve quality."[1] If you as a manager are reviewing every piece of work, you are dependent on your own inspection to achieve quality.

Managers in an Agile organization train people to understand customer expectations and to listen for both stated and unstated expectations. Managers articulate their own expectations, and rather than inspect work, they create the conditions and the processes that produce good work.

Frequency

Frequent decisions are not strategic decisions. If you repeatedly make the same kind of decision, ask yourself how you can push that decision, accompanied by guidelines for making good decisions, down in the organization.

Reserve your time for the infrequent, haven't-seen-that-before decisions; and even then, look for someone in the organization better positioned to make the call.

Risk

The greater the risk, the higher in the chain of command the decision must be made. While this seems like a truism, organizations looking to decentralize decisions must push the boundaries, by empowering those lower in the organization to make moderately risky decisions without fear. Is the decision irreversible? If so, then make it at the top. But most decisions aren't irreversible, and an organization can take smaller risks before making the big bet. Make it safe for people to fail; failure leads to learning.

How Do Decisions Get Made?

The traditional justification for top-down decision-making is that only top management has the experience to make the best decisions. Top management makes nearly all the decisions because decisions are based on "experience." There are two problems with that approach:

1. *Top management's experience likely is not current.* The market has changed from when their experience was gained.
2. *Experience is limited.* With everyone depending on them to make the right decisions everywhere, executives become overwhelmed. Time spent on issues that could be resolved lower in the food chain is time not available for focusing on strategies and decisions that do require their unique expertise.

Agile organizations replace experience-based decisions with data- and value-based decisions.

Data

In the third principle of Agile marketing, validated learning over opinions and conventions, and in our discussion of the shift from a campaign mentality to continuous improvement, we've seen the importance of making data-based decisions. Top managers can encourage data-based decisions by setting aside your belief in your own instincts. Do you ignore those instincts? No; if they're telling you something is wrong, step back; ask questions about the data: Where did it come from? What's the degree of uncertainty?

Values

Sometimes you don't have the data to make a decision. Should I do this for a particular customer or say no? Should I react to a particular competitor or

Figure 18.1   The values of Southwest Airlines
Courtesy of Southwest, Inc.

ignore the move? When data isn't available, having a well thought-out and articulated set of values can be invaluable in making decisions.

Southwest Airlines has enjoyed great success with values-based decision-making. Their values can be seen in Figure 18.1. All employees learn these values; they use them to make thousands of decisions every day, from how they give safety instructions to how they treat a difficult customer. Top management is freed up to make the strategic decisions that have kept Southwest profitable for 45 straight years and at the top of the heap, year after year, in customer satisfaction.[2]

How Quickly Do Decisions Get Made?

To achieve Agile, one last shift has to take place in decision-making: the speed with which decisions are made. Not every decision can be made in a few hours or a few days, but every decision must be made without unnecessary delays.

Routine decisions must be made in hours or a day, two days tops. More consequential decisions may take longer, and still without delay. The surest way to speed up decision-making is to reduce the length of the decision path. Can a decision be pushed down the organization so that it doesn't have to travel through multiple layers of management? Can a decision path be limited to touch only those departments or groups that are most impacted or most aware of the decision's consequences, rather than extended to touch every group?

As you examine the decision-making process in your organization, it may help to adopt a lean mentality. Are there parts of the decision-making process that can be eliminated because they don't deliver value to the customer or the organization? How lean can the process get and still result in good decisions?

Advantages of Decentralized Decision-Making

If information doesn't need to flow up and decisions don't need to flow down, and if endless approval cycles are eliminated, decisions get made faster. Other benefits include the following:

- *Improved customer responsiveness*. If frontline employees are authorized to make certain decisions, within limits, according to the values of the organization, customer responsiveness and customer satisfaction go up. The employees of Ritz-Carlton hotels are authorized to spend up to $2,000 per incident to resolve a bad customer experience. Employees don't abuse this trust; instead, they are core to delivering one of the highest levels of customer loyalty in the industry.
- *Greater creativity and harnessing of talent*. Decentralizing decision-making harnesses the talents, expertise, and creativity of everyone in the organization, not just the strengths (and weaknesses) of top management. And it frees up management to focus on those areas that only they can own.
- *More accountability*. Employees who are trained and authorized to make decisions on behalf of the organization are more likely to take accountability for those decisions and ensure the success of the decision.
- *Improved morale*. People work harder if they feel a sense of ownership and some control over the decisions, and hence the results, of their work. Compare the morale of frontline employees at Southwest Airlines or Ritz-Carlton with that of their peers; whom do you imagine has the greater job satisfaction?

Getting Off the Approval Treadmill

The next time you're about to review a piece of content, stop and ask yourself what qualities you are looking for in your review: Is it something simple, like correct spelling and grammar? Is it alignment with certain customer expectations? Whatever internal rules you apply to reviewing content, make them explicit, turn them into a checklist, and then make the checklist part of the process. Now, when someone gives you something to review, you respond by asking, "Show me the quality checklist." Your reviews suddenly take much less time, because the deliverables were created to meet your criteria. In Agile terms, these criteria are known as process policies.

If you are a team member blocked by approval delays, work with the reviewers to develop your own quality checklist. If they don't or won't help, reverse engineer a quality checklist based on their behavior. Examine the comments from the last several things they reviewed, looking for patterns. Codify these into a quality checklist.

Making the Transition

The shift in who makes decisions requires us to push information and strategic imperatives to lower levels. To make good decisions, people need information and context. For example, if you find yourself overruling decisions because individual contributors aren't considering the impact on profitability of their decisions, give them the information they need so that they *do* know how their decisions affect profits. If people make poor decisions because they haven't considered the impact of their decisions within the broader context, provide that broader context.

Pushing decisions down in an organization requires behavior change not only on the part of leaders but also on the part of individual contributors. Many individual contributors, when presented with the opportunity to make decisions, show reluctance. They hesitate. They ask the leaders to take responsibility for the final decisions. They don't feel safe.

What can leaders do to encourage individual contributors and those further down in the organization to make decisions and assume the mantle of accountability that comes with being the final decision maker?

- Ensure that people understand that it's okay to fail, particularly if they've followed a good decision-making process.
- Make decisions smaller by breaking them into smaller bets, each carrying little risk. For example, rather than make a large investment in a new product area, make many small, testable investments first.
- Give lower-level decision makers a broad perspective. Ask, "What decision would the customer want us to make?" "What decision would the CFO want us to make?" "How does the cost/risk fit into the bigger picture of what we're trying to do?"
- Introduce wider time horizons: Look at a decision, consider all alternatives, and then look out 6 to 12 months to anticipate the impact or potential impact of each choice.

Challenges

When I talk with organizations about making the shift from top-down decision-making to decentralized decision-making, I often find the following dichotomy: Individual contributors and first-line managers tell me, "Management won't let go. They talk about decentralizing decisions and simultaneously insist on approving everything that goes out." Managers tell me, "My people aren't ready to make these decisions. They don't have the experience and the training."

They may both be right.

If management wants to decentralize decision-making and then go home at night without the burden of feeling that they have to either make or check every decision, then management must ensure that their people have the information, the context, and the training to make good decisions. That doesn't mean that their team will make the same decisions they might make. In many cases, they'll make better decisions. And the team, for whatever reason, will eventually make a bad decision. It's a learning opportunity! I've never met the management team that, with hindsight, could claim to have a perfect record of good decisions.

Part IV

Succeeding with Agile Marketing

Your journey of transformation to Agile marketing will not be linear. You will revisit certain stages. Management will change, and you must enroll new management in supporting Agile marketing. You will continuously improve the process by which you market. You will become skilled at quickly responding and effectively adapting to change.

Ever-changing and always challenging—isn't this what makes marketing so fascinating?

In "Succeeding with Agile Marketing," I cover some of the issues that organizations encounter as they adopt Agile marketing:

- How to build support for Agile marketing
- How to hire Agile marketers
- How to integrate Agile marketing with more traditional marketing practices
- How to scale Agile marketing

I conclude with a look into Agile marketing's future.

Chapter 19

Building Support for Agile Marketing

Teamwork is the ability to work together toward a common vision. The ability to direct individual accomplishments toward organizational objectives. It is the fuel that allows common people to attain uncommon results.
    —*Andrew Carnegie, American industrialist and philanthropist*

I have seen many successful implementations of Agile marketing, and I have seen some failures. Failed implementations tend to happen for the following reasons:

- Management—especially at the middle layers—does not fully commit to Agile. Mid-level managers most directly feel the impact of the shift to Agile. When asked to give up day-to-day decision-making authority in favor of long-term strategic projects and the building of Agile teams and an Agile culture, they may react with resistance and rejection.
- Before Agile marketing is fully implemented, a key manager leaves and a new manager comes in. If the new manager is unfamiliar with Agile

191

marketing practices, he or she may, consciously or unconsciously, sabotage the implementation.

• Companies equate Agile marketing with implementing processes, usually Scrum, Kanban, or a hybrid approach. After initially achieving modest success, they lose focus and they lose momentum. They never make the Four Shifts, they stop practicing their process, they fail to realize the expected benefits, and they declare Agile marketing a failure.

In fact, Agile, whether in software development or in marketing, is much more than implementing processes like Scrum or Kanban. It is a mindset and a set of disciplines. Agile marketing itself must be implemented in an Agile fashion—gradually and with iterative improvements.

Sustaining Agile marketing requires that companies solve for a number of issues not part of the Six Disciplines. For example, companies must integrate Agile with traditional marketing methodologies, as not all groups will (or should) move to Agile. Companies must scale Agile to fit their business, whether large, small, or in between. Companies must build an Agile culture, and one of the keys to building a successful Agile culture is to hire Agile people.

Building Support

Why Build Support?

Most Agile transformations start with middle management, and all involve change: change in the way teams work, change in roles, and change in the culture.

Most people are more comfortable with the status quo, no matter how dysfunctional or painful, than they are with change. A given way of doing things and a given culture in an organization have momentum. The culture resists change. Changing that organizational momentum more closely resembles reversing the direction of a powerful, spinning flywheel than it does turning a battleship. Battleships don't resist turning, they're simply slow to turn. Flywheels resist changes in direction and momentum.

This is where organizational transformations can fail. Those who seek change underestimate the momentum forces at play in the status quo, and they fail to take into account what people like about the status quo.

Every year, VersionOne surveys the global software-development community to determine the "State of Agile." The 2019 report included a section on the leading challenges to successful adoption of Agile. Keeping

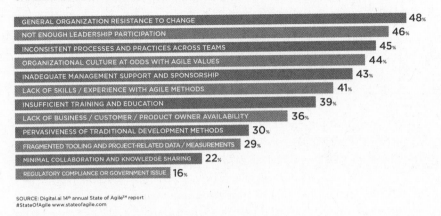

Figure 19.1 Leading causes of failed agile projects
State Of Agile, www.stateofagile.com

in mind that the respondents are software developers, not marketers, the results are instructive.[1]

As shown in Figure 19.1, the leading challenge is about resistance to change. The second and the fifth challenges is inadequate management support and sponsorship. And if you look at the typical Agile marketing training, the material addresses only the sixth challenge: lack of skills and experience with Agile methods.

So how do we build support for Agile and overcome the natural resistance to change? Let's start with building support from management.

Building Support from Management

To begin building support from management, start with a decision: Are you likely to find a receptive audience for Agile transformation from management? Your strategy for building support hinges on the answer to this question.

Management Is Receptive

If you are likely to find a receptive audience for Agile transformation from management, then building support entails following six steps:

1. *Educate them.* Start by educating management on the basics of Agile Marketing:
   - What is Agile marketing?
   - What are the benefits of Agile marketing?
   - Who else, particularly in my industry, is practicing Agile marketing?

   Answer their questions and make sure that they have a good understanding of Agile marketing. In Chapter 20, we'll cover a few exercises to use in enrolling management and the importance of getting them formal training and coaching.

2. *Align with their vision and goals.* Does any aspect of management's goals align with the goals of Agile? How does implementing Agile help achieve something that is important to management? Remember, everyone operates from "What's in it for me?"—also known as the WIIFM principle.

   Also give some thought to the fourth challenge in the VersionOne survey above: organizational culture at odds with Agile values. How must the company culture change to align with Agile values? Is management willing to support that change? What actions by management would support cultural transition?

3. *Ask managers to sponsor the Agile transformation in a visible way.* You want the managers to be invested in the success of the Agile transformation. You also want everyone else to see that management is behind the Agile transformation. Don't simply have the highest level manager publicly sponsor and support the Agile transformation. Make sure that middle management also support and are invested in the success of Agile. Some will resist. Dig into why and work with them to overcome their objections and get their full support.

4. *Set realistic expectations.* Don't set the expectation that you will achieve a 40 percent improvement in marketing throughput in the first two-week Sprint. Set the expectation that learning Agile is like learning a new golf swing: It will be awkward at first and it may take time before you see the full benefits. Set modest expectations with your initial attempts at Agile marketing. If you sense that management is not fully committed to Agile, position whatever you do as a trial, something that provides the evidence for you to continue.

5. *Start small and spread the word.* Don't start the Agile transformation with a huge, bet-the-company project. Start small, achieve some success, and spread the word. You want it to be very cool to be on the first team to adopt Agile, such that other teams clamor to be the next to be trained.

6. *Encourage management to practice Agile.* Habits die hard. You can expect to encounter managers who support applying Agile to software development, or perhaps even to marketing, and who continue to live in a world of annual budgets, annual strategic planning, annual personnel reviews, and strictly hierarchical leadership. And you can help them see that it makes no sense to live simultaneously in both worlds.

Management must also *be* Agile. Managers can increase the probability of achieving organizational agility by applying the precepts of Agile to their own work. They can regularly prioritize the most important projects, just as they would in a Scrum planning meeting; they can track progress through standups and Kanban boards; they can form self-managing teams to address the toughest, most recalcitrant problems; and they can put in place processes to enable quick reaction to threats and opportunities.

Management Is Not Receptive

If you expect management to resist Agile, your best bet is to change jobs or to move to another manager who is more likely to be receptive. That may sound facetious, but I'm serious. In my experience, it is easier to change jobs than to change a nonreceptive manager to support Agile.

For many people, however, changing managers or changing jobs is not an option. In that case, take these steps to build support for Agile:

1. *Don't call it Agile.* Don't call the initial project an Agile transformation. Don't use Agile terms like Scrum or Kanban or Sprints. Don't educate them on Agile marketing or its benefits. Don't tell them who else is practicing Agile. Instead, say, "We are testing some new tools to track our work," or "We scheduled some regular status meetings to make sure everything is kept on track." Find another way to describe whatever Agile processes you put in place.
2. *Align with their vision and goals.* When managers don't support an Agile transformation, you must even more explicitly align with their vision and goals. Even the most recalcitrant manager gets "What's in it for me?"
3. *Don't set any expectations, but measure improvement.* Instead of setting realistic expectations, set none at all. Capture baseline data so that you can later demonstrate improvements in throughput, quality, or the effectiveness of your marketing. Once you have data or anecdotes that support continuing an Agile experiment, share it with management.

4. *Build allies.* As you get some successes under your belt, champions will emerge. Build allies and allow your allies to speak for you. Educate allies about Agile marketing, about its benefits, and about who else is practicing it. You may find it easiest to find allies in the business units that benefit from your early efforts at Agile marketing. Let them speak for you, both to your management and to their peers.

Build Support Within the Culture

If you look at the VersionOne survey results above, one of the leading causes of failed Agile projects is not lack of management support; it's introducing Agile into a culture at odds with Agile values. In at least some cultures, you must have support for change to the culture itself. That support, and the change, must come from more than management.

How do you change a culture? This is one of the most difficult tasks in business. Here are several observations from my experience of helping more than 60 companies adopt Agile.

Meet People Where They Are

Chapter 5 introduced an exercise called Find Your Why. This exercise accomplishes several things. It honors the working parts of the current culture. Rather than telling your organization that we have all these problems and so we have to change (meaning "*you* have to change"), this approach asks them to identify what is working well—that is, aspects of the culture that we don't want to lose—and those areas with room for improvement. That is much less threatening than being told what's wrong and being told that you have to change. And third, it personalizes the change. It allows people to describe the benefits of change in ways that are personally beneficial—again, the WIFM principle.

Implement Agile in an Agile Fashion

In other words, don't worry about getting it perfect the first time. Plunge in, do your work using the methodologies and practices that seem easiest to implement at first, and then iterate as often as necessary to achieve an improved Agile practice. Learn by doing, not by planning.

Give People a Say

People support what they help to build. Conversely, they tend to reject something that, as they perceive it, is forced on them. Provide the people practicing Agile marketing the opportunity to determine the pace of adoption, determine which practices of methods like Kanban and Scrum they want to adopt, and determine what does and doesn't work for them. Encourage them to self-organize. If you are using a Scrum Master, allow them to select the person; they are much more likely to listen to someone that they choose than to listen to someone forced on them.

Balance Consistency and Flexibility

The champions of Agile and management must balance consistency and flexibility. What do I mean by that? And when do you decide to be consistent and when do you decide to be flexible?

Be consistent with the values and the goals of Agile and be flexible in terms of the process. For example, you want to be consistent in pushing down decision-making to the lowest level of the organization where it makes sense. You want to be consistent in valuing data over opinions when making decisions. And you want to be flexible in terms of how often the team holds standups, whether they use Kanban or Scrum or Scrumban, and the length of a Sprint.

Highlight Early Examples of Desirable Behaviors

Highlight and celebrate early examples of the behaviors that you want to create. If you want to create leadership at every level, acknowledge people who lead from below or from middle management. If you want a culture of decision-making based on metrics that matter, put the spotlight on early examples of this behavior.

Set Achievable Milestones

Adopting Agile marketing is like adopting a new exercise regimen. If you do too much too soon, your muscles ache and you struggle to continue. Better to start off gradually, setting reasonable milestones for long-term success. Make sure that you can succeed in your early efforts and build on them.

Reinforce Cultural Values Through Hiring and Promotions

If you say you value collaboration and then promote the lone wolf, everyone in the organization gets the message. Hire to your new cultural values. In Chapter 21 on sustaining Agile marketing, I'll show you what this looks like.

Walk the Talk

If you're an executive, overcome the habit of making all the decisions. Practice Agile yourself. Let it be okay to fail; if you're not failing occasionally, you're not stretching yourself. Ask for data, and make sure that decisions are based on that data, not on opinions or hunches.

Building support for Agile marketing is not a one-time thing. It's not something that you do at the beginning of an Agile marketing adoption and never do again. Like everything Agile, it is iterative and requires that you improve over time. Don't take support for granted.

You have support for an Agile marketing implementation. How do you start in such a way that you improve your odds of sustaining Agile marketing? That's the subject of the next chapter.

Chapter 20

Agile Kickoff: The First Six Months

If you don't know where you are going, any road will get you there.
—Lewis Carroll, English writer of children's fiction

How does a team or an organization get started with Agile to ensure sustainability? Do you start small or make a large, public commitment and reorganize everyone from the start into cross-functional teams? What training and coaching do you need? What do the first six months look like?

Creating the Vision

Lewis Carroll summed it up years ago, but many organizations still start the journey to Agile marketing with only a vague idea of where they want to go. They want better, faster, and more responsive—without looking at what these adjectives mean for their organizations.

199

The leader, with the help of the team, creates a vision—a desired future state—for Agile marketing. It is aspirational. It's a departure, in clearly defined ways, from the current state. The vision must answer three questions:

1. What problems do we want to solve?
2. What does success look like?
3. How do we know we're improving?

The Find Your Why exercise in Chapter 5 helped your organization answer the first two questions. The following exercise will help you boil down the results of that exercise into a poster.

The Poster Exercise

The leadership team creates a poster, a visual, to describe their vision for Agile marketing. It is informed by the Find Your Why exercise in Chapter 5, and the Beliefs and Behaviors exercise in Chapter 22. (I don't recommend listing the results of those exercises directly.) Someone passing the poster or looking at it quickly online must be able to scan it and make sense of it. Many teams use three or four large circles or boxes to describe the most important characteristics of their vision. Others show it graphically in other ways (a wheel with spokes, a road, etc.).

Write at least part of your vision on the poster—the part that describes what success looks like and perhaps the problems you want to solve. See Figure 20.1.

The purpose of the poster is, of course, to communicate your vision for Agile marketing to your organization. It can be used literally as a poster on the walls of your offices. It can also be used in communications, both within and outside the marketing group. Most marketing teams have access to graphic artists who can help create a polished version of this poster from the draft you create in this exercise.

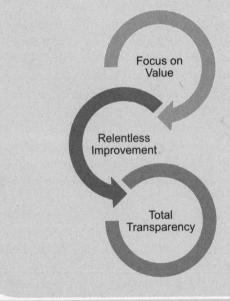

Figure 20.1   Sample agile marketing vision poster

Start Small

Should you begin your Agile marketing journey by making a large, public commitment and reorganizing everyone into cross-functional teams? Or do you start small? I recommend starting small.

One of my favorite books of 2019 was *Tiny Habits: The Small Changes That Change Everything* by B. J. Fogg, a Stanford professor who spent 10 years researching how people change behaviors. Fogg recommends starting not just small, but tiny. For example, if you don't floss your teeth regularly and you want to make it a habit, he recommends you start by flossing just one tooth! He focused on making this tiny habit automatic and then, once that tiny habit was established, he expanded it to flossing all of his teeth. His research shows that success breeds success and that you want to begin with something where you *know* that you can succeed.

How do we apply this to Agile marketing? Start where you know the team can succeed. For example, if you adopt Scrum, start with a Sprint backlog that is unquestionably achievable. Don't implement everything—burndown charts, velocity measures, and Portfolio Kanban (see Chapter 9)—in your first week.

If You're Practicing Scrum

- Start with one cross-functional team or no cross-functional teams.
- Create a small Agile marketing backlog of 10–20 items that are delivery increments or tasks. Don't list everything.
- Write a user story for each item.
- Hold a one- or two-hour Sprint planning session to create your first Sprint backlog. Undercommit—floss one tooth! The team must be 100 percent sure that they can finish all the items in the Sprint backlog.
- Create the simplest possible Kanban board, one with only three columns: To Do, Doing, and Done.
- Hold daily standups. Limit them to 15 minutes. Answer only the three questions.
- Add no work to the Sprint backlog during the Sprint. If work comes up, have a plan to direct that work to people other than the ones on the first Agile team.
- Those who finish early help others on the team finish what they're working on. If everyone finishes early, add just enough items to keep them busy for the time remaining. Be cautious: You want to make sure that you finish 100 percent of the work in the first Sprint.

If You're Practicing Kanban

- Kanban teams may or may not be cross-functional. If you form a cross-functional team, form only one. Either way, get started with just one team.
- Start with the first two principles of Kanban:
  1. Visualize the flow.
  2. Limit the work in process (WIP).
- Create a Kanban board that represents the flow of work through your existing process. Limit the board to five columns plus a Ready column and a Done column. Fewer is better. Think about bottlenecks as you build your flow and design the flow such that you can identify the bottlenecks. For example, if you expect a bottleneck in the approval stage, create a column called Approval.
- Establish one or two WIP limits—wherever you think you may have a bottleneck. Establish the smallest WIP limit you think possible. You can always increase it, but smaller WIP limits identify bottlenecks quickly and provide the incentive to fix them.
- Hold daily Kanban board reviews of no more than 15 minutes, identifying any bottlenecks or any work items that aren't moving smoothly through the flow.

The goals behind starting small are to build confidence, learn skills, and ingrain habits. You can't do this if you take on too much at once.

Training and Coaching

What kind of training is appropriate for Agile marketing? Some people begin with training to prepare themselves for the Certified Scrum Master exam. While this is somewhat helpful for the few people who will serve as scrum masters, most of your organization will not be scrum masters. And all of the Certified Scrum Master training currently available is designed to train scrum masters for software development teams.

I recommend marketing-specific, experiential Agile training. Lectures must take up no more than 30 percent of the training time, with the bulk devoted to simulations and real-world exercises. The training must also be appropriate to your organization's size and type. Training an 800-person marketing team within a Fortune 500 company bears little resemblance to training a team of five at a small startup.

You may also want to consider Agile marketing certification, provided by the International Consortium for Agile.[1] This training, designed by experts in Agile marketing, provides clearly defined learning outcomes. Again, the course material must be experiential and must balance lecture and exercises. Trainers must be approved to deliver the course. IC-Agile examines student scores from previously delivered courses to ensure quality and appropriateness.

You may also require training specific to managers. The role of the manager is critical to the success of Agile marketing, and at least a couple of organizations offer training specific to Agile marketing managers.

Consider, in addition to training, budgeting for coaching. No class can anticipate all of the issues that your team will run into as you adopt Agile. An experienced Agile marketing coach can save you time, money, and heartache, and increase the probability that your adoption of Agile marketing will be successful.

Here are a few things to look for in an Agile marketing coach:

- *Marketing background.* Can you imagine a software development team hiring an Agile coach who has no experience in software development? And yet Agile marketing teams sometimes hire coaches without marketing experience. You want a coach who can translate Agile concepts into the marketing context and who has already seen the marketing-specific problems and patterns.
- *Listening skills.* Coaches are not there to provide all of the answers, but to listen, ask questions, and help you find your own answers.
- *Experience with your kind of organization.* A marketing coach who hasn't helped a large organization adopt Agile marketing is unlikely to have run into the issues specific to large organizations. Similarly, a coach whose only experiences are in large organizations, and who has never worked at or coached small businesses or startups, will not understand the unique issues of small organizations. Size is probably the most important differentiator, and there are others. Issues facing marketing agencies differ from those facing brands. Nonprofits, educational institutions, and government institutions have unique issues. I'm less convinced that Agile coaches need to understand specific verticals— health care, insurance, financial, etc. Although every industry has its jargon, legal considerations, and competitive pressures, these can be quickly picked up if they are, in fact, relevant to the adoption of Agile.

The First Six Months

Start small. Get some successes under your belt. Develop skills, habits, and confidence. In terms of the Six Disciplines, focus, during the first six months, only on the first four disciplines and on the Four Shifts. To this strong foundation you can then add responding to change and creating remarkable customer experiences.

In particular, increase the pace of your validated learning. At its heart, Agile is iterative, and the faster you iterate, the faster you learn. If you don't generally test your campaigns today, start with one or two tests per week and grow from there. Set an achievable goal, reach it, and build on that success.

Review and retrospect often. What's holding you back? Of the Four Shifts, where are you making progress and where are you stuck? Where is Agile not being adopted? Why?

You've achieved some success with Agile marketing. How do you sustain this success? That's the subject of our next chapter.

Chapter 21

Sustaining Agile Marketing

Patience and perseverance have a magical effect before which difficulties disappear and obstacles vanish.
—John Quincy Adams, sixth president of the United States

T he good news is that Agile tends to stick around. Somewhere between 70 percent and 80 percent of the organizations I've trained still, after as many as 8 years, practice Agile marketing. That said, it takes work to sustain Agile marketing.

Organizations that focus on the following four issues are most likely to sustain Agile marketing.

Relentless Improvement

Improving your Agile practice requires a relentless commitment to improvement. Organizations that create this learning environment and the

206

mindset that we're always improving what we deliver to customers and how we deliver it, inoculate themselves against the diseases that lead to Agile failures.

What are these diseases? There are more than I can list. Here are a few:

- *Lack of transparency.* Marketing isn't willing to engage with the business groups, allow them to see marketing for what it is, warts and all, and accept accountability.
- *Doing Agile rather than being Agile.* Focusing too much on the process (standups, Sprint planning, etc.) and not enough on the outcomes. This is also known as Agile Theater or Agile for Show.
- *Dependency on personalities rather than culture.* A dynamic leader brings in Agile; when that leader leaves, Agile, if it hasn't become embedded in the culture, leaves too.

The cure for these diseases is to do the opposite of what leads to the disease. Be transparent. Focus on outcomes and the Four Shifts. Build an Agile culture that isn't dependent on individual personalities.

Radical Transparency

Marketing departments are accustomed to product groups or business units that toss marketing requests over the wall and expect marketing to toss back campaigns. When the campaigns are done, marketing writes glowing reports about how well the campaigns worked, chock full of vanity metrics that product groups and business units don't value.

To build trust and long-term support for Agile, marketers must engage with the product groups, sales teams, and business units, welcoming them to come behind the curtain. These groups may see at first that marketing does not have all the answers, but if they see a team that is relentless in improving their work to reach the right answer, they will support it.

Marketing teams must publish metrics that matter, even when the news is not good. Executives and managers of the marketing team must create a safe environment where people understand they're not going to be fired or reprimanded if an experiment doesn't pan out. We learn through experiments, whether the experiments prove or disprove our hypotheses.

Focus on Outcomes, Not Process

Teams that focus too much on the processes of Agile do not succeed like those who see the processes as a means to achieve better outcomes. No manager argues with success. When the outcomes steadily improve, management is won over, and Agile becomes sustainable.

Better outcomes also motivate the marketing team. These outcomes get celebrated, and most marketers know the difference between hiding behind vanity metrics and genuine success. They want to contribute to better outcomes and better customer experiences.

Embed Agile in the Culture

This is easier than it may seem. You don't need a change management or culture guru to embed Agile in the culture. Simply put, make Agile a part of the way that work gets done.

Establish all of the Agile ceremonies (Sprint planning sessions, standups, Sprint reviews, Sprint retrospectives) as a regular way of doing business. Establish quarterly business reviews and planning sessions. Create cross-functional teams to focus on business outcomes. Use Portfolio Kanban (see Chapter 9) to manage your marketing investments. Hire Agile coaches. Modify your recruiting and onboarding to hire and train for Agile. Give awards for marketing or business agility within your company. Encourage people to present at conferences about the successes you've achieved.

The Second Six Months

In Chapter 20, I covered what to do during the first six months of your Agile adoption. Here are some suggestions about what to do in your second six months.

Cross-Pollinate

Ask the people who initially adopted Agile to teach people from other teams. Perhaps move a few of them into teams that are starting to adopt Agile and move people who haven't yet experienced Agile into the teams that have already done so.

Hone the First Four Disciplines

Focus only on the first four disciplines during the first six months: alignment, structure, process management, and validated learning. In the second six months, hone those disciplines. Modify the processes to work in your environment. Adopt more of Agile if you've simplified it to begin with. And keep the focus on improving the outcomes. Modify the processes only to produce better outcomes.

Add the Additional Disciplines

Think about how to adopt the last two disciplines, adapting to change and creating remarkable customer experiences. Establish a team to respond to brand-damaging events and to fleeting opportunities. Establish another team to think through threats, short-term and long-term, and come up with contingency plans to handle them.

Establish a project to improve one customer experience, to make it remarkable, so much so that your customers tell other people about it.

The Four Shifts

Evaluate where you are on making the Four Shifts:

- A shift from a focus on outputs to a focus on outcomes
- A shift from a campaign mentality to continuous improvement
- A shift from an internal focus to a customer focus
- A shift from top-down decision-making to decentralized decision-making

I can guarantee you haven't gone as far as you'd like on all four of them in just six months. There is never an end to this journey; you can constantly improve on these Four Shifts. Decide where you most need to improve and come up with actions to move your team further along this dimension.

Handling Management Change

Sometimes an executive or a manager who championed Agile in the organization leaves and a new executive or manager comes in who is not familiar with Agile. This can be a threat to the sustainability of Agile in the organization. What can teams do when this happens?

If you have embedded Agile deep in the culture, as described in this chapter, and you're focused on outcomes over process, that can certainly help. I find that the most effective way to inoculate the Agile practice against management change is radical transparency and, in particular, developing partners and advocates in parts of the business other than marketing who can speak for you. Few new marketing executives are going to eliminate an approach that his or her peers have found very valuable. If the business units and the product team see the value of Agile marketing in terms of improved business outcomes, they can advocate for you far more effectively than you can advocate for yourself.

Implementing and sustaining Agile marketing takes leadership. What is the role of leaders in implementing and sustaining Agile marketing? How does their role change as Agile becomes adopted in marketing and more widely in the organization? Those questions are the subject of our next chapter.

Chapter 22

The Role of the
Agile Leader

Great leaders are almost always great simplifiers, who can cut through argument,
debate and doubt, to offer a solution everybody can understand.
        —*Colin Powell, American military leader and statesman*

In Chapter 20, we talked about the importance of creating a vision.
That vision, created by the leader with the help of the team, answers
three questions:

1. What problems do we want to solve?
2. What does success look like?
3. How do we know we're improving?

While the vision is necessary and helpful, leaders also need to make the
vision tangible by diving down into the beliefs and behaviors that make up
an Agile mindset.

Exercise: Defining Your Beliefs and Behaviors

Agile marketing isn't just the adoption of new methodologies and practices—Scrum, Kanban, Sprints, user stories, and so forth. It requires a change in beliefs and behaviors; many people refer to this as adopting an Agile mindset. This exercise will help you and your team define the beliefs and behaviors you aspire to (your Agile mindset) and discover those you hold today.

Begin by asking each person on the team to think of a few people they see as excellent marketers, people whom they'd hire in a heartbeat to add to the team. These are likely people that they've worked with; they could be public personalities. They don't have to be people who you actually hire.

What beliefs or values make these people outstanding marketers? What behaviors? Have each team member make a list. For example, here are the beliefs and behaviors of two outstanding marketers I know:

Beliefs:

Customers are at the center of everything we do.
The best marketing is word-of-mouth marketing.
Good execution beats good strategy.

Behaviors:

They are consistent in quantity and quality of their marketing. As bloggers, they publish regularly and provide high quality content. Same for their longer-form content.
They constantly test their assumptions and refine their marketing.
They constantly look for data to make decisions. They spend more time executing than planning or strategizing.

Note that the first belief (customers are at the center of everything we do) doesn't relate to the first behavior (consistency).

When everyone's lists are complete, create two "common" lists—one of beliefs you aspire to and the other of behaviors—by calling on people to contribute to them.

Rank the top three to five beliefs and the top three to five behaviors, based on discussion or the number of votes each belief or behavior has from the team.

For each top belief and each top behavior, assess, through discussion, where your marketing organization stands with regard to that characteristic today. For example, if the top beliefs and behaviors are the ones I listed, you'll create a chart that looks like Figure 22.1.

Beliefs Today	Beliefs We Aspire To
We say that we're customer centric, but we don't get out and spend enough time with customers; we don't do enough customer research; and financial considerations sometimes keep us from doing the right thing for customers.	Customers are at the center of everything we do.
We think of word-of-mouth marketing as something the social media people do. We don't have programs for fans, and we don't encourage referrals.	The best marketing is word-of-mouth marketing.
We spend too much time in meetings figuring out our strategy, and then we have to rush execution.	Good execution beats good strategy.

Behaviors Today	Behaviors We Aspire To
We're inconsistent in how often we blog, provide content, and update our marketing materials and campaigns.	We're consistent in quantity and quality.
We too often make assumptions and don't do enough testing. Many of our campaigns are one and done.	We constantly test our assumptions and refine our marketing.
We're not data driven. Most decisions are made by the highest paid person's opinion (aka the HIPPO method).	We are data driven.

Figure 22.1 Charting behaviors you recognize and behaviors you aspire to

At the end, you'll have a chart of the most important beliefs and behaviors for successful marketing and you'll see where you need to improve.

Creating an Agile Environment

What kind of environment is most likely to lead to the best execution of the vision? In my experience, there are four key considerations.

Physical Environment

Maximizing face-to-face communication maximizes productivity. Where possible, co-locate everyone on each Scrum team. It's not absolutely necessary, and some teams make it work with people in various locations and time zones. Where teams are located in an open floor plan, make small meeting rooms, often called huddles, available for standups and informal gatherings. Most organizations also have informal, open meeting spaces scattered throughout their open space for meetings of a few people.

Some teams form pods, with workspaces around a table in the center. Some teams work around a large table all day. Whatever works, as long as the team is connected and can communicate and do heads-down work.

Whiteboards, wall-mounted and free-standing, as well as projectors, must be available in each meeting room. Some teams use portable projectors, enabling them to project upon and write on free-standing whiteboards.

Tools

I recommend that, as teams move to Agile marketing, they also evaluate the tools they use to manage the marketing process. Many tools were created pre-Agile, and although many of them now support viewing tasks in a Kanban board, they are, at their core, ticket based. That may not sound bad but, in practice, ticket-based systems lead to ticket-based behavior (check it off and close the ticket rather than focus on achieving the best outcome). Choose tools created specifically for Agile.

- *Ease of use.* One company I worked with used a popular, development-oriented, pre-Agile tool that allowed a Kanban view. IT had to create every new Kanban board. Marketing couldn't create their own new boards; they could only add cards to an existing board. Needless to say, this greatly affected the flexibility and the speed with which marketing could respond to new needs.
- *Visual, flow-based.* Good agile tools facilitate visualizing the flow of work through a process. They also show cards that are blocked or delayed.

They support the use of colors to indicate categories of work and of filters and virtual boards to present customer views to each user.

- *Strong support for Kanban practices.* Kanban practices like work-in-progress (WIP) limits, process policies, swim lanes, Portfolio Kanban, and the measurement of flow through cumulative flow diagrams have strong support in native Kanban tools. When a Kanban view is applied to a ticket-based system, support for these fundamental Kanban practices is usually limited.

Whatever tool you use must promote communication within teams, between teams, and to management. Physical Kanban boards in an open environment are great for this, where many people pass by the Kanban board every day. Electronic Kanban boards, displayed on large screens, also improve communication. Of course, if your team is not physically co-located, electronic Kanban boards are the way to go.

Meetings

Many times, when adopting Agile, marketing teams add daily standups, Sprint planning meetings, Sprint reviews, and Sprint retrospectives to an already full slate of meetings. Have these Agile meetings eliminate other regular scheduled meetings! Agile teams, with deliberate intention and cooperation from the leadership team, create an environment of fewer and shorter meetings.

Approval Loops

If asked to identify one source of frustration, delays, and lack of agility in many organizations, I'd point to overlong and unnecessary approval loops. Here are five ways to shorten approval loops:

1. *Make the customer the ultimate arbiter of value.* If the focus is on pleasing the customer rather than pleasing management, and if every deliverable is measured in terms of its customer value and receptivity, the emphasis is on getting something of reasonable quality out to customers quickly, where it can be tested and improved.
2. *Be explicit about acceptance criteria.* If managers review everything that goes out to customers, internal or external, what do they review it for? Can they state what high quality work looks like up front, so that quality can be baked into the deliverable, rather than inspected through an approval loop?

3. *Establish process policies.* Once these acceptance criteria are established and well known, what process policies can be established to ensure that every deliverable meets the criteria?
4. *Establish WIP limits and SLAs for the approval stage.* Many documents sit in the approval stage for days, and sometimes weeks or months, waiting for the executive to make the approval a priority. Establish strict work-in-progress (WIP) limits for this stage, and an expectation of a service-level agreement (SLA). For example, you might establish a service-level agreement that approvals take no longer than 48 hours.
5. *Push approval (and accountability) down.* If people know that management reviews every deliverable, they may depend on management to ensure quality, rather than taking accountability themselves. Push the approval and the accountability to the lowest level of the organization commensurate with the importance of the deliverable.

Reducing approval loops also increases morale and reduces turnover, particularly among creative people. Nothing is more soul sucking than a dozen revisions of a creative document crawling through six levels of approval loops.

Hiring and Forming the Teams

Can you hire for Agile marketing? What characteristics do you look for in hiring marketers who will thrive in an Agile environment?

Hire T-Shaped People

IDEO CEO Tim Brown has popularized the term "T-shaped people."[1] This describes people who are deep in their discipline (content marketing, social media marketing, etc.) and who also have a breadth of knowledge of other disciplines. This is important for several reasons:

- *It makes them more empathetic.* Because they understand both the capabilities and the limits of other disciplines, it makes them great teammates and great communicators, whether they are on skill-set teams or cross-functional teams.
- *It gives the team more flexibility.* Those with cross-functional skills can fill in for people who have the depth skills in another area when those

people are out, or they can take on some of the tasks that might be assigned to others when the demand for a particular skill is greater than the current capacity.

- *It often makes them more creative.* Some of the best insights come from applying the methods and insights of established disciplines in new ways.

When interviewing people, ask questions like "If you weren't [their area of expertise], what kind of marketer would you be? If you weren't a marketer, what would be your profession? Why? What have you learned from [the other discipline]? How have you applied that in your work?"

Hire Pi-Shaped People

Ashley Friedlein[2] and Scott Brinker[3] have talked about hiring pi-shaped people, those who possess what are sometimes known as right-brained skills and left-brained skills. As Ashley describes it: "They are both analytical and data-driven, yet understand brands, storytelling, and experiential marketing."

It can be difficult to find these people, and they're very valuable to the team. When interviewing, alternate your questions between "left-brain" and "right-brain" topics. For example, if someone describes a "right-brain" creative brand strategy, ask what led to that decision. Did they find data that supported the decision? If someone is describing a "left-brain" data insight, ask what they did with that insight. Listen for storytelling skills.

Hire for Your Values

If you've completed the earlier exercise on beliefs and behaviors, you have a set of values for your Agile marketing team. Hire for those values. If one of your values is customer centricity, look for examples of customer empathy, creating customer value, and other examples of customer centricity. Customer centricity, by the way, is best determined indirectly, as you ask other questions, rather than directly. For example, rather than saying "Tell me about a time where you were customer-centric," you're better off asking "Tell me about your greatest success at your last job" or something more general, and then listening for examples of customer centricity, or asking follow-up questions like "What was the value of that success to the customer?"

Hire Lifelong Learners

I've always thought it important to hire lifelong learners, but it is particularly important for Agile marketing. Agile marketing itself is a learning journey. You want people who are open to learning and who are flexible in their thinking.

Hire a Few Rebels

One team I was on at Microsoft was led by Dan (not his real name). Dan was a rebel. He almost always rejected conventional wisdom, and rules just didn't seem to apply to him. Reporters loved him because he could always be counted on for a good quote, particularly in regard to our competitors. The central PR team hated him, because he ignored their guidelines.

Dan performed an important function on our marketing team—he never let us get complacent. He challenged our thinking and the thinking of the leader. He was fearless and would challenge anyone.

The Dans of the world are like adding salt or spice to a dish: Having a few can enhance the food, but too many can be overwhelming and ruin the dish. Hire a few rebels and give them freedom.

Providing Context and Clarity

One of my favorite leadership gurus is David Marquet. His book *Turn the Ship Around!* and his "Greatness" video[4] should be required reading and viewing for every leader.

According to Marquet, it is the leader's job to provide context and clarity for every major initiative. This is particularly true for Agile marketing initiatives. Rather than spending time reviewing work, cheerleading the troops, and telling people exactly what to do, leaders must provide context ("Why are we doing this?") and clarity ("What does success look like?").

Leaders then get out of the way and let the teams use their skills and creativity to implement a solution. This approach empowers the team and prepares them for accountability. Accountability without the power to implement your own solution and without any knowledge of the criteria by which accountability is to be measured is deeply frustrating.

I recommend that leaders provide clarity by answering the following questions:

- *Purpose.* Why are we doing this initiative? What problem are we solving? Why is it important to solve this problem? How does it compare in importance to other initiatives we may be doing? How does it help the customer? How does it help the organization?
- *Scope.* What is the scope of the initiative? What is within scope? What is out of scope?
- *Resources.* What resources—people and budget—are available? What is the time frame for the initiative? What's the process for requesting more resources?
- *Success criteria.* What does success, qualitative and quantitative, look like? How were the measurements for success determined? Were they plucked out of thin air or based on existing metrics?
- *Expectations.* Are there implicit or explicit expectations? Has anything been promised, either to the customer or to another internal department? What are the leader's expectations?

Removing Obstacles

It is critical that Agile marketing managers remove obstacles for their teams. At every standup, team members have the opportunity to report obstacles; these must be recorded by the scrum master. The scrum master, working with other team members and other teams, should be able to eliminate most of the obstacles. But some obstacles require management intervention to solve.

The leadership team meets at least once every two weeks to review the progress of the Agile marketing implementation, to review the work of the teams, and to hear about any obstacles that are holding the teams back. This meeting is not run by the most senior marketing leader; it is run by the midlevel managers who have been appointed to lead the Agile marketing initiative.

Who should lead the Agile marketing initiative? Appoint the people who are most critical to its success, even if—especially if—they do not support the initiative! Tie the success of the Agile marketing initiative to their performance evaluations.

A typical agenda of the leadership team might include:

- *Review of completed work.* A high level Sprint review to discuss how the work is meeting business objectives.
- *Plans for future work.* A short discussion with emphasis on how this work impacts business objectives.
- *Obstacles.* This critical part of the meeting gives teams the opportunity to make everyone aware of obstacles. Unless an obstacle can be resolved in less than a minute, assign someone on the leadership team responsibility for resolving it outside the meeting.
- *Progress toward the vision.* What progress is being made toward your vision of Agile marketing? What beliefs and behaviors are changing? How are you measuring progress toward the vision, and where do those metrics stand?

If this emphasis on removing obstacles sounds like servant leadership, that's intentional. I encourage Agile marketing managers to learn more about servant leadership and the work of Robert K. Greenleaf.[5]

Celebrating Successes

How important is it to celebrate early successes in the adoption of Agile marketing? Research by behavioral scientists Marcial Losada and Emily Heaphy suggest that it's very important. They found that in high-performing teams, the ratio of positive interactions to negative interactions was 5.6 (that is, nearly 6 positive interactions or comments for each negative one). By contrast, low-performing teams had a positive-to-negative ratio of 0.36 (that is, nearly 3 negative interactions for each positive one).[6]

Acknowledgment of success makes a critical difference during the early stages of the adoption of Agile in marketing. Managers must celebrate the first daily Scrum or standup, the completion of the first Sprint, the first results coming out of Agile teams, and anything else that looks like success.

A Day in the Life of a Manager

Agile marketing can dramatically change the day-to-day work of a leader in a marketing organization. The following scenario describes the before-and-after days of one manager.

Before

Emily spent most of her day in meetings—planning meetings, status meetings, and review meetings—and answering email or responding to Slack. And she was a production bottleneck for her team—work sat in her email box, waiting to be approved, sometimes for weeks. Although she was aware of the impact of this way of working, she saw no alternative to examining all the work that went out in her department's name: She had what she considered an inexperienced team, and their work had to meet her standards. When other department managers had a problem with her group's work, they came to Emily. She was the one they yelled at.

Emily was on the verge of burnout—working 50, 60, 70 hours a week and still not keeping up. Her team was frustrated and kept talking about empowerment. But how does she empower the team if they don't make the "right" decisions and produce the quality of work she expects?

After

Emily now spends less than half of her time in meetings and answering emails. She spent a lot of time up front developing the vision for their Agile marketing implementation, refining the vision with her team, and selling her team on the concept.

For each project or initiative, Emily does as much as she can to provide context and clarity. She trains all of her people to think like the CMO, or sometimes even better than the CMO; they are, after all, closer to the customer and closer to the work. Instead of reviewing all the work that goes out, she describes up front how that work will be evaluated, and then she asks questions to confirm that the team takes responsibility for meeting the standards.

Emily also spends at least a couple hours each day coaching. Not managing, but coaching—asking questions, not giving answers. She has discovered that she likes this style of management. So do her people.

Now, much of Emily's daily time goes to removing obstacles and celebrating successes. The team knows that she has high standards, and they know that she supports them and contributes to their success by removing obstacles and providing them with the resources they need to do a good job.

How do you integrate teams that are practicing Agile marketing with other teams who may not be practicing Agile marketing? That's the topic of our next chapter.

Chapter 23

Integrating Agile with Traditional Marketing Methods

Change your opinions, keep to your principles; change your leaves, keep intact your roots.

—Victor Hugo, French poet, novelist, and dramatist

A s an organization embarks on the Agile marketing journey, some part or parts of the organization will continue to use traditional marketing methods. Even where Agile practice is established, some marketing projects and functions do not practice Agile methodologies.

So how do you integrate Agile and traditional marketing methods? Although it's not that difficult, you can employ a few tips and tricks to make it as straightforward as possible.

Which Marketing Functions Lend Themselves to Agile?

We can classify marketing functions by whether they can be planned for or not, and by whether it makes sense to deliver outputs and measure outcomes at regular intervals. Those functions that satisfy both criteria tend to lend themselves to Scrum. Those that cannot be planned and those with output delivered as a steady stream of work lend themselves to the Kanban model. And a few marketing functions lend themselves to traditional methodologies, as shown in Figure 23.1.

Think of this mapping as guidance. On the ground, each team selects a method that works for them. Teams sometimes use Scrum to manage events. They have a well thought-out process for each event (a webinar, say) and they implement parts of the process in Sprints before and after the event. Other teams will use Kanban or Scrumban to manage events. And many teams will continue to use traditional methods to manage events. Adopt what works best based on empirical evidence.

Integrating Agile Teams with Non-Agile Teams

What if one department or team practices Agile while everyone else stays with traditional methods? This may or may not be a problem. If few dependencies exist between teams, or if the traditional team delivers with speed and quality sufficient to satisfy the Agile team, then it doesn't matter what methods it uses.

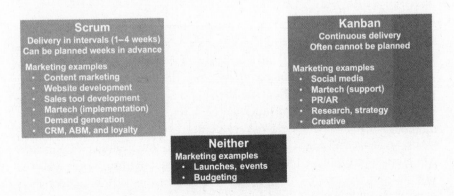

Figure 23.1 Marketing functions and agile

Problems arise when Agile teams depend on teams that can't deliver at the speed needed by the Agile team.

To address this, look at the constraints the other team is working under and establish an understanding of what you're trying to do together. Ask them for service-level agreements (SLAs) based on established process policies, and build the time specified by these SLAs into your process. Form a cross-functional team and request that someone with the skill set of the non–Agile function be assigned to the cross-functional team. If all else fails, reduce your dependencies on the other team by outsourcing or hiring your own people to deliver on the needed function.

Lastly, don't assume that Agile can't be applied to traditional marketing methods. If you are using nondigital marketing channels and they're effective for your business, they can still be managed by Agile marketing practices. There may be more external dependencies (printers, for example), but you can manage these external dependencies by building in lead time for them or finding external providers who can move at the speed of Agile.

Applying Agile principles to traditional marketing methods may be difficult initially. The most commonly cited issue is in measuring the effectiveness of nondigital campaigns. Don't accept this difficulty as inevitable. Use unique phone numbers or links to measure the effectiveness of nondigital media. Ask your vendors for best practices in measuring their media. They have almost certainly experienced skepticism of the effectiveness of their media compared to digital methods and know how to demonstrate the return on investment (ROI) of their media.

How to Budget for Agile

Annual budgets tend to be an exercise in hope over experience. Accountants hope that they are accurate, but experience tells us that changing circumstances influence spending and budgets and that they are seldom if ever accurate. When revenue exceeds budget, spending might expand to exceed budget. If revenue doesn't meet budget, spending will be cut. When opportunity knocks or when companies merge, budgets change.

Provide an annual budget and revise it quarterly. Redistribute spending based on what you learn about what works and what doesn't. If you find something promising and need more budget, recruit partners on the business side to argue the case for more budget. A marketing department effective in generating leads, revenue, profitability, or tremendous customer satisfaction does not get reprimanded for slightly exceeding its annual marketing budget.

Annual Marketing Plans

What if senior executives still want annual marketing plans? In addition to the annual budget, many companies require an annual marketing plan. Annual planning is not a terrible exercise as long as the planners are aware of its limitations.

Here are some guidelines for writing an annual marketing plan in an Agile world:

- *Keep it short.* I gravitated toward Agile initially because I found the annual planning function dysfunctional at some of the larger organizations where I worked. I still have one of those annual marketing plans, which consisted of 155 extremely dense PowerPoint slides. The day after that plan was presented, it went into a drawer and I didn't look at it again until I was leaving the company and cleaning out my drawers. No one reads long plans. Keep yours short (five to six pages at most).
- *Write marketing plans as a document rather than a presentation.* PowerPoint and similar tools support ambiguity and hand waving. Writing out a plan in prose, with paragraphs and sentences and a sufficient level of detail, creates a better plan. Amazon is just one of many companies that enforces this in their planning.
- *Focus on outcomes and strategies to reach those outcomes over outputs.* We've talked about how important it is to focus on outcomes (business results) over outputs. In your annual marketing plan, focus on the outcomes and how you intend to produce them from a strategic, not a tactical, approach. Strategies tend to remain constant; tactics shift. Further, executives care more about outcomes and strategies than about tactics. If you must get into tactics, describe some of your proposed experiments to achieve the outcomes, and your process for refining these tactics or changing course if these tactics don't work.
- *Identify and ROAM the risks to your plan.* Use the ROAM model (see Chapter 12) to describe how you're going to address risks to your plan.
- *Actively solicit feedback on critical issues.* Identify areas—the sooner the better—about which you seek feedback from executives.

How do you scale Agile? How do you take a methodology that was designed for smaller teams and apply it to larger organizations? That's the topic of our next chapter.

Chapter 24

Scaling Agile Marketing to Large Teams

Why fit in when you were born to stand out?

—*Dr. Seuss (Theodor Seuss Geisel)*

A gile was designed for small teams. In "*The Scrum Guide,*" Jeff Sutherland and Ken Schwaber, the creators of Scrum, describe the ideal Agile team as six people, plus or minus three.[1] Small teams are inherently more agile. They spend less time coordinating among their members. They tend to have greater engagement. They can achieve a better balance of autonomy and accountability.

How do you scale Agile to larger teams? How do you coordinate the efforts of a hundred marketers? A thousand?

Let's look at some of the ways that developers have found to scale Agile and whether these techniques might apply to marketing.

The Scaled Agile Framework (SAFe®) is the most popular approach used by software developers to scale Agile.[2] We'll take a look at it, not because it has strong applicability to scaling Agile marketing, but because many organizations use SAFe, and marketers need to understand their role in SAFe.

We'll also look at the approach taken by the music-streaming service Spotify, because it has served as a model not only for many technology companies but also companies like ING, the British banking giant. Although technically it is not a framework, it has been very influential, and marketers do well to understand it.

Scaled Agile Framework (SAFe)

The Scaled Agile Framework grew out of Dean Leffingwell's book, *Agile Software Requirements*, and a compendium of best practices of Scrum, Kanban, and Lean and Extreme Programming, especially for large organizations.

SAFe comes in four flavors of increasing complexity: Essential SAFe, Large Solution SAFe, Portfolio SAFe, and Full SAFe. Each includes unique practices to support the specification, building, and deployment of software at scale.

I'm somewhat skeptical about applying SAFe directly to marketing. There are some components of the newest version of SAFe, version 5.0, that try to address business agility. However, these components are not mature. Let's first take a look at some of the components and terminology of SAFe.

Essential SAFe

Essential SAFe, shown in Figure 24.1, is the foundation for the other SAFe configurations. Essential SAFe contains the minimal set of roles, events, and artifacts required to continuously deliver business solutions. Without these roles and practices, an organization can be SAFe-like or SAFe-light but isn't really doing SAFe.

Program increment planning, often referred to as *Big Room planning,* is a valuable way for organizations to coordinate across teams, sometimes known as coordinating at a "team of teams" level. In many ways, PI or Big Room planning constitutes SAFe's secret sauce for scaling Agile.

Essential SAFe is appropriate for teams of between 30 and 125 members. Above 125 members, more coordination is needed in the form of Large Solution SAFe. At this size, multiple Agile Release Trains (ARTs) are required to deliver value for a customer, which requires additional coordination.

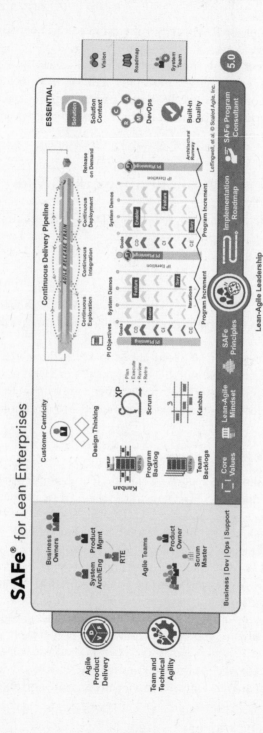

Figure 24.1 Essential SAFe

Source: From Scaled Agile provider of SAFe; Essential SAFe © Scaled Agile, Inc.

The Agile Release Train (ART) is a long-lived set of teams oriented toward the delivery of a value stream to a customer. Planning happens at least quarterly, with each team responsible for planning its iterations. An iteration in SAFe is equivalent to a Sprint (roughly two weeks). The delivery of software is decoupled from its development. Agile Release Trains deliver value to customers in program increments (PIs). Typically, these PIs are 8–12 weeks long, consisting of a series of development iterations followed by a planning iteration.

Large Solution SAFe

Large Solution SAFe, shown in Figure 24.2, adds a level of coordination for Enterprise Solution Delivery to coordinate multiple Agile Release Trains and external suppliers. If you think of Boeing delivering a new jetliner or Ford delivering a new automobile model, these scenarios require Large Solution SAFe. It consists of a set of best practices and competencies to deliver very large systems involving hundreds to thousands of developers and complex integration and regulation-compliance requirements.

Portfolio SAFe

Portfolio SAFe, shown in Figure 24.3, is the basis of business agility. Portfolio SAFe ensures that the value streams represented by the ARTs are aligned with the strategic themes of the organization. It also provides a methodology for budgeting value streams and ensuring that the ARTs are delivering customer and business value.

At the portfolio level, the business funds a portfolio of value streams that deliver on the strategic themes. For example, if one of the strategic themes is "Frictionless eCommerce" (make it as easy as possible to do business online), various value streams could be funded to allow customers to search for products that fit their needs, to evaluate and compare products, and to purchase the products. Each value stream is funded not for a project or iteration but for a period (quarter, year, biennium) consistent with the organization's budgeting needs.

Note the emphasis on building a portfolio of value streams focused on what customers want to accomplish and the value they want to achieve—not on the business and its goals. Value streams use customer language as much as possible and clearly define the value to the customer. For example, a wireless carrier could identify a value stream around "How much could I save by switching?" rather than "new customer acquisition."

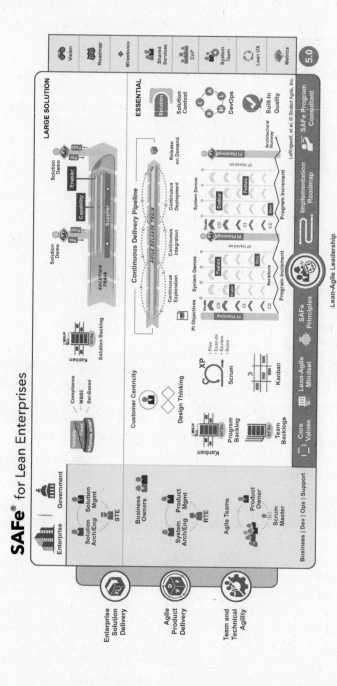

Figure 24.2 Large solution SAFe

Source: From Scaled Agile provider of SAFe; Large Solution SAFe © Scaled Agile, Inc.

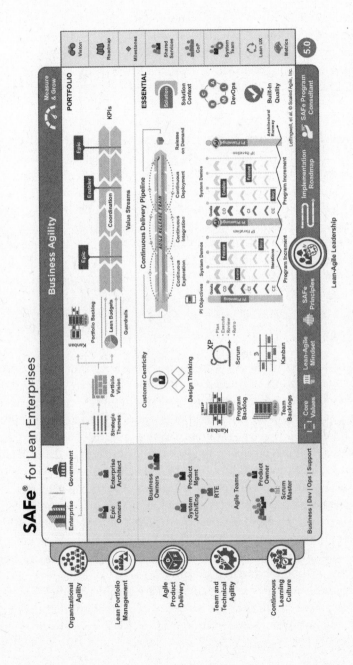

Figure 24.3 Portfolio SAFe

Source: From Scaled Agile provider of SAFe; Portfolio SAFe © Scaled Agile, Inc.

Full SAFe

Full SAFe, shown in Figure 24.4, combines Essential SAFe, Large Solution SAFe, and Portfolio SAFe. It is meant for large solutions that also require the practices and competencies of the Portfolio level. It does not add anything that is not included in Essential SAFe, Large Solution SAFe, or Portfolio SAFe.

What Marketers Need to Know About SAFe

SAFe came into being to scale large software projects. SAFe version 5.0, shown in Figure 24.5, includes significant support for business (including marketing) agility. SAFe 5.0 introduced two new competencies, Organizational Agility and Continuous Learning Culture. There is also a new emphasis on what SAFe calls "measure and grow assessment and practices," what we've referred to as validated learning (see Chapter 11).

Marketers who find themselves in organizations practicing SAFe should engage at four levels.

Portfolio Planning

At the strategic level, marketers wanting to influence product direction in a SAFe environment must participate in portfolio planning. They can submit Epics into the funnel for portfolio review, although in my experience, marketing Epics are seldom prioritized high enough to make the roadmap. SAFe developers tend to see portfolio planning as a series of epics and deliverables on a six- to nine-month-long roadmap. It can seem, and may be, the antithesis of Agile, with few discussions of rapid delivery, and roadmap items delivered too late to meet business needs and too late to be changed.

Marketers must shape portfolio planning in a SAFe environment. They must prioritize customer and business needs in the portfolio at least as high as IT needs or operational needs. They must ensure that the backlog includes innovation, and the risk that comes with it, along with the risk-free items that currently provide the revenue stream.

Getting involved at this level requires political capital. Either by virtue of positional power (the CMO) or by virtue of reputation, the marketing representative must be empowered to significantly influence the portfolio.

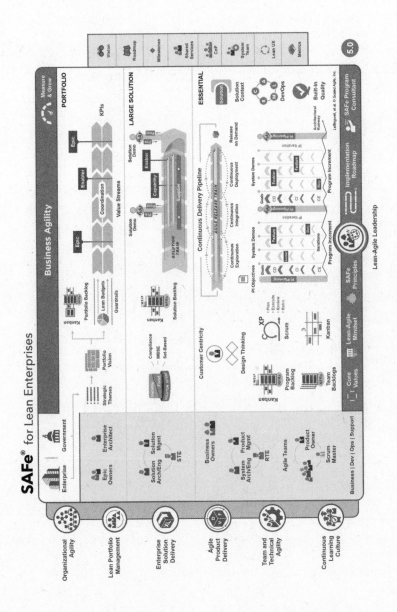

Figure 24.4 Full SAFe

Source: From Scaled Agile provider of SAFe; Full SAFe© Scaled Agile, Inc.

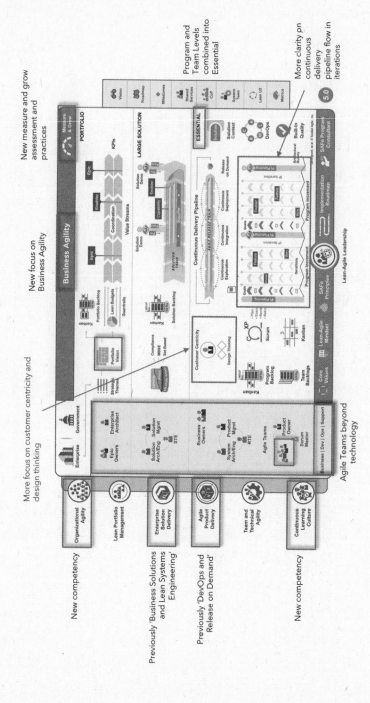

Figure 24.5 Overview of SAFe 5.0

Source: From Scaled Agile provider of SAFe; Overview of SAFe 5.0 © Scaled Agile, Inc.

234

Program Increment (Big Room) Planning

PI or Big Room planning sessions typically occur quarterly and often exclude marketing. You'll be told, "These meetings are boring, impossibly technical, and a waste of your time." Boring and technical, possibly. But these sessions determine which features and functions will be implemented over the next quarter or two. If you're not invited, or even if you're encouraged to stay away, be there. By being there, you can influence the deliverables in ways that benefit the customer and the business.

User Stories

Although PI planning meetings determine what gets implemented when, the details are typically worked out later, either in backlog grooming sessions or by the product owner. You won't be able to influence every user story, nor will you want to. Developers write user stories at a level of detail unheard of in marketing.

    Product owners should consult marketing for critical user stories and to take advantage of marketing's unique understanding of the voice of the customer. Ask to review the backlog with the product owner and talk to him or her about user stories that are important to the customer and to marketing. Get their perspective and make sure they get yours. Develop a good working relationship with the product owner, so that you *are* in the room when decisions about critical details are made.

System Demo

The System Demo is SAFe's equivalent to the Sprint review of Scrum, but at a higher (systems) level, as the name suggests. It is an opportunity for stakeholders to assess the system's current state and to provide feedback. Marketers who have an interest in functionality provided by a particular ART should attend their System demos.

The Spotify Model

Spotify, the music streaming service, started out using Scrum methodology and building their software using Scrum teams of six or seven people. Spotify didn't have to transition to Agile—it's all they've known. They did, however, outgrow the Scrum model for managing the complexity of multiple Scrum teams, so they came up with their own approach to scaling Agile[3] (see Figure 24.6).

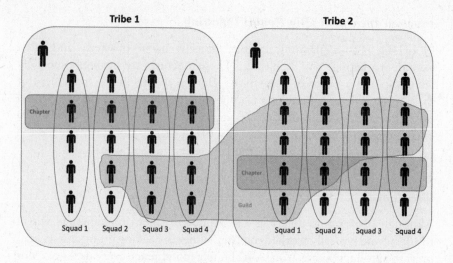

Figure 24.6 The spotify model

How the Spotify Model Is Organized

At the lowest level, Spotify organized into squads. Squads are the same size as Scrum teams, differing in that they have autonomy around one mission or component of their software. As autonomous teams, they do not have to practice Scrum; they can choose the methodology (Scrum, Kanban, Scrumban, or something else) that works best for them. They are also free to decide how to satisfy their mission and build their software.

Squads may or may not have a squad leader, but they do have a product owner who feeds the user stories to the squad. Rather than have a scrum master, squads have Agile coaches. The squad leader/product owner ensures the achievement of the desired outcomes and a focus on the mission. The Agile coaches help the squads be as Agile and productive as possible, ensuring that best practices are followed and shielding the team from interruptions and distractions.

The squads sit together, and they are semi-permanent. Each squad has a work area, a lounge or meeting area, and sometimes a few small huddle rooms.

Squads are organized into tribes—loose groups representing a business unit, an application, or a large piece of the product. Tribes are colocated, usually in the same building, certainly in the same geography. A tribe rarely comprises more than 100 people.

A tribe leader provides the appropriate tools and environment for the squads and facilitates any necessary coordination between squads. Tribes may have informal team-building or culture-building events or activities.

Chapters organize the individuals in the tribe with similar skill sets. Imagine four teams, each with a product manager, a designer, a copywriter, and a web developer. You could then create four chapters—product management, design, copywriting, and web development—and designate a chapter lead for each. The chapter lead sets salary levels and provides professional development for the chapter members. The lead does not prioritize the work or determine how it's done—that's the job of the product owner and the squad. Often, chapter lead is a part-time job. The chapter lead is part of a squad, working as a lead and as a contributor in his or her area of expertise.

The guild is an informal, organization-wide group for people with a shared interest. For example, the organization might have a guild of people interested in Adobe tools like Photoshop and Illustrator. People freely join or leave guilds at any time. Guilds hold informal events to share knowledge and best practices.

How to Apply the Spotify Model to Marketing

The Spotify model was never intended to be a framework (like SAFe). It was one company's approach to scaling Agile. Also, what most people know as the Spotify model is based on a 2012 paper by Henrik Kniberg and Anders Ivarsson. As you would expect, Spotify has continued to evolve that model. The 2012 version is no longer practiced.

The Spotify model does suggest some patterns and ideas that may be useful to organizations looking to scale Agile marketing. As long as they look to the model for these patterns and work out empirically whether they help their organization scale Agile, it can be useful. Don't apply the model literally.

One approach maps the customer experience and builds cross-functional squads with missions to improve discrete portions of the customer experience. The organization creates tribes by business unit, product, or some other logical grouping of squads.

Chapters are the easiest to identify; most marketing departments are essentially organized by skill sets, which translate to chapters. It may make sense to create chapter leads who set salary levels and provide professional development for the chapter members.

The typical guilds form quickly; others appear as squad members discover shared areas of interest.

Another approach looks across the lead pipeline and applies systems thinking, rather than local optimization, to improving the throughput and efficiency of the pipeline. The tribe might form squads to optimize handoffs between stages of the pipeline or individual stages of the pipeline, and, rather than optimizing each step (local optimization), the tribe views the pipeline as a system and measures their success through high level metrics.

For example, in 2014, Mike Volpe, then the head of marketing at marketing automation provider HubSpot, made recommendations for structuring a marketing team to any size.[4] He presented the following slide, which was the most-requested slide by conference attendees (see Figure 24.7).

Let's focus on the rightmost column, with a team size of 18. Note that the teams aren't organized by skill-set silos. Nor are they organized by customer experience. They are organized by squads: an attract squad, a convert squad, and a close squad. Each squad has a unique skill set (bloggers, SEO/SEM experts, designers, and people who generate attractive offers) based on the kinds of work delivered by that squad.

As the organization grows or in larger organizations, you can imagine the marketing organization forming into tribes, organized by product, by geography, or by business unit. The squads might well stay the same in each tribe.

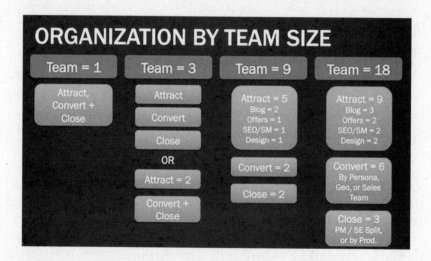

Figure 24.7   HubSpot team size recommendations
Source: From Mike Volpe, *How to Structure a Marketing Team of Any Size,* © Hubspot (blog), entry posted November 14, 2014, accessed April 13, 2020.

Voices from the Field: Scaling Agile

Melissa Reeve is vice president of marketing at Scaled Agile, Inc., the organization behind the Scaled Agile Framework (SAFe). Melissa has practiced Agile marketing since 2016.

Jim: Tell me about your challenges at Scaled Agile in scaling your marketing team. What have you implemented to address the challenges?

Melissa: One of the challenges is getting marketers with I-shaped skills—going deep in one area, like graphic design, digital marketing, or analytics—to adopt a T-shaped mindset. Instead of writing I-centered stories—such as the graphic designer writing a story about graphics creation—getting the team to think about the entirety of the story and writing a story that includes all of the pieces and parts needed to deliver value. We have copywriting, graphic design, campaign development and need to write the story from that point of view, rather than an individual's viewpoint. While the topic is much broader than story-writing, it exemplifies the shift that needs to take place. Getting that shift in mindset from individual to team can be difficult. Ways we have found to address this include writing stories as a group in iteration planning and encouraging pairing, to build out the team's cross-functional skills.

A second challenge we've faced is how I, as a Lean-Agile leader, transformed my traditional leadership mindset into a mindset of team empowerment. Both my education and experience reinforced my role was that of a conductor and knowledge specialist. Moving from a mindset where my main role was to conduct and review activity to a mindset where decision-making is decentralized and I am a servant leader to the team was quite a journey. Letting go of that mindset wasn't as difficult as really understanding my role in this new context. Working for Scaled Agile, where I am surrounded by individuals modeling this new behavior, made it easier to adopt.

Jim: How large is your team?

Melissa: We're about 30 people.

(continued)

(*Continued*)

Jim: Are you organized in multiple subteams?

Melissa: Yes. An events team, a marketing-solutions team focused on growth, and a marketing-ops team.

Jim: Any cross-functional teams?

Melissa: When I think cross-functional, it's "Do I have everyone I need to design, build, refine, and deploy my thing?" In marketing, I believe there are two levels to being cross-functional. The first is to be cross-functional within marketing. Do I have everyone I need to deploy a marketing-contained asset, like a social media post? Our marketing-ops team has this—copywriters, graphic designers, social media specialists. The second level is to think cross-functionally across the entire organization. Often times, if we are supporting a new campaign, we need to align with people outside of marketing. For this, we rely on our marketing-solutions team, which has representatives and relationships with each part of the business: partners, community building, and enterprise. They pull in people from across the organization to ensure alignment, and make sure we have the right people involved to deliver business value.

Jim: What processes do you use to coordinate the work of the three teams?

Melissa: The processes tie in to SAFe because we run the company on SAFe. We plan, with the 30 people on the marketing team, every two weeks. We meet, first, to understand our joint objectives for the next two weeks. Then we break into smaller teams to think about how those objectives impact the work across those three teams. Having everyone in one room creates synergies. If the campaign people propose an idea, the entire marketing team is together to work through the details of that idea.

Every quarter, we're in the bigger program increment (PI) planning meeting, which synchronizes the work of the three teams with the larger organization. In between PI planning sessions, we align with the larger organization through Scrum of Scrum, System Demo, and ART sync meetings.

Jim: How long is your every-two-weeks planning session?

Melissa: About two hours.

Jim: How does a marketing team, working in an organization that practices SAFe, work with other parts of the organization, particularly development? At what key times (meetings/processes) do they engage? And how?

Melissa: In addition to the previously mentioned ceremonies, the marketing team must look at the type of initiative being proposed and determine the level of involvement needed. Say that the development organization is re-doing an internal financial services application. Marketing may only need a light touch. The marketing team might want to review branding elements and have a say on how its marketing finances are tracked. In that scenario, you might have someone from marketing who attends PI Planning to understand how this financial application is being built; understands the key inputs needed from marketing; gets alignment with the enterprise about when that input is needed, about dependencies; and attends the regular systems demo every two weeks to monitor progress. That person, not dedicated to that Agile Release Train, acts more as a shared service.

That project differs from, say, an organization that decides to launch a promotional financing offer. In that situation, you need IT support to update systems and update websites supporting the offer, but you need much greater involvement from marketing to design and deliver an effective campaign. You might want a dedicated marketing team on the Agile Release Train to ensure alignment and synchronization between the technology and marketing teams.

Jim: Let's talk about SAFe 5.0 and its new core competencies to address business agility. How do you see them applying to marketing?

Melissa: We added two: the organizational-agility competency and the continuous-learning competency. With the latter, we're embracing a culture that says, "I may not have the answers, and I'm willing to learn." This gets us—the marketers—out of the opinion battles. We're moving instead into the hypothesis-driven mindset. What is the hypothesis and how can we test it? That's so valuable to marketers! Just as software has become so cheap to make, it's cheaper for us to run small campaigns and get a sense of how our messages land than it is to sit and debate the messages

(continued)

(Continued)

for eight hours. We can test easily. We can change messaging on the fly.

The Covid-19 context is exactly what the second new competency, organizational agility, is all about. Set your strategy and be nimble enough to change it on a dime. Watching commercials during the Covid-19 pandemic, I can tell who is able to adapt and who is struggling with agility. Think about all that must happen to adapt: The media buyer yanks the inappropriate ad; the marketing team must quickly produce new messaging along with a new commercial and get it in the right slot. All of this takes organizational agility.

Jim: Should marketing organizations scale using the SAFe methodology?

Melissa: I'm still regularly asking myself this question. Before scaling, you have to have some base level of team agility in order to get your teams exposed to team-level Agile principles and practices. Once your teams have a foundation of team level Agile, the CMO might want to take the entire marketing function Agile. Can SAFe be used for that? Yes, although I believe there are nuances to be worked out around how to implement SAFe in marketing organizations. Where is it really well aligned? Where does it break? How do we integrate it with the rest of the business? CEOs are looking to achieve business agility. If the marketing function goes Agile and the CEO doesn't bring in other parts of the organization, you don't have business agility; you have an Agile silo, so CMOs need to be aware of this and integrate with other parts of the business.

Will Agile become the way that most marketers organize and manage their work in the future? If so, what might cause that to happen? What tools and training will make it easier for organizations and teams to adopt Agile in their marketing practice and more broadly, into all aspects of business? We'll take a look at these questions and more in the next chapter.

Chapter 25

The Future of Agile Marketing

The future belongs to those who believe in the beauty of their dreams.
—*Eleanor Roosevelt, former First Lady of the United States*

What is the future of Agile marketing? What will it take to move Agile marketing further into the mainstream, to where it becomes the dominant approach to marketing, just as it has become the dominant approach to software development?

Expanding the Ecosystem

I began my marketing career in the early 1990s, about the same time that Geoffrey Moore published his seminal book *Crossing the Chasm: Marketing and Selling High-Tech Products to Mainstream Customers*. This book greatly influenced my thinking about how new products or concepts get adopted by mainstream customers.

In particular, Moore identified a key gap between what marketers promise and what the customer expects or needs in realizing the benefits of a product or service. He identified four levels of product completeness:

1. The generic product as provided by the vendor
2. The expected product, which includes the minimum set of capabilities, not all provided by the vendor, to make the product work
3. The augmented product, which goes beyond the minimum set of capabilities to provide augmented capabilities that the customer wants or needs
4. The potential product, which includes everything for the customer to realize the potential of the product

Agile marketing is, at the time of this writing, somewhere between a generic product and an expected product. It has some—not all—of the capabilities that a customer would expect, and it is missing some key capabilities. Figure 25.1 shows some of the ecosystem that must be available for Agile marketing to succeed.

The future of Agile marketing requires expanding the offerings in this ecosystem. We have books and case studies; customers need more books outlining how to adopt Agile marketing and describing some of its more nuanced and advanced capabilities. The Martech Conference has an Agile marketing track, and there is a dedicated Agile marketing conference planned for 2021 in the United States, but there are not enough conferences in enough geographies to support worldwide adoption. A handful of meetups of Agile marketers exist in a few geographies. There are business agility chapters that may include some Agile marketers. A small number of organizations offer training classes. Online training is limited. Certification is available from IC-Agile, but the number of people who are certified can be numbered in the hundreds.

Tools is an area where much work needs to be done. Agile developers have access to a wealth of tools. Kanban board tools are very useful for marketers, but the number of tools designed for Agile marketers is tiny. Traditional marketers have access to many tools, as evidenced by Scott Brinker's annual Martech Landscape Supergraphic mentioned in Chapter 1; few of these tools support Agile processes.

There are only a handful of Agile marketing consulting firms, along with small practices in the major management consulting firms like McKinsey. It is easy today to hire a contract developer who is familiar with Agile development practices; it is nearly impossible to hire the equivalent contract marketer who has experience with Agile practices.

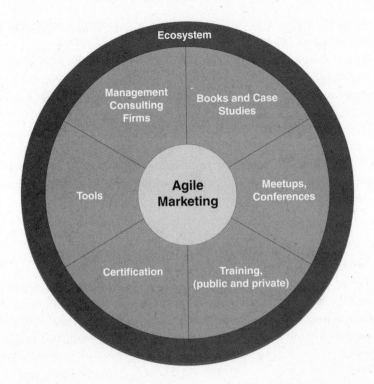

Figure 25.1 The whole product ecosystem for agile marketing

Only the expansion of each of these areas can guarantee the future of Agile marketing.

Breadth and Depth of Adoption

According to the 2020 3rd Annual State of Agile Marketing report, 42 percent of marketers are practicing some aspects of Agile.[1] This contrasts with 41 percent who follow a more traditional approach and 16 percent who have no specific methodology. This contrasts sharply with the breadth of adoption among developers, where 97 percent of organizations report that they are practicing Agile.[2]

More critical than breadth of adoption is the depth of adoption in marketing teams. While it's impossible to know from self-reported surveys like the State of Agile Marketing surveys, we have reason to believe that marketers have not adopted Agile in great depth. Certainly, we have not seen the widescale improvements in marketing efficiency that developers have seen in developer efficiency.

From my own experience, despite the documented successes of, and the enthusiasm by, individual contributors to the Agile approach, many marketing organizations that adopt Agile fall back into old habits as management personnel changes.

One Agile practice—the use of cross-functional teams—remains relatively rare in marketing. Until we see widespread adoption of practices like cross-functional teams, and until we see teams with years of Agile marketing experience, we won't have the depth of adoption to start seeing wholesale improvements in marketing efficiency.

Integration with Other Disciplines

The future of Agile marketing requires integration with other disciplines, and with product management and product development above all. The potential benefits of integrating these disciplines is huge and, informally, you can already see some of the best companies adopting this integrated approach.

To create remarkable customer experiences, product management and product development need the customer focus and the storytelling abilities that marketers bring to the table. When we can create customer experiences in an Agile fashion, iterating quickly, testing minimum viable products and small modifications until the result is something remarkable, then we will realize Agile marketing's potential.

Endnotes

Preface

1. Andrea Fryrear, *3rd Annual State of Agile Marketing Report*, April 2020, p. 11, accessed April 10, 2020, https://www.agilesherpas.com/state-of-agile-marketing-2020.
2. Steven Blank and Bob Dorf, *The Startup Owner's Manual: The Step-By-Step Guide for Building a Great Company* (Pescadero, CA: K & S Ranch, 2012), p. 31.

Chapter 1

1. Rick Fox, "Technology and Today's Agency: What You Need to Know," SlideShare, October 15, 2015, accessed April 8, 2020, https://www.slideshare.net/mobile/AgencyRevolution/technology-todays-agency-what-you-need-to-know-by-rick-fox.
2. Moz, comp., "Google Algorithm Update History: A History of Major Google Algorithm Updates from 2000–Present," January 22, 2020, accessed April 8, 2020, https://moz.com/google-algorithm-change.
3. J. Clement, "Share of Global Mobile Website Traffic 2015-2019," Statista, January 2020, https://www.statista.com/statistics/277125/share-of-website-traffic-coming-from-mobile-devices/.

4. Scott Brinker, "Marketing Technology Landscape Supergraphic (2019): Martech 5000 (actually 7,040)," *ChiefMarTech.com* (blog), entry posted April 4, 2019, accessed August 12, 2019, https://chiefmartec.com/2019/04/marketing-technology-landscape-supergraphic-2019/.

5. Google, "Zero Moment of Truth (ZMOT)," Think with Google, last modified 2011, accessed August 7, 2019, https://www.thinkwithgoogle.com/marketing-resources/micro-moments/zero-moment-truth/.

6. Kimberly Morrison, "81% of Shoppers Conduct Online Research Before Buying," *Adweek*, last modified November 28, 2014, accessed February 5, 2019, https://www.adweek.com/digital/81-shoppers-conduct-online-research-making-purchase-infographic/.

7. Oskar Lingqvist, Candace Lun Plotkin, and Jennifer Stanley, "Do You Really Understand How Your Business Customers Buy?" *McKinsey Quarterly*, February 2015, accessed February 2015, https://www.mckinsey.com/business-functions/marketing-and-sales/our-insights/do-you-really-understand-how-your-business-customers-buy.

8. Gartner "A Blueprint for B2B Content Marketing Success," Marketing Research Team, 6 June 2019.

9. Jeanine Poggi, "'Google Facebook Duopoly Set to Lose Some of Its Share of Ad Spend: And Amazon Will More Than Double Its Share," *Ad Age*, last modified February 2019, accessed August 7, 2019, https://adage.com/article/digital/duopoly-loses-share-ad-spend/316692.

10. Jillian D'Onfro, "Google and Facebook Extend Their Lead in Online Ads, and That's Reason for Investors to Be Cautious," CNBC, last modified December 20, 2017, accessed August 7, 2019, https://www.cnbc.com/2017/12/20/google-facebook-digital-ad-marketshare-growth-pivotal.html.

11. Marianne Wilson, "Amazon to Capture 47% of All U.S. Online Sales in 2019," *Chain Store Age*, last modified February 2019, accessed August 7, 2019, https://www.chainstoreage.com/technology/emarketer-amazon-to-capture-47-of-all-u-s-online-sales-in-2019/.

12. Geoffrey A. Moore, *Inside the Tornado: Strategies for Developing, Leveraging, and Surviving Hypergrowth Markets*, Collins Business Essentials (Harper Business, 2005), pp. 68–72.

13. "Consumer Market Outlook: Eyeware," Statista, last modified 2019, https://www.statista.com/outlook/12000000/109/eyewear/united-states#market-arpu.

14. Shelbi Gomez, "Workfront Survey Finds Majority of Marketers Are Overloaded and Understaffed When It Comes to Work," news release,

August 2015, accessed August 7, 2019, https://www.workfront.com/news/workfront-survey-finds-majority-of-marketers-are-overloaded-and-understaffed-when-it-comes-to -work.

Chapter 2

1. Kent Beck, Mike Beedle, and Arie van Bennekum et al., "Manifesto for Agile Software Development," *Agile Manifesto*, last modified February 2001, accessed August 7, 2019, http://www.agilemanifesto.org.

2. CollabNet VersionOne, "13th Annual State of Agile Report," press release, May 2019, p. 7, accessed August 7, 2019, https://www.stateofagile.com/#ufh-c-473508-state-of-agile-report.

3. Jim Ewel, John Cass, and Frank Days et al., *Agile Marketing Manifesto*, June 11, 2012, accessed August 7, 2019, https://www.agilemarketingmanifesto.org.

4. Andrea Fryrear, *3rd Annual State of Agile Marketing Report*, April 2020, p. 3, accessed April 10, 2020, https://resources.agilesherpas.com/3rd-annual-state-of-agile-marketing.

5. Sergio Zyman, *The End of Marketing as We Know It* (New York: HarperCollins, 1999), pp. 13–14.

6. Although the origin of the 70-20-10 rule is somewhat unclear, many people attribute its more recent use to Mehrdad Baghai, Steve Coley, and David White, *The Alchemy of Growth: Practical Insights for Building the Enduring Enterprise* (Basic Books, 2000). It is also a common practice in financial planning, where portfolios are allocated using some variant of the 70-20-10 ratio.

7. Cara Harshman, "The Homepage Is Dead: A Story of Website Personalization," Moz, last modified May 2017, accessed August 7, 2019, https://moz.com/blog/homepage-personalization.

Chapter 3

1. Seth Godin, *Purple Cow: Transform Your Business by Being Remarkable* (Gardners, 2005), pp. 2–3.

Chapter 5

1. Dr. Eliyahu M. Goldratt and Ilan Eshkoli, "Overcoming Resistance to Change—Isn't It Obvious," video, *YouTube*, July 2010, accessed August 8, 2019, https://www.youtube.com/watch?v=9T_WB--wAxU.

2. Eric Ries, *The Lean Startup: How Today's Entrepreneurs Use Continuous Innovation to Create Radically Successful Businesses* (Currency Publishers, 2011), pp. 128–130.

Chapter 6

1. Rajesh Sethi, Daniel C. Smith, and C. Whan Park, "Cross-Functional Product Development Teams, Creativity, and the Innovativeness of New Consumer Products," *Journal of Marketing Research* 38, no. 1 (February 1, 2001), accessed March 2020, https://journals.sagepub.com/doi/10.1509/jmkr.38.1.73.18833.

Chapter 7

1. Hirotaka Takeuchi and Ikujiro Nonaka, "The New New Product Development Game," *Harvard Business Review*, January 1986, https://hbr.org/1986/01/the-new-new-product-development-game.

2. Ken Schwaber, "Scrum Development Process," *Advanced Development Methods*, April 1995, accessed August 20, 2019, www.jeffsutherland.org/oopsla/schwapub.pdf.

Chapter 8

1. Erika Brooks, "Agile Retrospective Report Released (First Annual)," press release, August 2017, accessed May 4, 2020, https://www.retrium.com/press/retrium-releases-the-first-annual-agile-retrospective-report.

Chapter 10

1. Ladas, Corey, *Scrumban: And Other Essays on Kanban System for Lean Software Development* (Modus Cooperandi Press, 2009), p. 16.

Chapter 11

1. Ries, *The Lean Startup,* p. 143.
2. Paul Willard, "Agile Marketing Meetup—Satya Patel on Using the Scientific Method," video, YouTube, posted March 23, 2014, accessed August 8, 2019, https://www.youtube.com/watch?v=WALnvEuQ0mE. The pertinent question begins at the 57:39 mark in the video.
3. Sean Ellis, "Agile Marketing Meetup: Moving Beyond the Marketing Plan So You Remain Relevant," SlideShare, last modified September 2015, accessed August 8, 2019, https://www.slideshare.net/seanellis/agile-marketing-meetup-slideshare-52690997.
4. Andrew Chen, "How to Build a Growth Team—Lessons from Uber, Hubspot, and Others," *@AndrewChen* (blog), entry posted 2019, accessed February 12, 2020, https://andrewchen.co/how-to-build-a-growth-team/.
5. Brian Gregg, Hussein Kalaoui, and Joel Maynes et al., "Marketing's Holy Grail: Digital Personalization at Scale," *McKinsey Digital*, last modified November 2016, accessed August 8, 2019, https://www.mckinsey.com/business-functions/digital-mckinsey/our-insights/marketings-holy-grail-digital-personalization-at-scale.

Chapter 12

1. Tim Sykes, "Digitally Printed Packaging at the Tipping Point," *Packaging Europe*, last modified April 2018, accessed August 8, 2019, https://packagingeurope.com/digital-print-packaging-tipping-point-HP-Indigo-Scitex/.
2. "ROAM & Risk Management Under SAFe," Intland Software, last modified February 2015, accessed August 28, 2019, https://content.intland.com/blog/agile/safe/roam-risk-management-under-safe.

Chapter 13

1. Robert Rose and Carla Johnson, *Experiences: The 7th Era of Marketing* (Content Marketing Institute, 2015), p. 13.
2. Zarema Plaksij, "Customer Churn: 12 Ways to Stop Churn Immediately," *SuperOffice* (blog), entry posted March 6, 2020, accessed March 8, 2020, https://www.superoffice.com/blog/reduce-customer-churn/.

3. American Express, "#Well Actually, Americans Say Customer Service Is Better than Ever," *American Express Blog*, last modified December 2017, accessed August 8, 2019, https://about.americanexpress.com/press-release/wellactually-americans-say-customer-service-better-ever.

4. Spencer Reiss and Darren Jacoby, *Vail Resorts Creates Epic Experiences with Customer Intelligence*, May 2013, accessed March 18, 2020, https://www.sas.com/content/dam/SAS/en_us/doc/conclusionpaper1/vail-resorts-creates-epic-experiences-with-customer-intelligence-105852.pdf.

Chapter 14

1. Giselle Abramovich, "Forrester Consulting: It Pays to Be an Experience-Led Business," CMO.com, last modified February 2018, accessed March 18, 2020, https://cmo.adobe.com/articles/2018/4/forrester-consulting-it-pays-to-be-an-experience-led-business.html.

Chapter 15

1. Brian Knollenberg, "BECU Leverages Amplero to Increase Member Engagement, Promote Financial Health and Achieve Business KPIs," November 2019.

2. John Cutler, "Beyond Outcomes Over Outputs," *Hackernoon Blog*, entry posted May 2018, accessed March 18, 2020, https://hackernoon.com/beyond-outcomes-over-outputs-6b2677044214.

Chapter 17

1. Harley Manning, "Does Customer Experience Really Drive Business Success? The Relationship Between Superior Customer Experience and Growth," Forrester, July 15, 2015, accessed March 2019.

2. Gopal Srinivasan, Deepak Sharma, and Aishwarya Sharan et al., *Enterprise Customer Success (CS) Study and Outlook, Fostering an Organization-wide CS Mindset,* Deloitte, https://www2.deloitte.com/content/dam/Deloitte/us/Documents/consumer-business/2019-enterprise-customer-success-study-and-outlook.pdf.

3. Adele Revella, "Buyer Persona Expectations," Buyer Persona Institute, accessed March 19, 2019, https://www.buyerpersona.com/. A good place to learn more information about personas.

4. Sean Downey, "How Integrated Data and Technology Helped 3 Companies Transform Their Marketing," MIT SMR Custom Studio, last modified 2018, https://www.thinkwithgoogle.com/marketing-resources/customer-integrated-data-technology/.

5. Srinivasan et al., *Enterprise Customer.*

6. *NICE-BCG CX Survey; Survey Highlights*, 2016, accessed April 8, 2020, https://info.nice.com/rs/338-EJP-431/images/NICE-BCG%202016 %20Customer%20survey%20-%20survey%20PP%20for%20Hub%20V8.pdf.

Chapter 18

1. W. Edwards Deming, *Out of the Crises* (1982; Cambridge, MA: MIT Press, 2016), p. 23.

2. Southwest Airlines, "Purpose, Vision and The Southwest Way," Investor Relations, accessed March 2020, http://investors.southwest.com/our-company/purpose-vision-and-the-southwest-way. You can find the Southwest Airlines values on this page.

Chapter 19

1. CollabNet VersionOne, "13th Annual State of Agile Report," accessed March 2020, p. 12, https://www.stateofagile.com/#ufh-c-473508-state-of-agile-report. This is where you will find the latest version of the VersionOne survey.

Chapter 20

1. "Agility in Marketing," IC-Agile, https://www.icagile.com/Business-Agility/Operating-with-Agility/Agility-in-Marketing. More information on IC-Agile's Agile Marketing certification can be found here.

Chapter 22

1. Morten Hansen, "T-Shaped Stars: The Backbone of IDEO's Collaborative Culture," *Chief Executive*, https://chiefexecutive.net/ideo-ceo-tim-brown-t-shaped-stars-the-backbone-of-ideoaes-collaborative-culture__trashed.

2. Ashley Friedlin, "Why Modern Marketers Need to Be Pi-People," *Marketing Week*, last modified November 2012, accessed August 8, 2019, https://www.marketingweek.com/why-modern-marketers-need-to-be-pi-people.

3. Scott Brinker, "Econsultancy's CEO: Marketing Needs Pi-Shaped People," *ChiefMartec.com* (blog), entry posted November 8, 2012, accessed August 8, 2019, https://chiefmartec.com/2012/11/econsultancys-ceo-marketing-needs-pi-shaped-people.

4. "Inno-Versity Presents: 'Greatness' by David Marquet," video, 9:47, *YouTube*, posted October 8, 2013, accessed August 8, 2019, https://www.youtube.com/watch?v=OqmdLcyES_Q. This Inno-Versity Inno-Mation was adapted from Captain David Marquet's talk on Greatness, and is based on his book, *Turn the Ship Around!*

5. "Start Here: What Is Servant Leadership?" Robert Greenleaf: Center for Servant Leadership, accessed August 8, 2019, https://www.greenleaf.org/what-is-servant-leadership.

6. Marcial Losada and Emily Heaphy, "The Role of Positivity and Connectivity in the Performance of Business Teams: A Nonlinear Dynamics Model," *American Behavorial Scientist* 47, no. 6 (February 2004), accessed August 8, 2019, https://journals.sagepub.com/doi/abs/10.1177/0002764203260208.

Chapter 24

1. Ken Schwaber and John Sutherland, "The Scrum Guide," *Scrum Guides*, accessed April 13, 2020, https://www.scrumguides.org/scrum-guide.html. The latest version of the Scrum Guide is available here under a Creative Commons license.

2. "SAFe," Scaled Agile, accessed April 13, 2020, https://www.scaledagileframework.com/. For more information about the Scaled Agile Framework (SAFe).

3. The best descriptions of "The Spotify Model" can be found in the following paper by Henrik Kniberg and Anders Ivarsson, "Scaling Agile @ Spotify with Tribes, Squads, Chapters and Guilds," *Crisp's Blog*, entry posted October 2012, https://blog.crisp.se/wp-content/uploads/2012/11/SpotifyScaling.pdf; and the video, Spotify Training and Development, "Spotify Engineering Culture—part 1," video, 13:12, Vimeo, posted January 30, 2014, accessed April 13, 2020, https://vimeo.com/85490944.

4. Mike Volpe, "How to Structure a Marketing Team of Any Size," *Hubspot* (blog), entry posted November 14, 2014, accessed April 13, 2020, https://blog.hubspot.com/marketing/how-to-structure-marketing-team.

Chapter 25

1. Fryrear, *3rd Annual State of Agile Marketing Report*, p. 3.
2. CollabNet VersionOne, "13th Annual State of Agile Report."

Bibliography

Abramovich, Giselle. "Forrester Consulting: It Pays to Be an Experience—Led Business." CMO.com. Last modified February 2018. Accessed March 18, 2020. https://cmo.adobe.com/articles/2018/4/forrester-consulting-it-pays-to-be-an-experience-led-business.html.

The Agile Marketing Manifesto. June 27, 2012. Accessed April 8, 2020. http://agilemarketingmanifesto.org/.

Paul Willard, "Agile Marketing Meetup—Satya Patel on Using the Scientific Method." Video. YouTube. Posted March 23, 2014. Accessed August 8, 2019. https://www.youtube.com/watch?v=WALnvEuQ0mE.

"Agility in Marketing." IC-Agile. https://www.icagile.com/Business-Agility/Operating-with-Agility/Agility-in-Marketing.

American Express. "#Well Actually, Americans Say Customer Service Is Better Than Ever." *American Express Blog*. Last modified December 2017. Accessed August 8, 2019. https://about.americanexpress.com/press-release/wellactually-americans-say-customer-service-better-ever.

Anderson, David J. *Kanban: Successful Evolutionary Change in Your Technology Business*. Sequim, WA: Blue Hole Press, 2010.

Baghai, Mehrdad, Steve Coley, and David White. *The Alchemy of Growth: Practical Insights for Building the Enduring Enterprise*. Basic Books, 2000.

Beck, Kent, Mike Beedle, and Arie van Bennekum et al. "Manifesto for Agile Software Development." *Agile Manifesto*. Last modified February 2001. Accessed August 7, 2019. https://www.agilemanifesto.org.

Blank, Steven, and Bob Dorf. *The Startup Owner's Manual: The Step-By-Step Guide for Building a Great Company*. Pescadero, CA: K & S Ranch, 2012.

Brinker, Scott. "Econsultancy's CEO: Marketing Needs Pi-Shaped People." *ChiefMartec.com* (blog). Entry posted November 8, 2012. Accessed August 8, 2019. https://chiefmartec.com/2012/11/econsultancys-ceo-marketing-needs-pi-shaped-people.

———. "Marketing Technology Landscape Supergraphic (2019): Martech 5000 (actually 7,040)." *ChiefMarTech.com (blog)*. Entry posted April 4, 2019. Accessed August 12, 2019. https://chiefmartec.com/2019/04/marketing-technology-landscape-supergraphic-2019/.

CEB Marketing Leadership Council and Google. *The Digital Revolution in B2B Marketing*. 2012. Accessed August 12, 2019. https://www.cebglobal.com/content/dam/cebglobal/us/EN/best-practices-decision-support/marketing-communications/pdfs/CEB-Mktg-B2B-Digital-Evolution.pdf.

Chen, Andrew. "How to Build a Growth Team—Lessons from Uber, Hubspot, and Others." *@AndrewChen* (blog). Entry posted 2019. Accessed February 12, 2020. https://andrewchen.co/how-to-build-a-growth-team/.

Clement, J. "Share of Global Mobile Website Traffic 2015–2019." Statista. Last modified January 2020. https://www.statista.com/statistics/277125/share-of-website-traffic-coming-from-mobile-devices/.

CollabNet VersionOne. "*13th Annual State of Agile Report*." May 2019. Accessed August 7, 2019. https://www.stateofagile.com/#ufh-c-473508-state-of-agile-report.

"Consumer Market Outlook: Eyeware." Statista. Last modified 2019. https://www.statista.com/outlook/12000000/109/eyewear/united-states#market-arpu.

Cutler, John. "Beyond Outcomes over Outputs." *Herkernoon Blog*. Entry posted May 2018. Accessed March 18, 2020. https://hackernoon.com/beyond-outcomes-over-outputs-6b2677044214.

Deming, W. Edwards. *Out of the Crises*. 1982. Cambridge, MA: MIT Press, 2016.

D'Onfro, Jillian. "Google and Facebook Extend Their Lead in Online Ads, and That's Reason for Investors to Be Cautious." CNBC. *Last modified December* 20, 2017. Accessed August 7, 2019. https://www.cnbc.com/2017/12/20/google-facebook-digital-ad-marketshare-growth-pivotal.html.

Downey, Sean. "How Integrated Data and Technology Helped 3 Companies Transform Their Marketing." MIT SMR Custom Studio. Last modified 2018. https://www.thinkwithgoogle.com/marketing-resources/customer-integrated-data-technology/.

Ellis, Sean. "Agile Marketing Meetup: Moving Beyond the Marketing PlansSo You Remain Relevant." Speech. SlideShare. Last modified September 2015. Accessed August 8, 2019. https://www.slideshare.net/seanellis/agile-marketing-meetup-slideshare-52690997.

Dr. Eliyahu M. Goldratt and Ilan Eshkoli. "Overcoming Resistance to Change—Isn't It Obvious." Video. *YouTube*. Posted July 2010. Accessed August 8, 2019. https://www.youtube.com/watch?v=9T_WB–wAxU.

Ewel, Jim. "Persona Template." *AgileMarketing.net*. http://agilemarketing.net/download/2037.

Ewel, Jim, John Cass, and Frank Days. *Agile Marketing Manifesto*, *June* 11, 2012. Accessed August 7, 2019. https://www.agilemarketingmanifesto.org.

Fogg, B. J. *Tiny Habits: The Small Changes That Change Everything*. New York: Houghton Mifflin Harcourt, 2019.

Fox, Rick. "Technology and Today's Agency: What You Need to Know." SlideShare, October 15, 2015. *Last modified* October 2015. Accessed April 8, 2020. https://www.slideshare.net/mobile/AgencyRevolution/technology-todays-agency-what-you-need-to-know-by-rick-fox.

Friedlin, Ashley. "Why Modern Marketers Need to Be Pi-People." *Marketing Week*. Last modified November 2012. Accessed August 8, 2019. https://www.marketingweek.com/why-modern-marketers-need-to-be-pi-people.

Fryrear, Andrea. *3rd Annual State of Agile Marketing Report*. April 2020a. Accessed April 10, 2020. https://resources.agilesherpas.com/3rd-annual-state-of-agile-marketing.

———. *The 3rd Annual State of Agile Marketing Report*. Accessed April 10, 2020b. https://resources.agilesherpas.com/3rd-annual-state-of-agile-marketing.

Godin, Seth. *Purple Cow: Transform Your Business by Being Remarkable*. Gardners, 2005.

Gomez, Shelbi. "Workfront Survey Finds Majority of Marketers Are Overloaded and Understaffed When It Comes to Work." News release. August 2015. Accessed August 7, 2019. https://www.workfront.com/news/workfront-survey-finds-majority-of-marketers-are-overloaded-and-understaffed-when-it-comes-to-work.

Google. "Zero Moment of Truth (ZMOT)." *Think with Google*. Last modified 2011. Accessed August 7, 2019. https://www.thinkwithgoogle.com/marketing-resources/micro-moments/zero-moment-truth/.

Gregg, Brian, Hussein Kalaoui, Joel Maynes, and Gustavo Schuler. "Marketing's Holy Grail: Digital Personalization at Scale." *McKinsey Digital*. Last modified November 2016. Accessed August 8, 2019. https://www.mckinsey.com/business-functions/digital-mckinsey/our-insights/marketings-holy-grail-digital-personalization-at-scale.

Hansen, Morten. "T-Shaped Stars: The Backbone of IDEO's Collaborative Culture." *Chief Executive*. https://chiefexecutive.net/ideo-ceo-tim-brown-t-shaped-stars-the-backbone-of-ideoaes-collaborative-culture__trashed.

Harshman, Cara. "The Homepage Is Dead: A Story of Website Personalization." *Moz*. Last modified May 2017. Accessed August 7, 2019. https://moz.com/blog/homepage-personalization.

"Inno-Versity Presents: 'Greatness' by David Marquet." Video, 9:47. *YouTube*. Posted October 8, 2013. Accessed August 8, 2019. https://www.youtube.com/watch?v=OqmdLcyES_Q.

Kniberg, Henrik, and Anders Ivarsson. "Scaling Agile @ Spotify with Tribes, Squads Chapters and Guilds." *Crisp's Blog*. Entry posted October 2012. https://blog.crisp.se/wp-content/uploads/2012/11/SpotifyScaling.pdf.

Ladas, Corey. *Scrumban: And Other Essays on Kanban System for Lean Software Development*. Seattle, WA: Modus Cooperandi Press, 2009.

Leffingwell, Dean. *Agile Software Requirements: Lean Requirements Practices for Teams, Programs, and the Enterprise*. Agile Software Development Series. Boston, MA: Addison-Wesley Professional, 2011.

Lingqvist, Oskar, Candace Lun Plotkin, and Jennifer Stanley. "Do You Really Understand How Your Business Customers Buy?" *McKinsey Quarterly*, February 2015. Accessed February 2015. https://www.mckinsey.com/business-functions/marketing-and-sales/our-insights/do-you-really-understand-how-your-business-customers-buy.

Losada, Marcial, and Emily Heaphy. "The Role of Positivity and Connectivity in the Performance of Business Teams: A Nonlinear Model." *American Behavorial Scientist* 47, no. 6 (February 2004): 740–765. Accessed August 8, 2019. https://journals.sagepub.com/doi/abs/10.1177/0002764203260208.

Manning, Harley. "Does Customer Experience Really Drive Business Success? The Relationship Between Superior Customer Experience and Growth." Forrester, July 15, 2015, 1–23. Accessed March 2019.

McClure, Dave. "Startup Metrics for Pirates." Lecture presented at SlideShare. Last modified August 2007. Accessed August 8, 2019. https://www.slideshare.net/dmc500hats/startup-metrics-for-pirates-long-version.

Moore, Geoffrey A. *Inside the Tornado: Strategies for Developing, Leveraging, and Surviving Hypergrowth Markets.* Collins Business Essentials. Harper Business, 2005.

Morrison, Kimberly. "81% of Shoppers Conduct Online Research Before Buying." *Adweek.* Last modified November 28, 2014. Accessed February 5, 2019. https://www.adweek.com/digital/81-shoppers-conduct-online-research-making-purchase-infographic/.

Moz, comp. "Google Algorithm Update History: A History of Major Google Algorithm Updates from 2000–Present." January 22, 2020. Accessed April 8, 2020. https://moz.com/google-algorithm-change.

NICE-BCG CX Survey; Survey Highlights. 2016. Accessed April 8, 2020. https://info.nice.com/rs/338-EJP-431/images/NICE-BCG%202016%20Customer%20survey%20-%20survey%20PP%20for%20Hub%20V8.pdf.

Plaksij, Zarema. "Customer Churn: 12 Ways to Stop Churn Immediately." *SuperOffice* (blog). Entry posted March 6, 2020. Accessed March 8, 2020. https://www.superoffice.com/blog/reduce-customer-churn/.

Poggi, Jeanine. "'Google Facebook Duopoly Set to Lose Some of Its Share of Ad Spend: And Amazon Will More Than Double Its Share." *AdAge.* Last modified February 2019. Accessed August 7, 2019. https://adage.com/article/digital/duopoly-loses-share-ad-spend/316692.

Reddy, Ajay. *The Scrumban [R]Evolution: Getting the Most out of Agile, Scrum, and Lean Kanban*. New York: Addison-Wesley, 2016.

Reiss, Spencer, and Darren Jacoby. *Vail Resorts Creates Epic Experiences with Customer Intelligence*. May 2013. Insights from Forrester's Marketing Leadership Forum, "Experience of a Lifetime—How Vail Resorts Is Redefining Targeted Marketing with the Help of SAS." Accessed March 18, 2020. https://www.sas.com/content/dam/SAS/en_us/doc/conclusionpaper1/vail-resorts-creates-epic-experiences-with-customer-intelligence-105852.pdf.

Revella, Adele. "Buyer Persona Expectations." Buyer Persona Institute. Accessed March 19, 2019. https://www.buyerpersona.com/.

Ries, Eric. *The Lean Startup: How Today's Entrepreneurs Use Continuous Innovation to Create Radically Successful Businesses*. Currency Publishers, 2011.

"ROAM & Risk Management Under SAFe." Intland Software. Last modified February 2015. Accessed August 28, 2019. https://content.intland.com/blog/agile/safe/roam-risk-management-under-safe.

Rose, Robert, and Carla Johnson. *Experiences: The 7th Era of Marketing*. Content Marketing Institute, 2015.

"SAFe." Scaled Agile. Accessed April 13, 2020. https://www.scaledagileframework.com/.

Schwaber, Ken. "Scrum Development Process." *Advanced Development Methods*, April 1995, 1–23. Accessed August 20, 2019. http://www.jeffsutherland.org/oopsla/schwapub.pdf.

Schwaber, Ken, and John Sutherland. "The Scrum Guide." Scrum Guides. Accessed April 13, 2020. https://www.scrumguides.org/scrum-guide.html.

Scott, David Meerman. *Newsjacking: How to Inject Your Ideas into a Breaking News Story and Generate Tons of Media Coverage*. Hoboken, NJ: Wiley, 2011.

Sethi, Rajesh, Daniel C. Smith, and C. Whan Park. "Cross-Functional Product Development Teams, Creativity, and the Innovativeness of New Consumer Products." *Journal of Marketing Research* 38, no. 1 (February 1, 2001): 73–85. Accessed March 2020. https://journals.sagepub.com/doi/10.1509/jmkr.38.1.73.18833.

Southwest Airlines. "Purpose, Vision, and The Southwest Way." Investor Relations. Accessed March 2020. http://investors.southwest.com/our-company/purpose-vision-and-the-southwest-way.

Spotify Training and Development. "Spotify Engineering Culture—part 1." Video, 13:12. Vimeo. Posted January 30, 2014. Accessed April 13, 2020. https://vimeo.com/85490944.

Srinivasan, Gopal, Deepak Sharma, Sourabh Bhandari, and Anand Mohan. *Enterprise Customer Success (CS) Study and Outlook, Fostering an Organization-wide CS Mindset.* Deloitte. https://www2.deloitte.com/content/dam/Deloitte/us/Documents/consumer-business/2019-enterprise-customer-success-study-and-outlook.pdf.

"Start Here: What Is Servant Leadership?" Robert Greenleaf: Center for Servant Leadership. Accessed August 8, 2019. https://www.greenleaf.org/what-is-servant-leadership.

"State of Agile Report." CollabNet VersionOne. Accessed March 2020. https://www.stateofagile.com/#ufh-c-473508-state-of-agile-report.

Sykes, Tim. "Digitally Printed Packaging at the Tipping Point." *Packaging Europe.* Last modified April 2018. Accessed August 8, 2019. https://packagingeurope.com/digital-print-packaging-tipping-point-HP-Indigo-Scitex/.

Takeuchi, Hirotaka, and Ikujiro Nonaka. "The New New Product Development Game." *Harvard Business Review,* January 1986. https://hbr.org/1986/01/the-new-new-product-development-game.

Volpe, Mike. "How to Structure a Marketing Team of Any Size." *Hubspot* (blog). Entry posted November 14, 2014. Accessed April 13, 2020. https://blog.hubspot.com/marketing/how-to-structure-marketing-team.

Wilson, Marianne. "Amazon to Capture 47% of All U.S. Online Sales in 2019." *Chain Store Age.* Last modified February 2019. Accessed August 7, 2019. https://www.chainstoreage.com/technology/emarketer-amazon-to-capture-47-of-all-u-s-online-sales-in-2019/.

Zyman, Sergio. *The End of Marketing as We Know It.* New York: Harper-Collins, 1999.

Acknowledgments

There are way too many people to acknowledge, but here's a start. Thanks to Scott Brinker, who started me on this journey with his blog post, *Ideas for an Agile Marketing Manifesto*. Thanks to John Cass and Frank Days, along with Scott Brinker, for helping organize Sprint Zero, and Roland Smart for helping on SprintOne and all that he's taught me about Agile marketing. Thanks to Travis Arnold for building and hosting the Agile Marketing Manifesto site. Thanks to Yuval Yeret for all that he's taught me about SAFe and Agile in general. Thanks to Jascha Kaykas-Wolff for hosting both Sprint Zero and SprintOne.

Thanks to Evan Leybourn for the great work he does at the Business Agility Institute and for his response to the concept of the Six Disciplines, which helped me find focus for the book.

Thanks to everyone who I interviewed for the book: Eric Schmidt, Katie Lowell, Justin Schroepfer, Justin Zimmerman, Melissa Reeve, Roland Smart, and Tara Wilkinson.

Thanks to all my clients and students over the years; I've learned just as much from you as you from me. Special thanks to Peter Francis for bringing me in at T-Mobile and giving me the opportunity to work with that team for the better part of a year. A shout-out to Stephanie Hescock, May Yu, Bart Ons, and Anthony Patterson, all of whom shared that journey with me.

Thanks to my editors, Ray Johnston and Lynn Northrup, who greatly improved my prose as well as the organization, clarity, and consistency of the book. Any remaining errors or inconsistencies are mine. Thanks to Shannon

Vargo, Sally Baker, and the team at Wiley for taking on this book in a difficult time.

Thanks to all of my teachers over the years, but particularly to Ann Sharp, who taught me to write, and Charles Brewer, who held me to the highest standards.

And special thanks to my wife, Ann, who kept after me in the nicest possible way to finish the book and without whose support I wouldn't have been able to write this or to do so many other things in my life.

About the Author

Jim Ewel began blogging about Agile marketing in 2010 and is one of the leading bloggers on the topic (www.agilemarketing.net). He was the co-organizer of the first gathering of Agile marketers, called Sprint Zero, in June 2012, and is one of the authors of the Agile Marketing Manifesto. He is frequently asked to speak on the topic of Agile marketing at industry conferences, and he has helped companies as diverse as T–Mobile, Salesforce, Best Buy Canada, SpaceSaver, Great Dane Trailers, Northern Alberta Institute of Technology, and Zenprise learn about and adopt Agile marketing.

Jim is also an accomplished CEO and marketing executive. He spent 12 years at Microsoft, where he was VP of server marketing, working on products such as Windows NT Server, Microsoft SQL Server, and Windows 2000. He has also run emerging and very high–growth mid–market companies, including InDemand Interpreting, Adometry, and GoAhead Software.

Jim completed his BA, with honors, at Furman University and continued to graduate work at the University of Pennsylvania. He has also been an adjunct professor at the University of Washington. He resides in Kirkland, Washington, with his wife, and they have five children and six grandchildren. When he isn't writing, speaking, or teaching Agile marketing, he enjoys travel, photography, and cooking.

Index